The Politics of Policy Implementation

Library of Congress Catalog Card Number: 79-93406
Copyright © 1980 by St. Martin's Press, Inc.
All Rights Reserved.
Manufactured in the United States of America.
43210
fedcba
For information, write St. Martin's Press, Inc.,
175 Fifth Avenue, New York, N.Y. 10010

typography: Bernard Klein

cloth ISBN: 0-312-62779-3
paper ISBN: 0-312-62780-7

Dedicated to Jeff Pressman,
a teaching colleague and a wise and loyal friend

Preface

Social scientists have long been interested in the study of public policy. This interest has generally been pursued within the framework of specialized disciplines. Political scientists studying legislatures, for example, have attempted to explain how policies are passed, while public administrators and political sociologists have studied various organizations that further define and carry out policies. Economists have focused on the effects of policies on the individual's rational calculations and the implications of these calculations, in the aggregate, for society.

In recent years there has been increasing interest in policy-relevant research as a subject in its own right. Such an interest is demonstrated in the actions of both policy makers and scholars. Federal lawmakers, for example, have expanded their staffs of policy analysts and appropriated more money to support outside research on policy implementation and evaluation. In addition, they have initiated programs and created institutions with the express purpose of providing policy appraisals for more widespread dissemination. Scholarly interest can be gauged by increased efforts to develop both graduate and undergraduate courses in policy analysis, create new scholarly journals providing outlets for research, and establish new interdisciplinary associations providing forums for the discussion of specialized issues raised by a policy focus.

The study of policy, which is located at the intersection of the concerns of policy makers and scholars, involves a broadly based interdisciplinary approach. Not surprisingly the definition and rationale of policy studies are far from exact. There are fundamental differences over what is meant by policy, what variables can be used to explain its effects, and what criteria should be used in assessing its success and failure. Despite these differences, during recent years policy makers and scholars have increased their efforts to work together in the belief that a more integrated view will evolve from those efforts.

The case study literature on policy implementation has grown very rapidly. This book represents an attempt to integrate those case studies into a more general conceptual framework. In order to do this we found it necessary to relate the process of implementation to some of the other elements found in policy research. Specifically, implementation as a general phenomenon cannot be separated from the processes of formulating and evaluating the policies being implemented. This requires consideration of different views of the policy process developed by a diverse group of participants and observers, including policy makers, bureaucrats, and social scientists. In short, our purpose in writing this book has been to explore the politics of policy implementation.

This book is directed toward several audiences: students of policy implementation drawn from various disciplines; practitioners of policy making and evaluation whose work is influenced by what happens during the policy implementation process; and policy makers who are interested in a more explicit description of their implementation problems and alternatives.

While we realize that the book breaks new ground and will be subject to future revisions and reinterpretations, we hope it will contribute to a more effective understanding of some of the major forces that influence the politics of policy implementation.

Acknowledgments

This book originated in an experimental undergraduate seminar that the authors taught at Dartmouth College during the winter of 1978. The book was further refined in a second seminar taught in the winter of 1979.

After reviewing relevant literature and case studies one of the students in the first seminar, Adam Rowland, indicated an interest in developing a conceptual model of the implementation process, which the authors refined in chapter 2 of this study. During the spring term Rowland did further background research on implementation literature, and he deserves special credit for making a major contribution to both the form and the content of this work.

The other students in the two seminars also made substantial contributions to the book, some by preparing papers on various aspects of policy implementation, which are cited in the text, and others by providing thoughtful comments on drafts and redrafts of the manuscript.

Hence, additional thanks go to the following students in the two seminars: (1978) Walter Callender, Stephen M. Dorvee, Albert J. Edwards, Timothy J. McNamara, Stephen R. Munger, Charles F. Nadler, Adam B. Rowland, Jonathan P. Wendell, Mary L. Wong, Michael J. Yoshii, Mitchell Zeller; (1979) Helen A. Davis, Anthony C. Desir, Thomas R.

HILTON

hon—

There's another text on the same topic that's simpler & I think it's cited in one of the chapter notes of this text. Please return them to Linda.

Good luck.

Don

10-23

ALBANY HILTON
At Ten Eyck Plaza   State and Lodge Streets
Albany, New York 12210
518/462-6611

Dustin, David M. Frankel, David R. Joyce, David H. Klinges, Laurie J. Laidlaw, Leslie J. Mandel, Peter J. Monahan, Barbara A. Murphy, Robert B. Richards, Robert J. Schpoont, Robert J. Wasz, Maja C. Wessels, Maxwell C. West, Joseph H. Young.

In addition, the authors are grateful to a number of others who offered comments on various portions of the book, including Jonathan Brownell, Susan L. Smallwood, and Denis G. Sullivan. Special thanks also go to Barbara Pryce and Janet Allen of the Dartmouth Public Affairs Center, who helped type and edit the copy.

The authors are grateful for a grant from the Alfred P. Sloan Foundation to support Dartmouth's Policy Studies Program, which was used, in part, to help cover secretarial and other costs involved in the preparation of the manuscript. In addition, the Brookings Institution Guest Scholar Program provided facilities for Robert Nakamura during the spring of 1979.

We express our appreciation to each of the foregoing for their interest, support, and encouragement, with the understanding that final responsibility for any errors of fact or judgment is our own.

Robert T. Nakamura
Frank Smallwood

Contents

Introduction   1

Part 1   BACKGROUND

Chapter 1   Changing Perceptions of Policy Implementation   7
        The "Classical" Model of Administration   7
        Recent Studies of Implementation   7
        Summary   12

Chapter 2   Implementation and the Policy Process:
                A Conceptual Overview   21
        Elements: The Concept of Policy Environments   22
        Linkages   23
        Summary   27

Part 2   THE POLICY ENVIRONMENTS

Chapter 3   Policy Formation (Environment I)   31
        Actors and Arenas   31
        Policy Instructions and Directives   32
        Constraints on Clarity of Policy Statements   34
        Political Intensity: Signals and Cues   39
        Anticipating Systems Failure   42
        Summary   44

Chapter 4   Policy Implementation (Environment II)   46
        Actors and Arenas   46
        Organizational Structures and Bureaucratic Norms   53
        Communications Networks and Compliance
            Mechanism   59
        Summary   65

Chapter 5   Policy Evaluation (Environment III)   67
   Evaluation by Political Standards   68
   Technical Evaluation   72
   Political Obstacles to Technical Evaluation   78
   Program Termination   80
   Summary   82

Chapter 6   The Special Case of Judicial Implementation   85
   Judicial Policy Making   86
   Communication Linkages   88
   Judicial Policy Implementation   92
   Examples of Judicial Implementation   95
   Summary   107

Part 3   LINKAGES

Chapter 7   Implementation Linkages: Policy Makers and
              Implementers   111
   "Classical" Technocrats   112
   Instructed Delegates   118
   Bargainers   122
   Discretionary Experimenters   127
   Bureaucratic Entrepreneurs   133
   Summary   142

Chapter 8   Evaluation Linkages: Assessing Implementation
              Scenarios   145
   Evaluation Criteria   146
   Evaluating Implementation Scenarios   152
   Summary   159

Part 4   LEADERSHIP

Chapter 9   Policy Implementation and Leadership Styles   163
   Policy Implementation: The Eisenhower Presidency   163
   Comparative Leadership Styles   167
   Leadership Style: The Personal Component   169
   The Constraints of Overextension   171
   The Constraints of Undue Caution   173
   Conclusion: Leadership and Political Feasibility   175
   Postscript   179

Bibliography   183

Index   191

The Politics of
Policy Implementation

Introduction

In the early summer of 1952, before the heat of the campaign, President Truman used to contemplate the problems of the General-become-President should Eisenhower win the forthcoming election. "He'll sit here," Truman would remark (tapping his desk for emphasis), "and he'll say. Do this! Do that! *And nothing will happen*. Poor Ike—it won't be a bit like the Army. He'll find it very frustrating."

> Richard E. Neustadt
> *Presidential Power*[1]

Neustadt's anecdote about "poor Ike" highlights a fundamental fact of governmental life. Implementation—which we define in this book as the process of carrying out authoritative public policy directives—is neither easy nor automatic.

While this has long been apparent to virtually anyone who has worked in a bureaucratic setting, it was not until the early 1970s that the RAND Corporation organized the first major research conference designed to "focus analytic efforts on the problem of implementation."[2] A few years later, in 1973, Jeffrey Pressman and Aaron Wildavsky published their pathbreaking book, *Implementation*. In Appendix 2 of that book they concluded that "there is no analytic literature on implementation."[3]

Although some have argued that this assessment was too harsh, our understanding of the policy implementation process is still relatively limited, despite the flurry of articles and other publications that have appeared since Pressman and Wildavsky's book. As recently as 1975 Donald Van Meter and Carl Van Horn observed that "at present we know relatively little about the process of policy implementation,"[4] while Erwin C. Hargrove labeled this "The Missing Link"[5] in the study of social policy.

While these observations may have been true when they were written, the number of more recent studies has reached a point at which it is useful to pull together the various findings in an effort to broaden our understanding of the policy implementation process.

In terms of its central focus, this book is designed to fill a gap that was identified by Mark H. Moore and Graham T. Allison, Jr., in their introduction to a special issue of *Public Policy* (Spring 1978). According to Moore and Allison,

> In designing and advocating policies, we must be able to anticipate the actual performance of the government in adopting and implementing the proposed policy. This anticipating, in turn, requires analytic procedures that enable us to (1) outline the main features of the political and bureaucratic settings within which specific policy proposals will be considered, and (2) make reliable judgments about whether the setting is hospitable or inimical to the proposed policy. To help with the first problem we need explicit terms to use in calibrating the scale and complexity of the settings, and to suggest the kinds of relationships that can exist among the different actors within the setting.[6]

The basic objective of this book is to describe and analyze "the main features of the political and bureaucratic settings" within which policy proposals are—or are not—implemented, and to classify "the kinds of relationships that can exist among different actors" within these settings. Within this context, the book is concerned specifically with the following:

1. *Public policies* that are initiated in the governmental, rather than the private, sector.
2. The types of *"macro-implementation"* institutional settings that span the entire public policy sector from the federal to the local levels.[7]
3. The *political dimensions* of policy implementation within these institutional settings.

This emphasis on the politics of implementation does not imply that other considerations are unimportant or insignificant. Obviously, the implementation of policies is dependent on economic factors such as the availability of money and other resources, on geographic considerations such as territorial jurisdiction, and on sociological factors such as interpersonal work relationships.

Our major concern in this study, however, is with the political pressures and constraints which influence the processes of policy formation, implementation, and evaluation. In this regard it is important to clarify the fact that we are focusing on politics in the broadest sense of the term. We are not limiting ourselves to partisan politics—how one or another political party attempts to influence the policy process. Instead, we are concerned with the *conflicts over values* which permeate many, if not all, aspects of public life, and the role of politics in resolving these conflicts.

As a result, our interpretation closely parallels that of political scientist David Easton when he defines politics as "the authoritative allocation of values for a society":

> Political life concerns all those varieties of activity that influence significantly the kind of authoritative policy adopted for society and *the way it is put into practice.* We are said to be participating in political life when our activity relates in some way to the making *and executing* of policy for society. . . .
>
> A policy . . . consists of a web of decisions and actions that allocate values. . . . Arriving at a decision is the formal phase of establishing a policy. . . . *When we act to implement the decision, we enter the second, or effective, phase of a policy.*[8] (emphasis added)

In terms of general organization, the book is divided into four major sections:

- Part One provides a background summary and review of literature on policy implementation (chapter 1), which is followed by the presentation of a conceptual model (chapter 2) that serves as the central organizing focus for this study.
- Part Two examines major political constraints and forces at work in the three environments of policy formation, implementation, and evaluation (chapters 3, 4, and 5) before presenting a separate discussion of the special problems involved in the area of judicial implementation (chapter 6).
- Part Three analyzes different types of linkages between the three policy environments. Chapter 7 describes various scenarios to illustrate the diverse linkages which can exist between policy makers and implementers. Chapter 8 examines different ways evaluation criteria can be linked into the assessment of policy implementation performance.
- Part Four concludes with a discussion of leadership styles and analyzes the different roles leaders can play in helping to shape and guide the implementation of public policies.

While the formal study of the implementation of public policies is still a relatively new field of inquiry, it is hoped that the following analysis will clarify some of the major political constraints and forces that come into play when we attempt to implement the "effective phase of a policy."

Notes

1. Richard E. Neustadt, *Presidential Power* (New York: Wiley, 1960), p. 9.
2. Mark H. Moore and Graham T. Allison, Jr., "Introduction," *Public Policy*, Spring 1978, p. 154.

4 Introduction

3. Jeffrey L. Pressman and Aaron Wildavsky, *Implementation* (Berkeley: University of California Press, 1973), pp. 166–175.

4. Donald S. Van Meter and Carl E. Van Horn, "The Policy Implementation Process: A Conceptual Framework," *Administration and Society*, 6, no. 4 (February 1975), 449.

5. Erwin C. Hargrove, *The Missing Link* (Washington D.C.: Urban Institute, July 1975).

6. Moore and Allison, "Introduction," p. 154.

7. See Paul Berman, "The Study of Macro- and Micro-Implementation," *Public Policy*, Spring 1978, p. 164.

8. David Easton, *The Political System* (New York: Knopf, 1953), pp. 128–130.

PART 1

Background

Chapter 1

Changing Perceptions of Policy Implementation

During the 1930s a "classical" model of public administration based on the principles of scientific management gained widespread publicity in the United States. This model was grounded in an explicit set of assumptions that virtually excluded implementers from any significant role in the policy process. Since the "classical" model helped shape our earlier perceptions of policy implementation, it is important to understand the central components of this theory.

The "Classical" Model of Administration

The antecedents of "classical" theory reach back to the turn of the century, when a diverse group of social scientists developed an interrelated set of hypotheses about the nature of the administrative process. These hypotheses tended to view administration in terms of the mechanical, or "machine," metaphor that, as Dwight Waldo has pointed out, was "probably the most pervasive and important model in American administrative study in the Twentieth Century."[1] At least three basic concepts helped shape this "machine" analogy.

The structural components of administrative organizations were viewed in terms of a centralized, hierarchical pyramid, a concept that grew out of the work of Max Weber (1864–1920), "the first to attempt a systematic theory of bureaucratic organization."[2] Weber described the "ideal" bureaucracy as a highly rationalized, legalistic kind of authority and structure controlled at the top by a small group of decision makers whose policies were dutifully implemented by "subordinate administrators whose obedience to commands should be prompt, automatic, and unquestioning."[3] Weber's "ideal" bureaucracy—"a firmly ordered system . . . in which there is a supervision of the lower offices by the higher ones"[4]—constituted the organizational framework for the "classical" model of administration.

A second major concept was developed by political scientist (later President) Woodrow Wilson (1856–1924), who published an influential paper on "The Study of Administration" while teaching at Bryn Mawr and Wesleyan. Wilson's central thesis was clear-cut: Politics and administration are, and should be, two separate and distinct activities. In his words, "The broad plans of government action are not administrative; the detailed execution of such plans is administrative."[5] The key contribution that Wilson made to "classical" theory was a belief that administration, as a separate, neutral, professionalized, and nonpolitical activity, could be carried out on the basis of objective principles of scientific rationality.

A third major actor, Frederick W. Taylor, provided the rationale for these objective principles. In 1911 Taylor, an industrial engineer, published a book on *The Principles of Scientific Management*[6] that stressed "efficiency" (as measured in time–motion studies of worker productivity) as the basic criterion against which to evaluate administrative performance.

Following the publication of Taylor's book the different streams of "classical" theory began to fall into place. During the 1920s and 1930s public administrators integrated these three concepts—organizational hierarchy, the separation of politics and administration, and "efficiency"—into a comprehensive set of rational precepts to guide the administrative process. This "classical" approach was fully integrated in 1937, when Luther Gulick and Lyndall Urwick edited their celebrated *Papers on the Science of Administration*.[7] The new science was based on a rigid, machine-like hierarchical structure. As Amitai Etzioni explains,

> The classical approach rests firmly on the assumption that . . . the number of subordinates controlled by one superior defines his "span of control." What results is a pyramid of control leading up to one top executive. In this way, the whole organization can be controlled from one center of authority.[8]

Hence, the "classical" model minimized the significance of implementation in the policy process precisely because it was based on a top-down command structure that allowed very little discretionary authority, and certainly no political latitude, to subordinate administrators. As T. B. Smith has observed, "The assumption was that once a policy has been 'made,' the policy will be implemented and the results of the policy will be near those expected by the policy-makers."[9]

In retrospect it is clear that two central sets of assumptions characterized the "classical" model. The first dealt with decision making and the second with implementation. In his book on *The Policy-Making Process*, Charles E. Lindblom describes the steps involved in this rational–comprehensive approach to decision making as follows:

"Classical" Decision-Making
1. Faced with a given problem
2. a rational man first clarifies his goals, values, or objectives, and then ranks or otherwise organizes them in his mind;
3. he then lists all important possible ways of—policies for—achieving his goals
4. and investigates all the important consequences that would follow from each of the alternative policies,
5. at which point he is in a position to compare consequences of each policy with goals
6. and so choose the policy with consequences most closely matching his goals.[10]

We can add a few logical steps of our own to bring policy implementation into this "classical" model:

"Classical" Implementation
7. An agent to carry out the policy is chosen by the policy maker according to technical criteria (i.e., the perceived ability of the agent to employ the appropriate means to accomplish the policy goals).
8. The policy is communicated to the agent as a series of specific instructions.
9. The agent implements (carries out) the specific instructions according to the policy guidelines specified in the communication from the policy maker.

These last three steps fit closely into the "classical" formulation. As Francis E. Rourke points out, "In the traditional theory of public administration in the United States, it was assumed that the administrator's discretion extended only to decisions on means, while the ends or goals of administrative action were fixed by statute or by the directives of a responsible political official." [11] Hence, this approach can be depicted as follows:

"Classical" Hierarchical Model

Policy Formulators
    | (CHOOSE AND INSTRUCT)
    ↓
Policy Implementers
    | (DELIVER)
    ↓
Policy Outputs ———————→ (STOP)

As has been noted, this model rests on a number of preconceptions about both policy making and policy implementation. The major ones are as follows:

1. Policy making and policy implementation are bounded, separate, and sequential.
2. These boundaries exist between policy makers and policy implementers because
   a. there is a clear division of labor between policy makers, who set goals, and policy implementers, who carry out these goals.
   b. policy makers are capable of stating policies definitively because they can agree on a priority among different goals.
   c. policy implementers possess the technical capability, the obedience, and the will to carry out the policies specified by the policy makers.
3. Since both policy makers and implementers accept the boundaries between their tasks, the process of implementation unfolds in a chronological, sequential fashion in which policy making precedes policy implementation.
4. The decisions that are involved in the implementation of policies are *nonpolitical* and *technical* in nature. It is the responsibility of the implementer to carry out policies in a neutral, "objective," "rational," and "scientific" fashion.

It soon became obvious that many of the assumptions behind the "classical" model represented an oversimplified view of the policy process. At least three developments led to a reexamination of this approach.

First, a number of studies of decision making indicated that policy formation is more complex than the model indicated. Lindblom was at the forefront of this challenge when he suggested that many decisions are made through an incremental process of successive comparisons (labeled "muddling through") rather than by means of rational, comprehensive choices.[12] Other important works included Chester Barnard's *The Functions of the Executive* and Anthony Downs's *An Economic Theory of Democracy*, which indicated that the information costs involved in decision making can be so high that many decisions are made under conditions of extreme uncertainty.[13] These studies suggested that the initial decision-making step was, in many cases, too complex and subtle to involve the types of clear-cut priority choices and specificities that characterized the "classical" model.

Second, additional studies in public administration and organizational behavior indicated that the middle step—the implementation of policy—was also much more complex than had previously been thought. A major breakthrough here occurred in 1949, when Paul Appleby, dean of the Maxwell School, published his book on *Policy and Administration*. Appleby challenged the older concept that politics and administration are two separate and distinct activities. He argued that it was inaccurate to draw such a clean dichotomy because administrators are involved in the process of making policy when they apply policy "at successively less abstract levels."[14] Other studies by Herbert Simon, Amitai Etzioni, Warren Bennis, and Herbert Kaufman revealed that the process of administration is compounded by an intricate variety of psychological norms and bureaucratic pressures that take on a complex political life of their own.[15] Thus, investigations into the realms of decision making and administrative behavior indicated that these areas are considerably more complicated than the "classical" model implied.

The third, more recent development that has challenged the "classical" model originated in the world of action rather than that of theory. This third influence appeared in the mid-1960s in the form of the "Great Society" legislation that was pushed through Congress under the tutelage of Lyndon B. Johnson. When Johnson succeeded John F. Kennedy as president, he could draw upon his superb background as a legislative tactician, but he lacked extensive administrative experience. His strength, which he used with consummate skill, was in influencing Congress to pass his legislation. Within a short time Congress responded by approving a series of diffuse policies designed to alleviate major social problems such as poverty, juvenile delinquency, unemployment, urban decay, racial and sexual discrimination, and a host of other social concerns.

It was not long before disillusionment began to set in as it became apparent that it might be easier to "legitimize" social policy by passing ambiguous legislation than to carry out such policy by means of effective program implementation. By the late 1960s some political scientists, most notably Theodore Lowi, were calling for a return to a more rationalized and structured approach to policy formation. In *The End of Liberalism* Lowi pointed to the Interstate Commerce Act of 1887 as an example of "good" law: "The ICC was given the power to be flexible, but it was relatively well shackled by clear standards of public policy, as stated in the statute and as understood in common law."[16]

Lowi was concerned that democratic norms of accountability and responsibility were being undermined by the allocation of too much discretionary authority to administrative implementers. After analyzing the development of public policy in the United States, he indicated that the scope and objects of governmental regulation had evolved from the concrete and specific (the railroads under the Interstate Commerce Act of 1887) to the concrete and general (the Trusts under the Sherman Antitrust Act of 1890) to the abstract and general (unfair competition under the Clayton and Federal Trade Commission Acts of 1914). Lowi argued that this broadening of focus had continued throughout the twentieth century to a point that government was now attempting to control the more universal aspects of human behavior ("the environment of conduct") under such recent initiatives as the Civil Rights Acts of the 1960s and other Great Society legislation.

To Lowi, this increasingly broad expansion of governmental concerns had eroded clear standards of administrative accountability and led to a crisis of public authority. He expressed the fear that as government moved into ever more abstract areas of social concern it became difficult, if not impossible, to set precise legislative standards to guide the actions of those who were responsible for implementing public policy. As laws become more ambiguous and abstract, they were subject to attack and reinterpretation at all levels through the pluralistic chaos of "interest group liberalism." The solution, to Lowi, involved a return to a more structured system of policy formulation in which policy makers and the courts would be responsible for setting strict legislative standards to guide administrative behavior:

> A good law eliminates the political process at certain points. A good law made at the center of government focuses politics there and reduces interests elsewhere. The center means Congress, the President, and the courts. To make law at a central point is to centralize the political process.[17]

A number of other scholars confirmed the hard reality that the diffuse Great Society legislation was placing tremendous strains on program implementers. Case studies such as Daniel Moynihan's *Maximum Feasible Misunderstanding*, Jerome Murphy's "Title I of ESEA," Martha Derthick's *New Towns In-Town*, and Beryl Radin's *Implementation, Change, and the Federal Bureaucracy* all indicated serious breakdowns in the policy implementation process.[18]

Yet despite the potential attractiveness of reverting to the "classical" administrative model, once Pandora's box had been opened it was not easy to close it. The previously simplistic process of implementation would never look the same again. Instead of returning to "classical" administrative theory, a host of observers attempted to grapple with, clarify, and explain the complexities of the newly discovered world of policy implementation.

Recent Studies of Implementation

During the 1970s a growing number of publications appeared in an attempt to pin down what Erwin C. Hargrove has called "The Missing Link"[19] in social policy—the implementation process.

Although earlier papers, articles, and books had commented on selective aspects of what we now label "implementation studies," it was not until 1973 that such studies assumed major visibility with the publication of Jeffrey Pressman and Aaron Wildavsky's *Implementation*.

Subsequent works have attempted to refine our understanding of the implementation process. A summary review of these studies reveals a clear evolutionary trend.

Pressman and Wildavsky, "Implementation" (1973)

Pressman and Wildavsky presented a case study coupled with a series of prescriptive warnings, rather than a theoretical model of the implementation process. However, their work has been so central to the emerging field of implementation studies that it marks a logical starting point for any review of recent literature on this subject. At the outset the authors defined implementation in specific, and highly positive, terms: "Implementation, to us, means just what Webster and Roget say it does: to carry out, accomplish, fulfill, produce, complete."[20]

Hence, Pressman and Wildavsky began their study with the assumption that implementation means getting things done, and they proceeded to dissect the efforts of the Economic Development Administration (EDA) to produce jobs for the hard-core unemployed in Oakland, California, as an example of how not to get things done. After leading the reader through the veritable minefield of mishaps, misfortunes, and mistakes that plagued the EDA experiment, they concluded their analysis with a series of observations and warnings that took on prescriptive tones:

1. "Implementation should not be divorced from policy . . . and . . . must not be conceived as a process that takes place after, and independent of, the design of policy."
2. "Designers of policy [must] consider direct means for achieving their ends." The EDA experiment was plagued with implementation via intermediaries, and the multiplicity of decision points and clearances resulted in a "complexity of joint actions" that paralyzed the implementation process. Hence, "a second way of joining policy more closely with implementation would be to pay as much attention to the creation of organizational machinery for executing a program as for launching one."
3. Consider carefully the theory that underlies your actions. "Behind the seemingly endless number of roadblocks in the path of the EDA employment program in Oakland lay deficiencies in concept. The economic theory was faulty because it aimed at the wrong target—subsidizing the capital of business enterprises rather than their wage bill."
4. Continuity of leadership is important to successful implementation. The abrupt disappearance of key actors (such as Eugene C. Foley, the assistant secretary of commerce who started the EDA Oakland project) wreaked havoc on the program.
5. "Simplicity in policies is much to be desired . . . Simplicity can be ignored only at the peril of breakdown . . . If policy analysts carry bumper stickers, they should read, "Be Simple! Be Direct! or PAYMENT ON PERFORMANCE."[21]

Although Pressman and Wildavsky did not attempt to construct an explicit theoretical model of the implementation process, observations like those just listed provided a clear indication of some of the key elements that might have been included in any such model. They accepted the concept that the policy process was basically unidirectional (in which policies were first designed or formulated by leaders and then carried out through intermediary implementers), but their analysis broke with the "classical" dichotomy between politics and administration by stressing the close interrelationship between policy design and implementation. In this respect they went considerably beyond "classical" theory by calling for the integration, rather than the separation, of policy formation and policy implementation.

Van Meter and Van Horn, "The Policy Implementation Process" (1975)

In a 1975 article in *Administration and Society*, Donald S. Van Meter and Carl E. Van Horn defined policy implementation as "those actions by public and private individuals (or groups) that are directed at the achievement of objectives set forth in prior policy decisions."[22]

Hence, like Pressman and Wildavsky, they pictured implementation as a undirectional process mandated by prior policy decisions. Yet their study is especially useful for its review of organization theory and its emphasis on the human and psychological factors that influence behavior within the implementation arena. From their analysis they develop a model of the policy implementation process that is based on six "clusters of variables" that shape the linkage between policy and performance:

1. Policy
   a. Standards and objectives
   b. Resources
2. Linkage
   c. Interorganizational communication and enforcement activities
   d. Characteristics of the implementing agencies
   e. Economic, social, and political conditions
   f. The disposition of implementers
3. Performance

Once again, Van Meter and Van Horn's analysis pushed beyond earlier "classical" theory by highlighting and exploring some of the personal and psychological complexities that influence the actors in the implementation arena. These actors are no longer faceless automatons. Instead, they are seen as flesh-and-blood participants who can play a crucial role in shaping the policy process. In a follow-up paper political scientist James D. Sorg extended Van Meter and Van Horn's conceptual framework by refining various routines that characterize the implementation process once policies have been authorized.[23]

The weight of analysis has begun to shift dramatically by placing increasing emphasis on the personal, political, and organizational forces at work within the implementation arena itself as a key object of study.

McLaughlin, "Implementation as Mutual Adaptation" (1975)

Milbrey McLaughlin, using data collected from a RAND Corporation study of federal programs involving educational change, focused on the interpersonal relationships between implementers and policy formulators as a key factor in program success. Like Van Meter and Van Horn, McLaughlin was interested in the implementers' receptivity, or lack of receptivity, to policy change. She concluded that, within the implementation arena, "the amount of interest, commitment, and support evidenced by the principal actors had a major influence on the prospects for success."

As part of her analysis McLaughlin described three different types of potential interactions between policy makers and implementers:

1. *Mutual Adaptation* described successfully implemented projects. It involved both modification of the project design and changes in the local institutional setting and personnel during the course of implementation.
2. *Co-optation* signified adaptation of the project design, but no change on the part of the local staff or the institutional setting. When implementation of this nature occurred, project strategies simply were modified to conform in a pro forma fashion to the traditional practices the innovation was expected to replace, either because of resistance to change or inadequate help to implementers.
3. *Nonimplementation* described the experience of projects that either broke down during the course of implementation or simply were ignored by project participants.[24]

McLaughlin's analysis indicated that the implementers are crucial actors in the policy process. Under conditions of "mutual adaptation" they can be influenced to accept, and cooperate in, program implementation. Under other circumstances, however, they may either "take the money and run" (co-optation) or resist to a point at which the entire implementation process breaks down.

Bardach, "The Implementation Game" (1977), and Radin, "Implementation, Change, and the Federal Bureaucracy" (1977)

The role of the implementers in the policy process came into even sharper focus in Eugene Bardach's *The Implementation Game*. In this book Bardach defined implementation as "an assembly process . . . [which involves] . . . putting the machine together and making it run." Hence,

Bardach reverts to the machine analogy to characterize the administrative process, but the type of machine he describes is vastly more playful and human than the earlier "classical" model. In Bardach's analysis those who attempt to put the implementation machine together try to exercise "control" through

> bargaining, persuasion, and maneuvering under conditions of uncertainty. "Control," therefore, resolves into strategies and tactics—hence the appropriateness of "games" as the characterization of the "control" aspects of the process.
>
> The idea of "games," therefore, will serve principally as a master metaphor that directs attention and stimulates insight. It directs us to look at the players, what they regard as the stakes, their strategies and tactics, their resources, the rules of play (which stipulate the conditions for winning), the rules of "fair" play (which stipulate the boundaries beyond which lie fraud or illegitimacy), the nature of the communications (or lack of them) among the players, and the degree of uncertainty surrounding the possible outcomes. The game metaphor also directs our attention to who is not willing to play and for what reasons, and to who insists on changes in some of the game's parameters as a condition for playing.[25]

The metaphor of games led Bardach to focus on the conditions under which different strategies adopted by implementers can be recognized, classified, and resolved. In his book he discusses and analyzes a variety of games that implementers can use to divert resources, deflect goals, resist initiatives, and dissipate energies. The goal of Bardach's book is prescriptive: how to make better implementation machines. This can be accomplished in two ways: (1) Limit policy goals in recognition of the shortcomings of social theories and (2) plan around the pitfalls represented by the various implementation games. The second prescription is dealt with at length because Bardach assumes that many of the implementation games may be found in all complex policy areas.

At the same time that Bardach's book appeared, Beryl Radin published a comprehensive case study of attempts by the Department of Health, Education and Welfare (HEW) to implement desegregation policy between 1964 and 1968. Radin's analysis of the difficulties experienced by HEW paralleled many of the woes that Pressman and Wildavsky had revealed in their earlier study of EDA in Oakland. Her book also provided ample evidence that the types of games Bardach had classified are part of the real-life world of public policy implementation. A key focus in Radin's study involved Title VI (nondiscrimination in federally assisted programs), which was added almost as an afterthought to the Civil Rights Act of 1964. As she explained at the outset,

> The detailed descriptions of implementation efforts and policy decisions surrounding structural questions seek to convey the climate of ambiguity,

confusion, and political intrigue that characterized Title VI activities and to communicate the importance of the interplay between the literal and the symbolic within the policy setting.[26]

Hence, both Bardach and Radin continued the emerging trend of focusing on the political arena occupied by policy implementers as an area that deserved detailed analysis. This theme literally came full circle when two other political scientists attempted to place the implementation process in a theoretical perspective.

Rein and Rabinovitz, "Implementation: A Theoretical Perspective" (1978)

In an article in *American Politics and Public Policy*, Martin Rein and Francine Rabinovitz completed the process of revising the assumptions that underlay the "classical" hierarchical model of implementation. According to their analysis,

> One of the consequences of passing ambiguous and inconsistent legislation is that the arena of decision-making shifts to a lower level. The everyday practitioners become the ones who resolve the lack of consensus through their concrete actions . . . Interest group pressures are brought to bear largely after legislation is passed.[27]

Rein and Rabinovitz defined implementation as "(1) a declaration of government preferences (2) mediated by a number of actors who (3) create a circular process characterized by reciprocal power relations and negotiations." They indicated that this process of implementation is "dominated by three potentially conflicting imperatives":

1. *The Legal Imperative* (Respect for legal intent. To do what is legally required. This imperative stresses the importance of subordinate compliance to rules which derive from legislative mandates along the lines described by Lowi's "classical" theory).
2. *The Rational-Bureaucratic Imperative* (What from a bureaucratic point of view is a morally correct, administratively feasible, and intellectually defensible course of action. Emphasis here is on such bureaucratic norms as consistency of principles, workability, and concern for institutional maintenance, protection, and growth).
3. *The Consensual Imperative* (To do what is necessary to attract agreement among contending influential parties who have a stake in the outcome).[28]

Because of the need to reconcile these potentially conflicting imperatives, the entire implementation process is characterized by a "principle of circularity":

The process is not one of a graceful one-dimensional transition from legislation, to guidelines, and then to auditing and evaluation. It is, instead, circular or looping . . . No one participant in the process ever really is willing to stop intervening in the other parts of the process just because his stage has passed.[29]

With their "principle of circularity" Rein and Rabinovitz completed the break with the earlier hierarchical, unidirectional "classical" model. They also pushed their analysis one step beyond those of their predecessors. Whereas previous investigators had implied that implementers play an important role in the policy process, Rein and Rabinovitz place a direct and high priority on bureaucratic and consensual initiatives as two of the three basic "imperatives" that help to shape policy. If their interpretation is correct, it will be necessary to incorporate implementers as very key actors in the policy process.

Summary

The studies on policy implementation that have appeared during the 1970s have revealed a consistent and progressive shift away from the "classical" hierarchical model. As was noted at the outset, this earlier model was grounded in the assumption that policy implementation was a technical, nonpolitical activity that proceeded in response to directives from the top. Under this model policy makers provided concise instructions and neutral implementers carried out these instructions in an automatic fashion.

Beginning with Pressman and Wildavsky's call for an integration of policy design with implementation, successive studies have placed increasing emphasis on implementers as key actors in the policy process. Thus, Van Meter and Van Horn stressed the psychological and human factors that can influence implementers' behavior; McLaughlin emphasized a reciprocal process of "mutual adaptation" between policy makers and implementers; Bardach classified and analyzed a wide variety of "games" that implementers can play to impede, frustrate, and subvert policies; and Radin's case study depicted the political intrigue that can surround attempts to implement specific policies. Finally, Rein and Rabinovitz analyzed the circular nature of an implementation process that attempts to reconcile a potentially competing set of legal, bureaucratic, and consensual imperatives.

After reviewing this shift in emphasis away from policy makers and toward policy implementers, one might even suspect that the "classical" model had been turned upside-down, which is precisely what M.I.T.

political scientist Michael Lipsky suggests in an article entitled "Implementation on Its Head." According to Lipsky,

> There are many contexts in which the latitude of those charged with carrying out a policy is so substantial that studies of implementation should be turned on their heads. In these cases, policy is effectively "made" by the people who implement it.[30]

Each of these recent studies has produced a more circular view of the policy process. This process appears to be characterized by a fluid and reciprocal series of interrelationships between different groups of actors rather than a straight-line "classical" hierarchy that points directly from the top to the bottom.

Yet these new insights into circularity also pose a dilemma because, with all its faults, the "classical" model did have the virtue of simplicity. Now, however, the policy process has begun to unravel in an increasingly complex manner, with possibly no clear beginning or end points to define its parameters.

What is to be done, then, in light of Pressman and Wildavsky's admonition to policy analysts to carry bumper stickers that read "Be Simple! Be Direct!"? Is it possible to construct a meaningful model of policy implementation that captures the complexities of circularity in a manner that is both comprehensive and comprehensible?

"Tut, tut, child," said the Duchess to Alice. "Everything's got a moral if only you can find it."

Notes

1. Dwight Waldo, *Perspectives on Administration* (Tuscaloosa, Ala: University of Alabama Press, 1956), pp. 30–31.

2. Victor Thompson, *Modern Organization* (New York: Knopf, 1961).

3. Ibid., p. 11.

4. Max Weber, *Essays in Sociology*, ed. H. H. Gerth and C. Wright Mills (New York: Oxford University Press, 1946), pp. 196–198.

5. Woodrow Wilson, "The Study of Administration," *Political Science Quarterly*, 2 (June 1887), 212.

6. Frederick W. Taylor, *The Principles of Scientific Management* (New York: Harper & Row, 1911).

7. Luther Gulick and Lyndall Urwick, eds., *Papers on the Science of Administration* (New York: Institute of Public Administration, 1937).

8. Amitai Etzioni, *Modern Organizations* (Englewood Cliffs, N.J.: Prentice-Hall, 1964), pp. 22–23.

9. T. B. Smith, "The Policy Implementation Process," *Policy Sciences,* 4 (1973), 197–198.

10. Charles E. Lindblom, *The Policy-Making Process* (Englewood Cliffs, N.J.: Prentice-Hall, 1968), p. 13.

11. Francis E. Rourke, *Bureaucracy, Politics and Public Policy,* 2nd. ed. (Boston: Little, Brown, 1976), p. 33.

12. Charles E. Lindblom, "The Science of Muddling Through," *Public Administration Review,* 19 (Spring 1959), 79–88.

13. Chester I. Barnard, *The Functions of the Executive* (Cambridge: Harvard University Press, 1938); Anthony Downs, *An Economic Theory of Democracy* (New York: Harper & Row, 1957), pp. 77–279.

14. Paul Appleby, *Policy and Administration* (Tuscaloosa, Ala.: University of Alabama Press, 1949), p. 8.

15. Herbert A. Simon, *Administrative Behavior* (New York: Macmillan, 1947); Amitai Etzioni, *Modern Organizations;* Warren G. Bennis, *Changing Organizations* (New York: McGraw-Hill, 1966); Herbert Kaufman, *The Forest Ranger* (Baltimore: Johns Hopkins Press, 1960).

16. Theodore J. Lowi, *The End of Liberalism* (New York: Norton, 1969), p. 131.

17. Ibid., p. 127.

18. Daniel P. Moynihan, *Maximum Feasible Misunderstanding* (New York: Free Press, 1970); Jerome T. Murphy, "Title I of ESEA: The Politics of Implementing Federal Education Reform," *Harvard Educational Review,* 41, no. 1 (February 1971); Martha Derthick, *New Towns In-Town* (Washington, D.C.: Urban Institute, 1972); Beryl A. Radin, *Implementation. Change, and the Federal Bureaucracy* (New York: Teachers College Press, Columbia University, 1977).

19. Erwin C. Hargrove, *The Missing Link* (Washington, D.C.: Urban Institute, July 1975).

20. Jeffrey L. Pressman and Aaron Wildavsky, *Implementation* (Berkeley: University of California Press, 1973), p. xiii.

21. Ibid., pp. 143–149.

22. Donald S. Van Meter and Carl E. Van Horn, "The Policy Implementation Process: A Conceptual Framework," *Administration and Society,* 6, no. 4 (February 1975), 447.

23. James D. Sorg, "Extensions of Van Meter and Van Horn's Conceptual Framework of the Policy Implementation Process" (Tarrytown, N.Y.: Northeastern Political Science Association Conference, November 9-11, 1978).

24. Milbrey McLaughlin, "Implementation as Mutual Adaptation," in Walter Williams and Richard Elmore, eds., *Social Program Implementation* (New York: Academic Press, 1976), pp. 167–180.

25. Eugene Bardach, *The Implementation Game* (Cambridge, Mass.: M.I.T. Press, 1977), p. 56.

26. Radin, *Implementation, Change, and the Federal Bureaucracy,* p. 23.

27. Martin Rein and Francine F. Rabinovitz, "Implementation: A Theoretical Perspective," in Walter D. Burnham and Martha W. Weinberg, eds., *American Politics and Public Policy* (Cambridge, Mass.: M.I.T. Press, 1978).

28. Ibid., pp. 309–315.

29. Ibid., p. 322.

30. Michael M. Lipsky, "Implementation on Its Head," in Burnham and Weinberg, *American Politics and Public Policy,* pp. 390–402.

Chapter 2

Implementation and the Policy Process: A Conceptual Overview

The various studies discussed in chapter 1 have indicated that policy implementation cannot be analyzed in isolation. In order to understand what occurs when a policy is being implemented, it is necessary to explore the related stages of the policy process.[1]

The policy process is complex. Implementation is but one part of this process, and is inextricably related to, and interdependent with, the other parts. Considering implementation without reference to these other parts would be tantamount to studying election returns without reference to the personalities of the candidates or the composition of the electorate; only a limited depth of understanding could be attained. Thus, a conceptual overview of the entire policy process is required.

One useful way to study the implementation of a policy is to view the policy process as a system. A system is characterized by a set of interconnected elements, each directly or indirectly related to the other. The utility of a systems overview lies in its simplification of the policy process into a set of elements and linkages. If we can define and analyze these elements and linkages, we will be able to perceive where and how implementation fits into the life of a policy.

Elements: The Concept of Policy Environments

The key elements in the policy process can be viewed as sets of functional environments in which different aspects of the process take place. Within each of these environments there are a variety of arenas where actors interact. Two attributes of this concept explain the usefulness of this type of overview.

First, the use of environments minimizes the misleading tendency to characterize implementation solely as a unidirectional phenomenon, the kind of "top-down" heirarchical activity that characterized the earlier "classical" model described in the preceding chapter. Environments are always in flux. They are not mutually exclusive, since the same actors can participate in different roles in different environments. The concept of environments suggests there is some order in a policy's life, but that the ordered parts can be fluid rather than dominated by a single unidirectional movement from top to bottom.

Second, the concept of environments can encompass the wide variety of different actors who may attempt to influence the policy process. Anyone who may become involved in this process, not just the "legitimate" governmental actors, may be included in a policy environment. Hence, the concept of environments lends flexibility, yet underlying simplicity, to a complex process.

In this book we will view the policy process in terms of three interrelated functional environments, each of which contains various groups of actors and arenas:

Policy Environments	*Functions*
Environment I	Policy formation
Environment II	Policy implementation
Environment III	Policy evaluation

Environment I: Policy Formation

Historically, this environment has been viewed as the most formally structured of the three, centering on legally prescribed policy-making mechanisms. Key public actors include "legitimate" policy makers (e.g., the president, Congress, governors, state legislatures, etc.) plus other, nongovernmental individuals and/or groups that are capable of influencing these policy makers (e.g., interest groups, powerful constituents, etc.). A policy can originate in this environment in response to the interest of powerful governmental or nongovernmental actors (e.g., the president, committee chairpersons, the press, one or more lobbies, etc.) or in response to crisis situations (e.g., riots, depression, war, natural disasters, energy shortages, etc.) or because of more general public concerns and pressures (e.g., issues such as abortion, "Proposition 13" tax cuts, etc.). Technically, policy formation ends when a decision is legitimized by formal governmental policy makers (e.g., Congress passes a law, the president issues an executive order, etc.), although as we will attempt to demonstrate, policies can be reformulated in the other environments.

Environment II: Policy Implementation

The actors and structure of this environment vary depending on the type of policy under consideration. Although theoretically the actors in this environment are guided by the mandates legitimized by the policy makers in Environment I (i.e., Rein and Rabinovitz' "legal imperative"), they can also be influenced by their own perceptions and/or attempts to gather support for their implementation efforts (i.e., Rein and Rabinovitz' "bureaucratic and consensual imperatives"). Hence, implementation efforts can vary according to the composition, disposition, and interaction of the actors and the conditions of the environment. Activity in this environment technically ends when the policy is terminated by mandate of the formal policy makers who occupy the policy formation environment (owing to "success," "failure," "disinterest," etc.).

Environment III: Policy Evaluation

This environment is the most amorphous and abstract of the three. The actors involved in evaluation can include policy makers from Environment I, or implementers from Environment II, who engage in planning projections, oversight, or monitoring activities. On the other hand, if evaluation takes place on an "after-the-fact" basis, the actors might include social scientists or other academics, public interest groups, and the like who have no prior connection with policy formation or implementation. In virtually all cases the implementers become involved in evaluation because they generate much of the information on which evaluation is based. The process of evaluation usually has two objectives: to determine the "success" or "failure" of policies and/or to develop policy alternatives. Hence, new policies may originate in this environment that are ultimately legitimized by the policy makers in Environment I.

As the foregoing descriptions indicate, the three environments are interrelated. Actors, ideas, and policies can shift back and forth between the environments in accordance with the "principle of circularity" described by Rein and Rabinovitz.[2]

Linkages

Communication and compliance linkages between different actors in the three environments tie the policy system together. "Communication" presupposes a situation in which "each of two (or more) purposeful individuals . . . is aware that there is another such individual . . . in its environment and that the choices of the other can affect what will happen."[3]

In the policy system described here, communications linkages are especially important between Environment I policy makers and Environment II policy implementers because, as Edwards and Sharkansky point out in *The Policy Predicament,* "the first requirement for effective implementation is that those responsible for carrying out a decision must know what they are supposed to do . . . Orders to implement a policy must be consistent, clear, and accurate."[4]

Despite this admonition, communications linkages within any policy system can be replete with potential pitfalls. Mishaps can occur because of (1) garbled messages from the senders; (2) misinterpretations by the receivers; or (3) system failure in terms of transmission breakdowns, overload, "noise," and inadequate follow-through or compliance mechanisms.

The first potential difficulty—garbled messages from senders—can result from the limitations of verbal and written communication. Because of the potential ambiguity of language, coupled with other constraints that can dilute the content of a message (e.g., limited time allotted to communications, "forbidden" language based on etiquette, etc.), the complete essence of a communication may not be contained in the message. This can be especially true in policy messages in which policy makers use diffuse, ideological code words or phrases (e.g., to promote the "general welfare" or the "public interest"), which are very high on what S. I. Hayakawa has called the "abstraction ladder."[5] Such messages can be deliberately garbled as a result of the compromises that are required to gain political support for the adoption of the policy. For example, policy makers may reach consensus on very general goals, but they are unable to agree on the specifics of how those goals are to be achieved. The Great Society legislation mentioned in chapter 1 is full of examples of these kinds of diffuse policy messages. Because such messages can have a crucial impact on both the implementation and the evaluation of policies, this subject is covered at greater length in chapter 3.

The second potential communications pitfall—misinterpretation by the receivers—can be either unintentional or intentional. If the policy messages transmitted by senders are actually garbled, the receivers may simply not be able to interpret these messages as either implementation or evaluation instructions to be strictly followed. In addition, receivers can "misinterpret" a message because their own interests, perceptions, and purposes clash with those of the senders. Here we are dealing with the attitudes of implementers and the types of psychological influences and organizational norms that can shape their perceptions. Implementers may "misread" or ignore messages that are transmitted by policy makers

because those messages threaten various bureaucratic or personal prerogatives. Hence, implementer receptivity is another critical component of
the communications process and is discussed further in chapter 4.

Finally, the overall system can be subjected to communications
failures. The absence of effective machinery to transmit messages from
one environment to another can result in communications that are sent to
the wrong actors or not even transmitted at all. Edwards and Sharkansky,
for example, point out that "there are not regular channels of communications between courts and implementers" in the American political
system. As a result, "the transmission of judicial orders is very much a hit-
or-miss operation which depends heavily on interested private groups and
professional organizations. This open-ended system leaves a great deal of
room for ignorance and misinformation."[6]

A second kind of system breakdown can occur if an information
"overload" takes place owing to the fact that so many different messages
are being transmitted at the same time that the resultant "noise" and
"static" block out key communications.

A third, and very important, system failure can result from an
absence of follow-up and compliance mechanisms that can be used to
ensure that policy messages have been received (accurately) and that
implementers and/or evaluators are attempting to take appropriate
action in accordance with these messages. Here we are dealing with the
difficult challenge of how to use sanctions and/or incentives to ensure
that policy directives are actually being implemented once they have been
transmitted from one environment to another. Various case studies of
Great Society programs have indicated that breakdowns of compliance
linkages represent one of the thorniest problems of policy implementation. Since this represents another critical aspect of the policy process, it is
also discussed in more detail in chapter 4.

While linkages between the different environments constitute a vital
part of the policy system, they also present a variety of potentially difficult
problems. It is all well and good for Humpty Dumpty to tell Alice, "when
I use a word, it means just what I choose it to mean—neither more
nor less." In the complex world of public policy, where communications must link different actors from different environments, Humpty
Dumpty's optimistic assertion represents a blueprint for disaster.

A final component in any system, in addition to its environmental
elements and its communications linkages, consists of its entry and exit
points. In the case of a policy system, this raises the question of where
ideas for policies originate (i.e., how policies get into the system) and,
once begun, how programs are terminated (i.e., how policies get out of
the system).

The summary description of the policy formation environment at the beginning of this chapter touched briefly on *why* a policy may be initiated. The primary stimuli mentioned were the interests of powerful actors, crisis situations, and more diffuse public concerns and pressures. It is much more difficult to determine precisely *how* or *where* a policy may originate, and it appears possible for this to occur in any of the three environments, or even from sources completely outside these environments. For example, in *Maximum Feasible Misunderstanding* Daniel Moynihan indicates that many of the key elements in the Economic Opportunity Act of 1964 originated in academic treatises that were incorporated into a Ford Foundation experiment in New York City before they were finally transmitted to the White House and Congress.[7] Likewise, numerous studies have indicated that legislative policy can be formulated by executive agency implementers who propose modifications in existing laws as a result of their experience in carrying out these laws.

The most commonly acknowledged source of public policy, however, is the policy formation environment, where most people assume (incorrectly) that all policy originates. As a general rule, the actors in this environment perform the vital role of legitimizing policy initiatives (i.e., making them official via legal mandates). Hence, while it is possible for policy to originate in any environment, we will pay special attention in the next chapter to Environment I as the major source of policy initiatives.

If it is difficult to determine how policies get into the system, it can be even more frustrating to ascertain where, when, and how policies may eventually get out of the system. Since the need for, and conditions affecting, a policy can change over time, it appears logical to assume that many policies might be terminated at some point. Termination could result because a policy is so "successful" that it is no longer needed; or a policy is a "failure" and therefore is no longer feasible; or a policy needs to be renovated from scratch. Other reasons for the termination of a policy might be that the problem with which the policy was intended to deal disappears on its own or that resources to carry out the policy (especially financial support) are no longer available.

When all is said and done, however, many policies can display a stubborn persistence and remain in existence long after common sense would indicate that they should have been terminated. Peter DeLeon of RAND Corporation has identified a variety of obstacles to policy termination; these, too, are discussed in more detail in chapter 4.

Hence, once again, the process of policy termination can involve a complex series of interactions between actors from all three of the policy environments. The circular linkages between these different environments constitute the essence of the policy system.

Summary

Our overview of the policy process has indicated that this process can be conceived of as a system of functional environments—policy formation, policy implementation, and policy evaluation—each of which contains a variety of actors and arenas and each of which is connected to the others by various communications and compliance linkages. Unlike the earlier "classical" model, the policy system we have described is cyclical rather than hierarchical. It is characterized by what Rein and Rabinovitz have called the "principle of circularity" and can be envisioned as shown in Figure 2-1.

Although the system is cyclical, this does not mean that all the actors in the system have equal power to dominate the policy process. However, it does imply that actors within any one of the three environments can influence actors in other environments, often very significantly. In addition, the system is not closed; policies can originate either within or outside the system, and the actors can participate in different roles in different environments. As a result, the political and communications

Figure 2-1   *ENVIRONMENTS INFLUENCING IMPLEMENTATION*

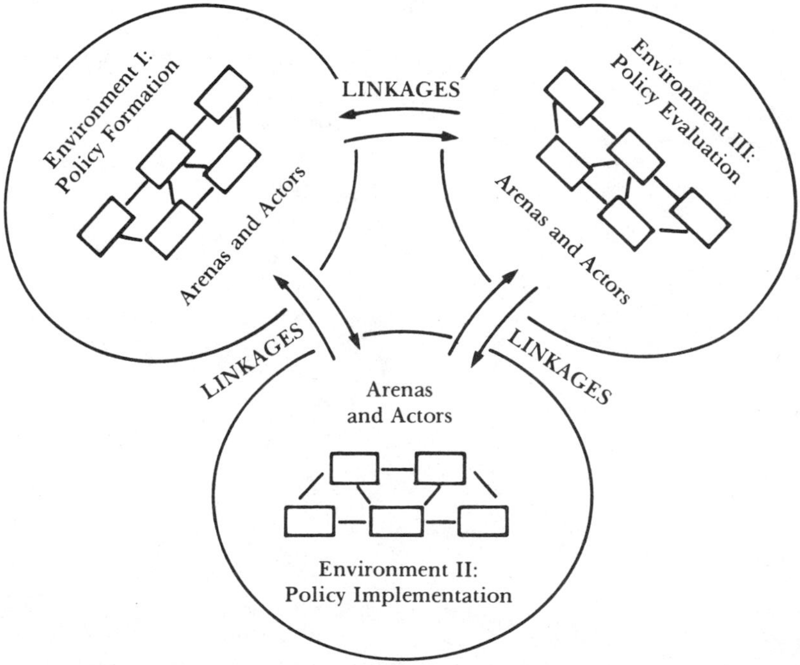

linkages that exist within, and between, the different environments and outside the system take on crucial importance.

In order to understand more fully how implementation fits into this policy system, we will explore each of these environments in depth in the next four chapters.

Notes

1. The authors are indebted to a seminar paper by Adam Rowland that outlined many of the concepts incorporated into this chapter.

2. Martin Rein and Francine F. Rabinovitz, "Implementation: A Theoretical Perspective," in Walter D. Burnham and Martha W. Weinberg, eds., *American Politics and Public Policy* (Cambridge, Mass.: M.I.T. Press, 1978), pp. 307–355.

3. Russell L. Ackoff and Fred E. Emory, *On Purposeful Systems* (Chicago: Aldine-Atherton, 1972), p. 141.

4. George C. Edwards and Ira Sharkansky, *The Policy Predicament* (San Francisco: W. H. Freeman, 1978), p. 295.

5. S. I. Hayakawa, *Language in Thought and Action*, 4th ed. (New York: Harcourt Brace Jovanovich, 1978), pp. 154–157.

6. Edwards and Sharkansky, *The Policy Predicament*, p. 296.

7. Daniel P. Moynihan, *Maximum Feasible Misunderstanding* (New York: Free Press, 1970).

8. Peter DeLeon, "Public Policy Terminations: An End and a Beginning," *Policy Analysis*, Summer 1978.

PART 2

The Policy Environments

Chapter 3

Policy Formation (Environment I)

According to Pressman and Wildavsky, implementation is the process of carrying out, accomplishing, fulfilling, producing, and completing a policy.[1] A policy can be thought of as a set of instructions from policy makers to policy implementers that spell out both goals and the means for achieving those goals. Experience shows that these instructions can range from precise "blueprints" to rather vague exhortations. The degree of specificity in policy instructions defines the amount of discretion enjoyed by implementers and evaluators.

It is appropriate to begin our investigation of the three policy environments by turning first to the formal policy makers in Environment I—the elected officials and other high-level actors who occupy positions of authority in the governmental arena. Our examination is focused specifically *on those conditions within the policy formation environment which most directly affect the actions of the implementers and evaluators.*

Actors and Arenas

In general, the principal actors in policy formation are the "legitimate," or formal, policy makers: people who occupy positions in the governmental arena that entitle them to authoritatively assign priorities and commit resources. These people include elected officials, legislators, and high-level administrative appointees, each of whom must follow prescribed paths to make policy. The requirements of making laws or administrative policy are spelled out in some detail, and under the American system of "checks and balances" these requirements usually involve securing the agreement of different sets of policy makers before a policy is formally approved. Since these formal policy makers represent diverse constituencies—electoral, administrative, and bureaucratic—the policy-making process offers many points of access through which interest groups and others from arenas outside government can exercise influence.

Thus, policy making usually involves a diverse set of authoritative, or formal, policy makers, who operate within the governmental arena, plus a diverse set of special interest and other constituency groups from outside arenas, who press their demands on these formal leaders.

Formal policy makers focus their major energies on setting priorities and determining the commitment of resources. Since there are many claims on their time and resources, policy makers are limited to only occasional forays into the implementation environment. As a result, policy makers usually do not implement policy themselves. Instead, they rely on another set of actors—the implementers and intermediaries who occupy Environment II—to actually carry out the policies they prescribe.

Hence, the directives and instructions that policy makers pass on to these implementers are crucially important. It is essential to understand the key factors in the policy-making environment that can influence the shape, nature, and clarity of these policy directives.

Policy Instructions and Directives

At a minimum, actors in Environment I start the policy process. Their initial statements of policy are expected to set the general boundaries within which implementation will occur by identifying

1. General policy goals, e.g.,
   a. the problem area
   b. the priority of specific problems over others
   c. a population to be benefited
2. General means to achieve policy goals, e.g.,
   a. suggested approaches by which goals are to be achieved
   b. the key actors who will carry out the policy
   c. resources to be expended in carrying out the policy
   d. possibly, suggest some indicators for measuring benefits

In this manner the policy makers set the strategic framework of rules under which the implementation process will occur. The initial statement of policy delineates the key cast of characters who will be involved in the implementation environment (directly, by designating actors to carry out policy, as well as indirectly, by providing resource incentives for others to make claims on the policy).

As the preceding chapter noted, the formal communication of

policies—as instructions about goals and means—from policy formulators to policy implementers can involve different breakdowns. We listed three sets of difficulties, or potential pitfalls, that can influence policy communications:

- Garbled messages from the senders.
- Misinterpretations by the receivers.
- System failure in terms of transmission breakdowns, overload and "noise," and inadequate follow-through or compliance mechanisms.

Actors in Environment I can increase or reduce these potential pitfalls in a number of ways. The most obvious way is by communicating a clear and concise set of instructions to implementers. While clarity does not ensure faithful compliance, it is a necessary first step toward effective implementation.

Clarity means being *specific* about both *what* is to be achieved and *how*. Both the goals of a policy and the means to achieve those goals must be stated in terms that are precise enough so that implementers know what they are supposed to do. In addition, policy directives should involve a statement of the implementers' responsibilities that is specific enough so that their performance can be assessed and they can be held accountable for their actions.

Since actors in both the implementation and evaluation environments enjoy discretion when their roles are left ambiguous by policy makers, clear definitions of roles and obligations reduce this discretion. Clear policy directives reduce the prospects for accidental misunderstanding of policy instructions on the part of recipients. They also, with less certainty, can increase the chances for responsible implementation and evaluation by

- reducing the possibility for implementer misinterpretation through a selective reading of ambiguous policies.
- reducing the chances that implementers' energies will be dissipated in disputes among themselves over the meaning of a policy.[2]
- aiding evaluators by presenting clear standards for assessing the extent to which a policy was actually implemented.

Yet, despite the obvious advantages of stating policy messages clearly and precisely, much of the literature on implementation has found that this often is not done. Policy makers do their work under a series of constraints, each of which can reduce the chances of producing a clear set of instructions to implementers. These limits include the following:

- Technical deficiencies—inadequate knowledge and information about the adequacy of alternative means for achieving goals.

- Conceptual complexity—limits on how well the problems are understood and defined.
- Political coalition-building considerations—limits that can result from the compromises needed to secure agreement for the approval of policies.

Since each of these constraints can have a significant influence on the clarity and content of policy directives, it is important to discuss them in more detail.

Constraints on Clarity of Policy Statements

Table 3-1 summarizes some of the factors that can affect the clarity of policy statements. It shows how particular policy maker characteristics can lead to constraints on clarity and produce several types of policy vagueness. In each instance resolution of ambiguities is left to implementers in Environment II.

Technical Limitations

or goal itself

It is difficult for policy makers to formulate clear instructions when they themselves are uncertain about what should be done. Vagueness, in this instance, will be lack of specificity about the means for achieving a goal. Moynihan argues that many of the problems encountered by the Community Action Program in the War on Poverty could be laid to an absence of reliable or proven techniques for achieving its ends:

> This is the essential fact: The Government did not know what it was doing. It had a theory. Or rather a set of theories. Nothing more. The U.S. Government at this time was no more in possession of a confident knowledge as to how to prevent delinquency, cure anomie, or overcome that midmorning sense of powerlessness than it was the possessor of a dependable formula for motivating Vietnamese villagers to fight communism.[3]

Banfield presents a similar characterization of problems in the Model Cities legislation:

> The new program would have been the product of (at best) the educated guesses of persons with experience and judgment but without any sort of technical expertise on the basis of which they could answer the really important questions. That the social and psychological approach would achieve worthwhile results, for example, was mere conjecture. No facts or tested theories existed from which a remedy for any of the ailments of the cities could have been derived.[4]

Table 3-1 *FACTORS THAT CAN AFFECT THE CLARITY OF POLICY STATEMENTS*

Policy Formation	Potential Constraints	Resulting Type of Vagueness
1. Policy makers are not technical specialists —active in many areas —sporadically involved in any single area	1. Technical limitations —inadequate information —complications when experts cannot agree on solutions using strictly technical criteria	1. Lack of specificity about means (e.g., Community Action Program, Model Cities)
2. Policy makers have diverse preferences	2a. Conceptual complexity —lack of agreement on how "problem" should be defined	2a. Lack of specificity about relationship of means to ends (e.g., guaranteed annual income)
	2b. Coalition-building considerations —vague goals can be used to build diverse coalitions —multiple (and contradictory) goals can be used to build coalitions	2b. Lack of specificity about goals or about the priority of goals to be achieved (e.g., Title I, ESEA)

In both the Community Action and Model Cities programs, limitations on available information led to unclear policy statements, which, in turn, resulted in significant conflicts during the implementation phase.

 Some writers argue that policy makers should not formulate policies when goals outstrip available knowledge. Amitai Etzioni, for example, writes:

> The "old-fashioned" mode of developing new programs, which is wasteful and alienating, limits the work that can be done. A program used to be launched, often on the hundred million, if not the billion, dollar level, on the basis of its political attractiveness and verbal and written arguments that it would work.[5]

Others simply note that this tendency is an inherent characteristic of political decision making. For example, James Schlesinger observes that

> the keynote of the Great Society has been the launching of new programs associated with substantial increases in government expenditures. Goals were announced (like the elimination of poverty) before any means of achieving them had been developed. Neither alternative policies nor the costs were studied until *after* a decision had been reached . . . My point here is neither to ascribe praise or blame to what is effective politics, nor . . . to raise questions regarding the merits of the programs themselves . . .[6]

Many politicians, argues Schlesinger, simply respond to demands for immediate action. They are more concerned with meeting those demands—by adopting a policy whose goals promise action—than they are with the requirements of finding policy means for actually achieving results.

 This is not to say that writing laws in which goals outstrip means is necessarily a cynical or fruitless activity. At a minimum, such policies commit societal resources to the search for technically feasible solutions. A student in the Dartmouth Seminar, Jonathan Wendell, analyzed the Clean Air Act of 1970. In his paper Wendell argued that the bill's sponsors understood the limitations on available means for achieving their goals but stated high goals anyway in the hope that the "technology-forcing" aspects of the act would encourage and clarify the subsequent understanding of appropriate means.[7] This is basically a variation on what Lindblom calls "incrementalism"—a decision-making strategy to cope with shortages of information—in which an action is undertaken because it is simultaneously a step toward a solution and a way of gathering better information for the next step.

Conceptual Complexity

In the preceding discussion we saw how vague policies could result from inadequate information about means for solving a commonly perceived problem. Another form of policy vagueness can grow out of the inability of policy makers to agree on the problem they are solving. When policy makers can clearly state the problem they want solved, such a statement guides implementers by establishing the proper relationship between a goal (the problem to be solved) and the means for reaching it. However, when the statement of the problem is ambiguous, implementers must guess at how the means selected relate to the problem being solved. This, of course, raises a problem for policy implementers, who must devise solutions for unclear problems, and for evaluators, who must gauge the adequacy of those solutions.

Charles Lindblom has made an excellent statement of the types of conceptual complexities that can be involved in identifying and defining a policy problem:

> Policy-makers are not faced with a *given* problem. Instead they have to identify and formulate their problem. Rioting breaks out in dozens of American cities. What is the problem? Maintaining law and order? Racial discrimination? Impatience of the Negroes with the pace of reform now that reform has gone far enough to give them hope? Incipient revolution? Black power? Low income? Lawlessness at the fringe of an otherwise relatively peaceful reform movement? Urban disorganization? Alienation?[8]

The causes of conceptual complexity in identifying policy problems are numerous. They can include the following:

- Such personal and psychological factors as the perceptual screen posed by differing ideological, constituency, and value perspectives.
- The relative ease of getting many political groups mobilized behind a vaguely stated problem ("urban crisis" or "environmental crisis") as compared with the narrower appeals of more precisely stated problems ("housing loan programs" or "solid-waste disposal").
- Societal concern with particularly complex problems that may be subject to many plausible interpretations.

Moynihan gives us a good example of how these conditions of conceptual complexity can operate simultaneously. In *The Politics of Guaranteed Annual Income*,[9] he cites a general problem—an increase in "welfare dependency"—that is subsequently reinterpreted as three different "problems" by policy makers with diverse ideological and organizational backgrounds and interests. The Department of Health, Education and Welfare conceived of it as a social service problem that required increased education and counseling activities. The Department of Labor viewed it as an unemployment problem that required job training programs. The White House Domestic Council believed it was an income strategy problem that required a presidential initiative in behalf of a guaranteed annual income.

Such diverse interpretations resulted from the conceptual complexities involved in defining the root causes of "welfare dependency." In turn, the consequences of these different interpretations provided each agency with incentives—organizational growth and maintenance, responsiveness to societal concerns, and the like—to arrive at its own unique interpretation of how to deal with the problem. While each could agree that the increase in welfare dependency was a real symptom, the nature of the illness was so poorly understood that each could use it as a justification for enhancing its own interests.

Coalition Building

Politics is normally thought of as a way of resolving conflicts that cannot be resolved by other means. In problem areas in which technical information about how best to achieve goals, or a consensus on the goals themselves, does not exist, disputes are resolved by recourse to political power. When no clear majority exists for a particular approach, political "solutions" will result from the coalition-building efforts of policy makers who try to get many diverse interests to agree on a common policy. When the requirements of building political coalitions conflict with the requirements of clear policy—when people making demands on politicians want different things—clear policy usually suffers.

The most basic political problem confronting policy makers in a pluralist system is the need to secure enough agreement among themselves, and among relevant interest groups, to gain approval of policies. Passing a law, for example, requires concurrent majorities in Congress and the agreement of the president. Since Congress and the executive are complex arenas, each offers multiple points of access for the many groups that can seek to influence policy making. The challenge facing the policy makers thus becomes one of satisfying as many of the people who are making demands on government as possible. Under these circumstances the test of "good" policy, Lindblom argues, is often reduced to its usefulness in gaining the support of policy makers who do not necessarily agree on either the problem they are solving or the ends they seek to achieve.[10]

Thus, for the policy maker the job of getting people to agree on a policy can become a goal in itself. It can also be viewed as a means of achieving good policy:

> Speaker O'Neill likes to tell the story of a little boy whose father made jigsaw puzzles for him by cutting up pictures in magazines. One day the father took a picture of the globe and ripped it into many pieces. The little boy put the puzzle together in a short time, surprising the father with the boy's speed.

The father asked how the boy was able to put the map of the world together so quickly. The boy responded that the other side of the picture of the world had on it a picture of a little boy's face. The boy simply put the face together and turned it over to form the picture of the world. The moral to this story is if you get people together, the world will take care of itself.[11]

A vague statement of policy can help the coalition-building process in several ways. It is often easier to get agreement on an abstract statement of principles—such as "equality of educational opportunity"—than it is to reach agreement on more concrete statements that involve difficult trade-offs among values. Furthermore, vagueness may be regarded by interest groups as a further opportunity to influence the shape of policy once it leaves the formal policy-making arena of Environment I. For example, different parts of the school lobby could accept the vague language of the Elementary and Secondary Education Act because each viewed this as contributing to its ability to influence this legislation during the implementation stage. In such cases vagueness becomes a way of postponing or rescheduling conflicting political demands so that they do not become due simultaneously, as they would if the formal statement of policy were definitive.

Two kinds of policy vagueness can result from the need for policy makers to build coalitions. Coalitions can be built around vague goals that sound good to participants for a variety of reasons. And coalitions can be built by offering to address many diverse and even conflicting goals, each of which is attractive to particular actors. In each instance the resulting policy statement offers unclear directions to implementers.

While coalition building is a necessary step in policy making, it is not a step that requires genuine consensus among participants. Instead, policy makers can agree on a general policy without agreeing on the details of what it actually means. Thus, the grounds for future interpretive conflicts during implementation are often laid by the ambiguous directions of policy-making majorities that are profoundly divided, transient, unaware of the ultimate consequences of their actions, or a combination of all these things.

Political Intensity: Signals and Cues

Even if the constraints on clarity just discussed can be surmounted, there remains the chance that a policy message will be misinterpreted, or reinterpreted, by implementers. This occurs because, as the next chapter indicates, policy implementers are faced with organizational, informational, and political problems that are different from those facing the actors in Environment I.

Communication is not restricted to written messages such as laws, executive orders, administrative directives, and regulations. Since implementers are often political actors in their own right, they pay attention to *both* the written directives *and* other political cues in assessing how they are expected to interpret their instructions.

One important cue to policy implementers relates to the strength of the policy-making coalition that is sending the message. Strength is assessed by

- The size of the coalition.
- Its stability.
- The degree of consensus within the coalition on the meaning of the policy instruction.

Specific demonstrations of strength can include

- Continuous monitoring by interested constituencies to back up a specific interpretation of a policy, including follow-up messages that reiterate, or clarify, the original policy.
- Intervention by policy makers during implementation to reinforce a specific interpretation of a policy.
- Credit claiming by policy makers in order to associate themselves with a policy during its implementation phase.

A series of examples will illustrate how each of these demonstrations of strength can influence the attitudes of policy implementers toward policy instructions.

Monitoring

A rather direct message to implementers that a policy-making coalition persists is found in the continuous transmission of messages from interested constituencies about how a policy should be interpreted. Messages to implementers from coalitions whose strength is demonstrated repeatedly are likely to be taken seriously.

The Supreme Court's policy on voting rights is an example of how constituency monitoring can affect recipient interpretations. When the initial implementers of this policy—political officials in the South—chose to ignore the original policy directives, repeated challenges by civil rights groups and other interested parties ultimately wore down the possibility of either selective interpretation or subterfuge. These challenges led to further specificity in the policy—striking down particular subterfuges such as racial gerrymandering—which reduced the scope of misinterpretation. The capacity of the Court to marshal repeated majorities to reaffirm and clarify the original policy also reduced hopes that the policy was a transient one.

Evidence that monitoring activities are very important in the interpretation of policies can be found in cases in which recalcitrant implementers have ignored clear policy directives in order to distort policies in favor of particularly active constituency groups who opposed those directives. Clayton Koppes's analysis of the Newlands Reclamation Act of 1902 is a case in point.[12] Basically, this act placed a very clear limit on recipients of federally subsidized water, with each recipient eligible to receive such water for a maximum of 160 acres. The policy makers' intent was to encourage the development of relatively small farms and to restrict the subsidy to small landowners. The means to accomplish this policy goal—the 160-acre limitation—was specified very precisely in the act. Despite its clarity, the Department of the Interior has consistently chosen not to implement this limitation, and large landholders, particularly in California's Central Valley, have benefited from projects covered by the act. In short, the Interior Department consistently refused to accept the full meaning of the act. Its intransigence was supported by a coalition of large landowners who repeatedly sent messages that influenced implementers to reinterpret the policy in favor of large agricultural interests. Small farmers were less agressive in monitoring implementation and protecting their interests. While Congress has, on occasion, declined to repeal the limitation, neither has it encouraged Interior to actually carry out the implementation as originally stipulated.

Intervention

In addition to constituency monitoring, there are other ways of influencing how implementers interpret policy messages. While monitoring involves follow-up action by outside constituencies, intervention is often the act of individual policy makers. Here an interested policy maker influences the degree of attention paid to the message. A powerful policy maker who intervenes in behalf of a particular interpretation of a policy helps clarify the message to the implementer. Of course, the message may range from "Carry out the policy faithfully as written" to "Selectively interpret it my way."

Eugene Bardach gives us the example of a legislator who repeatedly intervened in the implementation of a bill he had sponsored. Assemblyman Frank Lanterman, author of a reform in California mental health laws, served the role of a "fixer" who worked with policy implementers to ensure that the policy was faithfully understood and implemented.[13]

Jerome Murphy's description of the role of the Johnson White House in the implementation of the Elementary and Secondary Education Act forms a counterpoint to Bardach's example. When Commissioner of Education Francis Keppel delayed the granting of education funds to Chicago because he was concerned that city's interpretation of the Act was inconsistent with its stated intent of increasing educational opportunities to the disadvantaged, the White House overruled him and intervened in Mayor Daley's behalf. Funds were released, and Commissioner Keppel resigned some months later.[14] This signal, of course, did not have the effect of encouraging strict interpretation of that title of ESEA by other implementers.

Credit Claiming

Another cue for policy implementers about continued political support for a particular interpretation of a policy is the willingness of politicians to associate themselves with a program by claiming credit for its accomplishments. For example, the Social Security Administration used to get constant reassurance that its mission of aiding the elderly through a faithful interpretation of Medicare is appreciated and supported by politicians. On the other hand, the Medical Services Administration, which is responsible for Medicaid, receives little such encouragement in aiding its welfare recipient clients. Former Medicaid Commissioner Howard Newman noted the difference as symbolized in references by members of Congress during appropriations hearings to Medicare's "beneficiaries" as opposed to Medicaid's "recipients."[15]

Anticipating Systems Failure

In the preceding chapter we introduced the rather general concept of systems failure to cover a large category of pitfalls encountered during implementation. Examples of such failure include the absence of effective communications mechanisms to transmit messages from one environment to another, the general level of "noise" in the communications system because of message overload, and the absence of follow-up, or compliance, mechanisms. The contributions that policy makers can make to ameliorate these pitfalls are largely—although not entirely—confined to anticipating them in the design of policies.

A policy instruction is basically a design that indicates what must occur before a goal can be achieved. A poor design can lead to systems failure in a number of ways:

1. Designation of inappropriate organizations to carry out the policy:
   a. Organizations whose priorities conflict with those of the policy,

creating problems of "selective interpretation," "tokenism," and "diversion of resources."[16]
   b. Organizations lacking the technical competence to carry out the policy.[17]
2. Making the design too complex to achieve results in a timely fashion by requiring the serial approval and action of many disparate actors.
3. Failure to commit adequate resources to the tasks assigned:
   a. Insufficient money (spreading funds too thinly, as in Model Cities, or not allocating enough as in the compliance staff at HEW for Title IX of the Civil Rights Act).[18]
   b. Insufficient time (the demand for immediate results led the Job Corps to recruit volunteers prior to the creation of adequate facilities).

The capacity of policy makers to plan around these pitfalls is constrained by the amount of information available to them. These limits are both "political" and "technical":

1. Political limits can include the "unrepresentativeness" of policy coalitions:
   a. The constellation of groups making demands on policy makers is often distinct from the constellation of groups that will be active during implementation.
   b. As a result, the information policy makers receive in Environment I may be incomplete or biased about what is likely to happen during implementation in Environment II.
2. Technical limits on information:
   a. Good designs require the specification of proven and implementable means.
   b. For many popular policy goals these means are not certain.

Despite these constraints, there are things that policy makers can do to reduce the chances of systems failure. A number of writers have suggested partial remedies for each of the faults just outlined. Bardach, for example, advised policy makers to plan for implementer intransigence by making use of a variety of specific techniques whose titles suggest their substance: Do without; create substitutes; foster competition; buy off or co-opt opponents; build and maintain countervailing groups.[19] Amitai Etzioni points out that technical limits are not insurmountable. Our ignorance, he notes, is not uniform. By picking goals for which means are known, one can make an accurate calibration of expectations and resources.[20] Furthermore, each policy initiative, as Donald Campbell notes, is an opportunity for improving our store of technical knowledge, making further gains possible in the next round.[21]

Summary

A number of different conditions in the policy formation environment can have a significant influence on the implementation and evaluation of policies.

A key factor is the clarity, or lack of it, in policy instructions and directives. Clarity can be affected by a variety of constraints, such as inadequate information, the conceptual complexities involved in identifying and defining policy problems, the usefulness of ambiguity in forming majority coalitions, and the existence of miscellaneous signals and cues that further specify or confuse the meaning of policy. Policy makers can ameliorate systems failure through remedial initiatives.

The manner in which the policy makers deal with each of these factors will have a direct impact on what takes place in the implementation and evaluation environments. In addition, each of these environments is guided by its own internal dynamics, which can further influence the processes of policy implementation and evaluation.

Notes

1. Jeffrey L. Pressman and Aaron Wildavsky, *Implementation* (Berkeley: University of California Press, 1973), p. xiii.

2. Robert T. Nakamura and Dianne M. Pinderhughes, "Changing Anacostia: Definition and Implementation," paper delivered at the American Educational Research Association Meeting, Toronto, March 1978.

3. Daniel P. Moynihan, *Maximum Feasible Misunderstanding* (New York: Free Press, 1970), p. 170.

4. Edward C. Banfield, "Making a New Federal Program," in Alan P. Sindler, *Policy and Politics in America* (Boston: Little, Brown, 1973), p. 155.

5. Amitai Etzioni, "Societal Overload," *Political Science Quarterly*, Winter 1977–78, p. 626.

6. James Schlesinger, "Systems Analysis and the Political Process," *Journal of Law and Economics* (1966), pp. 281–298.

7. Jonathan Wendell, "Implementation of Title II of the 1970 Clean Air Act Amendments," Dartmouth College, Government 83, 1978. See also Charles Jones, *An Introduction to the Study of Public Policy* (Belmont, Calif.: Wadsworth, 1970), pp. 61–65.

8. Charles E. Lindblom, *The Policy-Making Process* (Englewood Cliffs, N.J.: Prentice-Hall, 1968), p. 13.

9. Daniel P. Moynihan, *The Politics of Guaranteed Annual Income* (New York: Vintage, 1973).

10. Lindblom, *The Policy-Making Process*, p. 13.

11. Paraphrased from Martin Tolchin, "An Old Pol Takes on the New President," *New York Times Magazine*, July 24, 1977.

12. Clayton R. Koppes, "Public Water, Private Land Origins of the Acreage Limitation Controversy, 1933–53," *Pacific Historical Review*, 47 (November 1978).

13. Eugene Bardach, *The Implementation Game* (Cambridge, Mass.: M.I.T. Press, 1977).

14. Jerome Murphy, "The Education Bureaucracies Implement Novel Policy: The Politics of Title I of ESEA, 1965–72," in Sindler, *Policy and Politics in America.*

15. Howard Newman, former commissioner, HEW Medical Services Administration, in a talk to students in policy implementation seminar, Dartmouth College, Government 83, 1978.

16. See, e.g., Koppes's discussion of the Department of the Interior and the 160-acre limitation; Murphy on the Office of Education and ESEA (both cited earlier). See also Grant McConnell, "Preemption: The Politics of Land and Water," in his book *Private Power and American Democracy* (New York: Vintage, 1966).

17. For a discussion of the sources of organizational incompetence, see Bardach, *The Implementation Game*, on obstacles to implementation.

18. Michael Yoshii, research paper on affirmative action policy, Dartmouth College, Government 83, 1978.

19. Bardach, *The Implementation Game.*

20. Etzioni, "Societal Overload."

21. Donald Campbell, "Reforms as Experiments," *American Psychologist*, April 1969.

Chapter 4

Policy Implementation (Environment II)

In a special issue of *Policy Analysis*, the guest editor, Walter Williams, observed that "there is a Kafkaesque aspect to the implementation area . . . It is a crucial area, yet people act as if it didn't exist."[1] As was noted in the opening chapter, this is due, in part, to the fact that many observers who endorsed the earlier "classical" dichotomy between policy and administration assumed that the major political battles were over once a policy was formally adopted. Recent studies have indicated, however, that political pressures within the implementation environment can be extremely lively, dynamic, and complex.

A variety of different forces can shape the implementation process once policy has been formulated. Our analysis will focus on three key influences within the implementation environment: (1) actors and arenas, (2) organizational structures and bureaucratic norms, and (3) communications networks and compliance mechanisms.

Actors and Arenas

Many different actors, operating out of diverse arenas, can attempt to exercise political leverage within the implementation environment. These actors can include policy makers, formal implementers, intermediaries, administrative lobbies, powerful individuals, policy recipients or "consumers," the mass media, and other interested parties.

Policy Makers

As the previous chapter has emphasized, in addition to formulating policy, policy makers from Environment I can attempt to influence actors in the implementation environment by monitoring, intervening, and/or credit claiming. The signals they transmit through their activities can have a significant political impact on the implementation process.

Formal Implementers

Formal implementers consist of those actors in the governmental arena who are expressly granted the legal authority, responsibility, and public resources to carry out policy directives. Such implementers can include administrators within departments, agencies, bureaus, and regulatory commissions at the federal level, or their counterparts in state, regional, or local governments. Since these individuals carry the burden of the implementation process, their actions will be analyzed in more detail in subsequent parts of this chapter.

Intermediaries*

As defined in this study, intermediaries are individuals or groups that are delegated responsibility by formal implementers to assist in carrying out public policies. Hence, if the federal government is implementing a policy, intermediaries could consist of state and/or local officials who, under other circumstances, might serve as formal implementers in their own right. In addition, American governmental officials at all levels often make use of private sector intermediaries to carry out public policies.

Two new variations in this historical pattern of intermediary utilization have occurred during recent decades. The first has involved a rapidly growing delegation of responsibility by the federal government to state and local intermediaries to carry out the day-to-day implementation of federal programs. As Williams has pointed out, under this kind of "mixed model"

> the federal government [is] involved in varying degrees in the specification of the priorities and objectives, the determination of the nature of the process

*Different terminology has been used in various works to describe this group of actors: *intermediaries, providers, secondary implementers, third-sector organizations,* and the like.

through which decisions are made at the local and state levels, and/or the monitoring and evaluation of projects and programs.[2]

Because this approach relies very heavily on state and local intermediaries to deliver services, it has led to the creation of multiple arenas of implementation within the governmental sector itself. Since the implementation of public policies under these conditions can involve actors from all three levels of government simultaneously, this can greatly increase the complexity of the process. At a minimum, such multiple arenas require the establishment of an expanded set of linkages *within* Environment II, between the federal implementers and state and local intermediaries.

If these linkages are not constructed carefully, the results can be chaotic. As Williams notes,

> Responsibility for implementation [can] slip between the cracks. Almost everyone assumes that specification and implementation are somebody else's task. Higher-ups see implementation as being a lower-level responsibility; but the lower levels look to higher echelons for specifications and guidance.[3]

In addition, this diffusion of intergovernmental responsibilities can allow the attitudes, norms, expectations, and perceptions of state and local intermediaries to shape policy implementation to meet these intermediaries' preconceptions of policy goals. Hence, the use of state and local intermediaries can pose difficult challenges to federal implementers.

A second major development in the use of intermediaries has involved growing governmental reliance on the private sector to provide an ever-widening and more diffuse array of "soft" social services. For many years governments have contracted with private sector intermediaries for "hardware" (e.g., aircraft, armored vechicles, and ships for the military services). While this may have produced abuses in the form of kickbacks and the like, there were generally clearly identifiable (and usually quantifiable) criteria that could be used to determine whether these private sector intermediaries were meeting their contractual obligations. Now, however, government is turning to doctors, hospitals, nursing homes, and other private professional groups to administer Medicare and Medicaid, and to private industry, unions, and universities to meet affirmative action goals, under much more uncertain and ambiguous criteria.

As emphasis has shifted to the use of state and local government, plus private sector, intermediaries to deliver federally funded public services, this has led to more linkages, more decision points, and more complexity, in addition to placing increased importance on the development of compliance mechanisms to move these intermediaries in desired directions.

Lobbies and Constituency Groups

In addition to the policy makers, formal implementers, and the intermediaries, a fourth group—administrative lobbies and other constituency groups—can constitute a powerful set of actors in the implementation environment. One of the most interesting discussions of the role of interest groups in implementation is found in Beryl Radin's book on civil rights enforcement by the Department of Health, Education and Welfare (HEW). Radin's study makes it clear that administrative lobbying can take two quite different forms.

The first occurs when outside groups attempt to pressure implementers to administer policies in ways that advance their perceived self-interest. Well-documented examples of this type of lobbying effort can be found in various studies of industry attempts to pressure regulatory agencies such as the Federal Communications Commission and the Civil Aeronautics Board to interpret governmental policies in a manner favorable to the industry's goals.

The key focus of Radin's analysis, however, is on a second, quite different type of administrative lobbying. Radin criticizes the failure of the Office of Education and the HEW civil rights staff to develop a strong interest group coalition to support HEW's own civil rights program initiatives. According to her,

> Nearly 80 organizations, crossing racial, economic, and religious lines, put together one of the most disciplined and effective lobbying efforts Congressional observers have recalled in order to press for the passage of the Civil Rights Act of 1964. But this activism failed to carry over into the implementation environment. Once the legislation was enacted, the Leadership Conference on Civil Rights, and other groups which had been active in the legislative arena, failed to develop a sustained program of administrative lobbying. The cathartic effect of seeing the legislation enacted pacified the lobby groups, despite the obvious wide latitude for interpretation (and misinterpretation) of the Act, particularly under Title VI.[4]

Radin makes it clear that implementers can deliberately encourage interest constituencies to intervene in administrative decisions in a manner that supports agency objectives. As Francis E. Rourke puts it,

> In an open system of politics, a vital source of power for administrative agencies is their ability to attract the support of outside groups. Strength in a constituency is no less an asset for an American administrator than it is for a politician, and some agencies have succeeded in building outside support as formidable as that of any political organization.[5]

A classic illustration of this approach to administrative lobbying is seen in Philip Selznick's description of the Tennessee Valley Authority's efforts to develop support for its programs during the 1930s.[6] A seminar paper written by Stephen Dorvee describes this "grassroots" approach as follows:

> There was ample reason for the Agricultural Relations Department to go to the grassroots . . . The use of the extension service was beneficial to ARD. The county extension agent had connections with local farmers . . . and was usually quite politically powerful on the local scene. Thus if the program was accepted by the agent, then it was more likely to be accepted by the population as a whole.
>
> By adopting the grassroots doctrine, the Department (and of course the TVA as a whole) was able to stand as the champion of the local institutions, and thus devise a viewpoint which could be used to justify its managerial autonomy within the federal system. In essence, the TVA agricultural program developed an administrative constituency . . . and, in times of need, the Authority had easily mobilizable support.[7]

In addition to lobbies and administrative coalitions, powerful individuals can have a decided influence on implementation outcomes, especially under the discretionary conditions described earlier.

There are numerous other examples of the role of interest groups in the implementation environment, but the cases already cited are sufficient to indicate that administrative constituencies can play a crucial role in shaping policy implementation.

Recipients and "Consumers"

Although many governmental policies are intended to benefit different groups of beneficiaries, some observers would argue that the policy "consumers" are the last to be included in the implementation process. This may well have been true historically, but as new policies have placed increased emphasis on a growing range of social concerns there has been a parallel movement to involve recipients more directly in the implementation of those policies.

Some of these new social initiatives have led to a pattern of program administration in which "consumers become implementers." This trend toward "consumer implementation" became most apparent in efforts to promote "citizen participation" under some of the Great Society legislative enactments of the 1960s. Section 202(a)(3) of the Economic Opportunity Act of 1964 marked a major move in this direction when it called for antipoverty programs that were to be "developed, conducted, and administered with the maximum feasible participation of the residents of the groups served." The Economic Opportunity Act's emphasis on "maximum feasible participation" led to a pattern of "consumer implementation" under which recipients were actually granted significant powers, including authority to establish relatively autonomous Community Action Agencies to implement antipoverty programs.

Another example that involves delegation of important implementation powers to policy "consumers" is described in a seminar paper by Mitchell Zeller. Zeller analyzes the Neighborhood Housing Services Program (NHS), which was administered by the Urban Reinvestment Task Force in cooperation with the Department of Housing and Urban Development and other federal agencies. This program, which began in Pittsburgh in 1967, involved a unique pattern of federal administration. Instead of attempting to dominate all policy planning, the federal administrators acted as "facilitators" in an effort to bring together neighborhood groups, local banks, and other parties in decaying sections of urban areas to reverse urban decline by providing support for improved housing. According to Zeller's study,

> Of all the actors in NHS, the residents play the most important role . . . In Pittsburgh they played the crucial role . . . Most of the local government officials agreed that without the commitment of the citizens, the program would not have succeeded. Therefore, any replication of NHS must have citizens as its base.[8]

As Zeller points out, the original NHS program enjoyed considerable success because of the participatory involvement of local citizens. The potential problem with this approach, however, is that it creates still another layer of intermediary actors—the consumers—and hence adds still another level of complexity to the implementation process. At a minimum, these new groups of participants call for the creation of additional linkages within the implementation environment.

The Media

"On the morning of April 25, 1966, the *Wall Street Journal* ran the following headline: URBAN AID KICKOFF: ADMINISTRATION SELECTS OAKLAND AS FIRST CITY IN REBUILDING PROGRAM."

Thus begins the opening chapter of Pressman and Wildavsky's *Implementation*. Other headlines appear later in the book that carry a less reassuring tone:

U.S. INVESTS $1,085,000 TO CREATE 43 OAKLAND JOBS
(*Oakland Tribune*, March, 1969)

OAKLAND MINORITY JOB PROGRAM LABELED A PRETTY BIG
DISASTER (*Los Angeles Times*, March, 1969)[9]

These headlines indicate the presence of a sixth set of powerful actors in
the implementation environment—the press and the other mass media
outlets, which report their own interpretations of program implementation and thereby shape the perceptions of the public, the policy makers,
and the policy implementers as well.

Because the media can influence these different groups, it has the
capacity to exercise tremendous leverage on the implementation process.
On the positive side, the press can perform the role of helping to keep
implementers honest in a variety of ways. First, aggressive reporting can
smoke out inflated reports of program accomplishments that implementers might foist onto the public, or their superiors, in an effort to gloss
over a mediocre performance. Second, the press can sound an early alarm
on potential program difficulties that implementers might try to disguise
in the hope that improvements are just around the corner. Third, the
press can dramatize legitimate accomplishments in order to enhance
support for successful implementation programs. Because of the media's
influence, most implementers go to great efforts to build and maintain a
strong media image.

In addition, however, the press can complicate the implementation
process and, under certain conditions, even influence performance in a
questionable manner. This is especially true in policy programs that are
highly visible and/or in which performance is relatively easy to publicize
on an almost continuous basis.

A seminar paper by Stephen Munger on the implementation of wage
and price controls under the Nixon administration focuses on the latter
problem. As Munger points out, a major characteristic of economic policy
implementation is

> the high visibility of its output . . . This is so for an obvious reason: the
> abundance of simple, numerical economic indicators. Every month, such
> figures as the rate of change in the Consumer Price Index (CPI) or the
> percentage of the work force unemployed are displayed with page one
> emphasis. This provides positive benefits in that progress toward "social"
> goals can be measured in such a way that agitation for movement toward
> these goals can take place in a continuous fashion.

Munger goes on to argue that there may be some negative aspects to
this high visibility:

> First, the indicators given most attention are rather imprecise . . . but the
> popular attention given to these figures may inflate their weight in the policy
> process . . .

A second problem caused by visibility on an almost continuous basis is that short-term considerations often take precedence over long-term ones. Popular support would probably swing to the President who says we are implementing a hard-hitting program to reduce the rate of inflation *now*, rather than to one who says we are initiating a program of long-term study and careful action to get at the structural roots of inflation.

Finally, because it creates "self-fulfilling" expectations, high visibility can build an inflationary basis into the economy. By "self-fulfilling" expectations is meant that if actors in economy anticipate inflation, they may act in such a way that, in the aggregate, will create more inflation.[10]

If Munger's warnings are correct, the press and the other media not only can serve to monitor and publicize implementation but also may have a direct impact on the outcome of implementation efforts.

Evaluators

A final group of actors who may intervene in the implementation environment are the evaluators who attempt to measure various aspects of program performance. Since the next chapter is devoted to a consideration of policy evaluation, it is not necessary here to elaborate on the actions of the evaluators beyond emphasizing the fact that they can have an important effect on policy implementation.

Summary

The implementation environment contains a variety of different actors, operating out of divergent arenas, who jockey back and forth in an attempt to influence the course of policy implementation. It is the job of the formal implementers to coordinate the activities of these actors in a way that will lead to successful and effective program performance. This is primarily a political challenge, since virtually none of the formal implementers have the dictatorial authority to order all of these diverse actors to conform to their commands, especially when these actors are located in outside arenas such as lobby groups or the press. As a result, the implementers must often rely very heavily on persuasion, negotiation, and compromise in their attempts to orchestrate the other actors who occupy the policy implementation environment.

Organizational Structures and Bureaucratic Norms

The particular organizations and institutions chosen to implement policies can significantly influence how those policies are carried out.

After reviewing relevant literature on organization theory, Richard Elmore identifies four distinct institutional models, each of which describes an alternative approach to the implementation process:[11]

- The "systems management model" views implementation as an ordered, goal-directed activity.
- The "bureaucratic process model" views implementation as a more routine process of continually controlling discretion.
- The "organizational development model" views implementation as a participatory process in which implementers shape policies and claim them as their own.
- The "conflict and bargaining model" views implementation as a conflict and bargaining process.

The first of these models relates most closely to the "classical" approach discussed at the outset of this study, and the final model fits more directly into the "principle of circularity" described by Rein and Rabinovitz. Whichever organizational alternative is chosen to carry out policies, implementers within these organizations must deal with a common set of issues that relate to internal organizational procedures, resource allocation, and bureaucratic norms.

Internal Procedures

A variety of organizational factors can influence an institution's implementation efforts. One of the most crucial of these involves the communications procedures that are relied upon to hold the organization together.

Some observers tend to evaluate communications solely in terms of clarity and accuracy—are messages and commands precise enough to be understood by those who are responsible for carrying them out? However, other procedural considerations, in addition to clarity, are important. One such factor is speed. Is the response rapid enough to deal with the problem at hand? Actors in Elmore's "systems management" or "bureaucratic process" models, for example, may go to great lengths to ensure that messages are delineated clearly and precisely, but this procedure may take so long that the communications are no longer relevant by the time they have been transmitted. Another important factor is responsiveness. If messages are formulated solely by implementers at the top of a hierarchical structure, they may fail to incorporate the insights of intermediaries and/or "consumers" and, hence, may be unresponsive to the issues they are attempting to address.

In addition to communications, administrative distance can represent an important organizational influence. In an analysis of the implementation of the Comprehensive Employment and Training Act (CETA) of 1973, Williams identifies "the long process from policy to operations" as a critical problem. According to Williams,

> A vast distance in layers of bureaucracy stands between the major decisions made at the top of the policy sphere and ultimate service delivery at the bottom of the operations sphere... All along the way, many minor and perhaps some major choices are made that in sum can alter substantially a policy's original intent. Moreover, in the long process of movement from the policy sphere to the operations sphere, people may lose sight of who is responsible for implementing and carrying out policies.[12]

Complexity is still another important organizational factor. While Elmore's "conflict and bargaining" model may imply more complexity than a tighter "systems management" model, complexity can affect any of his four models. Key factors that tend to increase complexity relate to the internal decision-making structure of the organization itself (the more levels and clearances, the greater the complexity); the degree of reliance placed on the use of intermediaries (the more intermediaries, the greater the complexity); and the extent of what Bardach calls "piling on" (the more actors from all arenas who enter the process, and add their own goals, the greater the complexity).

Hence, procedures relating to communications, administrative distance, and complexity can affect all of the organizational models described by Elmore, and thereby influence the process of policy implementation.

Allocation of Resources

The allocation of—and potential constraints on—resources can have such an obvious and direct impact on the implementation process that it is hardly necessary to dwell upon this topic in detail.

Administrative resources can come in a wide variety of colors. One of them is green. Money is certainly a key resource for implementing policies, since it can be used to finance the workings of administrative agencies, to procure goods and services, as an incentive to move intermediary actors, and to provide cash benefits to policy "consumers."

Time is another critical resource that, paradoxically, can have at least two contradictory impacts on the implementation process. On the one hand, implementers can rush ahead and move very rapidly when time is running out on authorized appropriations. Conversely, implementers can cite lack of time as an excuse for inertia.

Time contraints can be particularly important during the initial stages of policy implementation, when plans may be formulated very quickly. A classic example of this is found in Pressman and Wildavsky's analysis of the initiation of the Economic Development Administration's unemployment program in Oakland by Assistant Secretary of Commerce Eugene P. Foley and his special representative Amory Bradford:

> Why did Foley and his aides choose to concentrate on one city? One constraint on this decision was surely the lack of available time in which to spend EDA's first appropriation . . . Only four months remained in which to process nearly $300 million worth of projects, since any not completed and approved by the end of May could not be funded out of the 1966 appropriation, which would expire June 30. Bradford pointed out that the agency had a certain incentive to spend its allotted funds, for if EDA failed to use all of its current appropriations, the next year's appropriation would almost certainly be cut by the Budget Bureau and Congress.[13]

Another key resource is the adequacy and competency of staff, which may or may not be dependent on the availability of money. An example of a case in which inadequate funding appears to have been a constraint on staff support is seen in HEW's efforts to administer the Medicaid program:

> While Congress finally approved a supplemental appropriation for additional staff, staffing continued to be minimal. On Commissioner [Howard] Newman's arrival in February 1970, the Medical Services Administration (MSA) had a total of 80 on its staff in Washington, including secretaries, with responsibility for disbursing over $2 billion in federal money . . . While additional appropriations provided for another 80 persons, there were still only 160 people in MSA in Washington, and these henceforth had the heavy duty of monitoring and managing Medicaid. As a note of comparison, there were about 800 people running Medi-Cal in Sacramento.[14]

Even when money is available, however, staff resources may be inadequate because of limited availability of qualified personnel. An illustration of this is provided in Jerome Murphy's study of the implementation of Title I ESEA education programs in Massachusetts:

> Although the state Title I director had been unsuccessfully trying to hire two additional staff members, his problem was not money. For several years, the state had been returning federal funds earmarked for state administration of the program; almost $100,000 was returned in 1969. The Title I director argued that a major problem was finding competent people willing to work for the Department.[15]

In addition to money, time, and staff, another critical administrative resource is power—the ability to move other actors to implement policy goals. Since this resource is so central to the implementation process, it is discussed at greater length in a later section of this chapter.

For the present it is important to recognize that knowledge and power are very closely interrelated in any bureaucratic setting. The original social theorist of bureaucracy, Max Weber, argued that "the decisive reason for the advance of bureaucratic organization has always been its purely technical superiority over any other form of organization."[16] A more recent administrative theorist, Francis E. Rourke of Johns Hopkins University, begins his latest book with the assertion that

> in all modern societies—whether democratic or nondemocratic—a first and fundamental source of power for bureaucratic organizations is the expertise they command—the fact that administrators bring to the policy process a wide variety of skills necessary both for making decisions on policy and for carrying out these decisions . . . Nothing contributes more to bureaucratic power than the ability of career officials to mold the views of other participants in the policy process.[17]

Hence, the organizational structures within which policy implementers operate constitute an important asset as well as a potential liability. On the one hand, this institutional framework gives a necessary degree of continuity and underlying stability to the implementation process. Conversely, however, the bureaucratic norms that characterize this institutional setting can also produce rigidities and inertia, which may distort the implementation of policy goals.

Psychological Motivations and Bureaucratic Norms

A third major factor that can influence administrative performance grows out of the psychological motivations of the implementers and the bureaucratic norms that permeate the agencies and institutions in which those implementers work.

In discussing psychological motivations Van Meter and Van Horn note that "implementers may screen out a clear message when the decision seems to contradict deeply cherished beliefs." In addition, the intensity of the implementers' dispositions may affect their performance. "Those holding intense negative preferences may be led to outright and open defiance of the program's objectives . . . Less intense attitudes may cause implementers to attempt surreptitious diversion and evasion."[18] Other psychological influences may be related less to disagreements over policy beliefs than to the personal work styles and self-interest of the implementers. For example, implementation can be subjected to "tokenism" efforts by implementers who play the "easy life" game described by Bardach.[19]

In addition to being affected by the motivations and beliefs of individual actors, bureaucratic institutions are guided by collective sets of internal social norms that define acceptable behavior. In an article on organizational structure as "myth and ceremony," two Stanford University sociologists, John W. Meyer and Brian Rowan, argue that ceremonial influences can be extremely important to the inner workings of any institution (such as a government agency) that places a high premium on conformity to ceremonial rules as an indicator of its effectiveness in the absence of clear-cut criteria that can be used to measure external efficiency.[20] Indeed, some institutions place such a high premium on these ceremonial rules that they can constitute the basis of the institution's internal reward structure.

One such rule, or norm, can involve "keeping the peace" (i.e., not rocking the boat). This norm, which favors gradual change over drastic change, places a high value on bureaucratic routine as a desirable end in itself. Other norms, which are cited as "bureaucratic imperatives" by Rein and Rabinovitz, relate to the long-range self-interest of the institution and involve "concern for institutional maintenance, protection, and growth."[21]

The study of bureaucratic norms represents such a rich and complex field of inquiry that it is impossible to cover every aspect of this subject in a discussion of the policy implementation environment. Many volumes have been written on what Charles Peters and Michael Nelson call "the culture of bureaucracy."[22] The important point is that the political environment that characterizes many implementing agencies can often take on a life of its own that may or may not coincide with the goals of the policy makers who inhabit Environment I. A clear illustration of this can be seen in Rourke's discussion of the "tendency of bureaucratic momentum to transform small-scale commitments into large ones." As he points out,

> The momentum of the organizations charged with putting a decision into effect may make it very difficult to stop or reverse gears once the bureaucratic machinery has been set into motion. Irreversibility may thus become a major hazard of policy decisions carried out through large organizations.
>
> A chief factor contributing to such irreversibility is the fact that large bureaucracies arrive at policy positions only after an elaborate process of consultation and accommodation among diverse organizational interests. Agreements negotiated with such painstaking effort resist change, because such change would require reopening the whole bargaining process with no guarantee that the trade-offs required might not yield a less effective policy outcome.[23]

The internal norms that influence the perceptions, and often the actions, of administrators can cut in different directions in terms of their impact on policy implementation. As Peter Blau and Marshall Meyer have observed in their book *Bureaucracy in Modern Society*,

> Social processes in bureaucracies modify their structures and operations. Some of these processes make the organization more flexible and responsive to changing conditions, such as the informal modifications of formal procedures . . . but other bureaucratic processes engender rigidities and resistance to change.
>
> One important organizational process that engenders rigidity is the tendency, in large bureaucracies, for organizational ideologies to develop that take precedence over original goals . . . and typically create resistance to change by sanctifying the existing state of affairs . . . Large organizations tend to develop distinctive ideologies that glorify them and their members and exaggerate their virtues . . . Such ideologies serve useful functions in transforming a collectivity of individuals with their separate goals into a working organization . . . However, glorifying myths can have serious dysfunctions.[24]

Hence, the formal implementers who occupy Environment II can inhabit bureaucratic arenas that represent a series of "closed worlds" guided by their own internal beliefs and dynamics. Yet, as James Anderson notes in his book *Public Policy-Making*, these bureaucratic settings are also part of a larger world that can be influenced by the chief executive, the Congress, other administrative agencies and units of government, interest groups, political parties, and the communications media.[25]

Because they inhabit these two worlds, the formal implementers are involved in a political balancing act in which they attempt to reconcile internal agency norms with the external pressures brought to bear on the implementation process by outside actors. In addition to attempting to move these other actors toward desired policy goals, the implementers are engaged in the continuous process of adjusting their own actions to those goals.

Communications Networks and Compliance Mechanisms

Since the implementation environment consists of so many different actors and institutions, linkages are necessary to hold this environment together and relate it to the policy makers and evaluators who occupy the other policy environments. These linkages consist of a series of crisscrossing communications networks between policy makers, implementers, intermediaries, recipients, lobbyists, and others who become involved in the implementation process. Since these different actors may attempt to resist or circumvent policy directives for a variety of reasons, a critical component in these networks consists of compliance mechanisms that are employed in an effort to move various actors to carry out policy instructions.

Here we come face to face with a central issue of politics. How can one set of actors influence another set of actors to carry out policy directives, particularly if there is disagreement over those directives?

In *Modern Political Analysis* Robert Dahl points out that "the notion of politics and a political system presupposes that words like control, power, authority, and influence have a definite meaning. The fact is, however, that these words are ambiguous; their meaning is elusive and complex." [26] In an effort to clarify these "influence terms," Dahl discusses power relationships between two individual actors. While his analysis indicates that influence relationships between two individuals are diverse and complicated, these relationships become even more complex when efforts are made to secure compliance within, or between, bureaucratic institutions or organizations that consist of many different actors. Amitai Etzioni has observed that "the means of control applied by an organization can be classified into three analytical categories": [27]

- Physical (coercive) power—the application, or the threat of application, of punitive sanctions.
- Material (utilitarian) power—the allocation of material resources such as goods and services (e.g., salaries, commissions, fringe benefits).
- Symbolic (normative) power—the allocation and manipulation of symbolic rewards and deprivations (e.g., prestige, esteem, love, acceptance).

Hence, Etzioni's classification indicates that different types of negative sanctions and positive rewards can be employed in an effort to secure compliance. While this is a difficult task under the best of circumstances, it has been compounded by the types of developments described at the outset of this chapter, namely, the increased use of autonomous intermediaries, enactment of more diffuse social policies, and the increasing complexity of the implementation environment as a result of "consumer participation" and other factors that have added to the number of actors involved in the implementation process.

Securing Compliance on the Part of Intermediaries

As was noted in the discussion of actors and arenas, the federal government has placed increasing reliance on intermediaries from the state, local, and private sectors to deliver services under its more recent social programs. Some of these intermediaries are providing services under vendor payment schemes, as is the case with Medicare and Medicaid. The utilization of intermediaries from other levels of government and from the private sector has complicated the compliance problem enormously. The complications have resulted from the fact that many of these intermediaries are independent of the federal government and, hence, are not subject to negative coercive threats. It is impossible, for example, for the federal government to abolish state and local governments (or private companies) if they fail to carry out federal policy directives, or to fire state and local (or private sector) employees who defy these directives. As a result of this autonomy, state and local, as well as private sector, intermediaries can, at times, literally ignore federal policy directives with impunity. In his article on the politics of federal education reform, Murphy describes this situation quite succinctly:

> In the federal system, states have no inherent reason for following federal directives. Since states receive their full entitlement for mere participation in Title I—as opposed to producing some specified result, or doing a good job— there are virtually no reasons to follow federal directives. State officials know that there will not be any major repercussions for ignoring federal directives even with the Office of Education's knowledge.[28]

The same holds true with many private sector programs. Even if the federal government had the power to coerce private intermediaries to obey its directives, the maze of intermediary networks that have been established to service such programs as Medicare and Medicaid makes this task exceedingly difficult. As Robert and Rosemary Stevens explain in their book, *Welfare Medicine in America,*

> The combinations of vendor-payment schemes and services provided by state, county, and city authorities created a web of enormous complexity . . . Once Medicaid had been signed into law, in July 1965, states could proceed to develop their plans instantly . . . The states, smelling easy federal money, began putting on the pressure for implementation. Even in the spring of 1966, it was clear that the total costs of Medicaid would be far greater than expected.[29]

Because compliance by intermediaries is increasingly important, political scientists and others have begun to study this phenomenon more closely. A recent paper by George E. Rawson "Implementation of Public Policy by Third Sector Organizations"[30] represents an important contribution to our understanding of this subject, but we still have a great deal to learn about the use of intermediaries in policy implementation.

Diffuse Performance Criteria

A second major compliance problem has resulted from the fact that many of the newer social policy initiatives are too vague to permit evaluation of intermediary performance by easily measurable criteria. As the preceding chapter pointed out, much recent social legislation has been written in such an ambiguous manner that it is hard to understand the intent of the policies, much less evaluate their implementation. While this problem would be hard to solve if all the implementation efforts were taking place within the federal arena, it becomes even more unmanageable when reliance is placed on outside intermediaries to achieve these diffuse goals. Unless performance can be evaluated in some reasonable fashion, it is difficult, if not impossible, to determine whether intermediaries are complying with policy goals.

Numerous examples of this problem could be cited, but perhaps the clearest illustration is to be found in the implementation of federal affirmative action programs. In Executive Order 10925, issued in 1961, John Kennedy was the first president to call for "affirmative steps" to hire minorities on the part of private contractors doing business with the federal government. This concept was expanded into "affirmative action" under Titles VI and VII of the Civil Rights Act of 1964 and by Executive Order 11246, which was signed by President Johnson in 1965.

Implementation of the program began in earnest in 1969, when the Department of Labor established the "Philadelphia plan," which provided for goals and timetables in minority recruitment in the Philadelphia building trades. Thereafter it spread to other private sector businesses and to colleges and universities that were receiving funding assistance from the federal government. Under Title IX of the Education Amendments Act of 1972, the concept was expanded to bar discrimination based on sex.

In a seminar paper, Michael Yoshii analyzes Dartmouth College's attempts to implement affirmative action under these various directives. Interestingly enough, Dartmouth was one of the first institutions of higher education in the country to approve an affirmative action plan (in April 1972). The plan was submitted for federal review and was endorsed by the Office of Civil Rights three and a half years later (in October 1975). Under this plan various affirmative action goals were to be implemented by "good-faith" recruiting efforts on the part of faculty, administrators, and employees.

Thus, as Yoshii points out in his paper, affirmative action became a process of self-regulation in that both the setting of goals and the efforts to achieve those goals were the responsibility of the College:

> Affirmative Action policy relies on the employer to determine the extent of any employment deficiencies, and to act to rectify any shortcomings. Peter Holmes, Director of the Office of Civil Rights until 1975, described the self-regulation process thusly: "Universities must be introspective; they must

analyze themselves." His successor, Martin Gerry, concurred: "Once a university determines that a problem exists, it should attempt to identify the source of the problem, and take appropriate action to correct it." . . . In short, the Office of Civil Rights has never issued uniform national standards as a way of implementing Executive and Congressional policy. Instead, institutions develop their own goals.

Even within the College Yoshii found disagreement over what constituted "good-faith" efforts to achieve the overall goals:

> When asked about the meaning of good faith efforts, the College's Affirmative Action Officer replied, "I *know* what good faith efforts are." The Chairpersons of both the Administrative and Staff Affirmative Action Review Committees concurred. However, a minority member of the Faculty Committee responded differently. According to him, there is a breakdown in nondiscrimination "at the point where words are translated into action."[31]

As Yoshii points out in his paper, "the degree of goal compliance hinges on the personal interpretations of those involved in implementing the directives." The problem is that these personal interpretations of goals and means may vary widely. As Etzioni has written,

> Affirmative Action runs into difficulties not just with opponents, but also with proponents who differ over modes of implementation. For example, what is the proper basis for quotas (or "goals") for hiring and promotion— the ethnic, racial, and sex distribution in a particular profession, institution, town, or state, or in the nation as a whole? Are courts or federal agencies, grievance procedures, or class action suits the most effective tools? Should Affirmative Action rely chiefly on persuasion, or on fines and jail terms for those not in compliance?[32]

Under such conditions the process of implementation becomes one of raising questions rather than carrying out concise policy directives.

Compliance Legitimacy

A third compliance problem grows out of limitations on the perceived legitimacy of the options that can be employed by those who are attempting to secure compliance. As has already been pointed out, since the federal government has limited authority over state, local, and private sector intermediaries, many of the negative sanctions that can be used within organizations (e.g., firing, pay cuts, etc.) are not appropriate ways to control these autonomous intermediaries. As a result, the federal government has been forced to place increasing reliance on positive incentives in an effort to secure compliance, with the major incentive being money. In fiscal year 1978 the cost of some 572 federally assisted programs affecting state and local governments was estimated at over $117 billion, with many of those programs, having no specific plans covering the details of implementation.[33]

Even when specific implementation plans exist, money is a tricky type of compliance incentive. The major problem is that while attempts can be made to secure compliance by withholding money, if money is actually withdrawn the *entire* implementation program can go down the drain. In other words, it is analogous to using an atomic bomb rather than a fly swatter to kill the flies in the kitchen. The bomb may well get rid of the flies, but it may also blow up the whole house, neighborhood, community, region, and territories beyond.

The drawbacks of relying on money as an incentive to secure compliance by intermediaries are illustrated very concisely in Pressman and Wildavsky's book. By mid-1968 the cost estimates on the World Airways Hangar, one of the key EDA employment projects in the Port of Oakland Authority, had jumped from $9 million to $13.4 million. EDA regional officials favored the request for additional funds provided that "the employment plan of World Airways . . . will assure that members of the hard-core poverty group in Oakland will be trained and hired" to work on the project. At this point a disagreement broke out within EDA over the advisability of this strategy:

> EDA officials in Washington, D.C., were much less enthusiastic at this time about World Airways' employment performance than were their counterparts in the field. A World Airways compliance report of June 1968 had indicated that, while total employment at World Airways had increased by 98 employees, the total number of minority employees dropped from 129 to 111.

Despite their skepticism, however, the Washington EDA officials were caught on the horns of a dilemma:

> At the end of 1969 they were considering the bleak alternatives open to them on the hangar project. If they approved funding for the overrun, the EDA would be still further committed to the project . . . If they denied the overrun, the whole project would be in stalemate. If they cancelled the project completely, the money that had been allocated would revert to the federal treasury. The project appeared to be bogged down in a quagmire from which there was no promising exit.[34]

In the Dartmouth seminar we dealt with case study after case study in which this dilemma was repeated. The usual response on the part of the implementers was to impose "token sanctions" against intermediaries in which they huffed and puffed their threats to cut off funds but failed to actually do so because this would have killed entire programs. As a result, their threats lost legitimacy in the eyes of the intermediary implementers, who perceived they would not be carried out in the final showdown. This, in turn, led to only limited compliance, or even noncompliance, on the part of these intermediaries.

Yet whatever potential strains the use of intermediary implementers may place on the implementation process, it appears that this practice is here to stay. In terms of many new social policy initiatives, the federal government has entered into problem areas in which it simply does not possess the expertise to implement its own policies without relying on outside assistance. The role that private health care professionals play in carrying out Medicare and Medicaid policies is a primary example. The same development seems to be taking place with respect to the use of state and local governmental intermediaries in such areas as education and welfare policy.

Unless there is a dramatic shift in public policies in the years ahead, the practice of relying on intermediaries to carry out these policies seems to have become permanent—and very important—part of the implementation process.

Summary

The implementation environment is characterized by a high degree of diversity, fluidity, and complexity in terms of actors, arenas, bureaucratic imperatives, linkages, and compliance mechanisms. The formal implementers face the task of attempting to coordinate and orchestrate this environment in an effort to carry out policy directives that can be ambiguous and diffuse. Their tasks can be compounded by the need to reconcile their implementation responsibilities with the internal norms that tend to influence behavior within their own institutional settings. Additional complexity results from the growing use of outside intermediaries who are relatively immune to many of the negative sanctions traditionally employed in an effort to ensure compliance. As a result, the implementation environment has become increasingly more political, and bargaining and other forms of negotiation have taken on growing importance in the implementation process.

Notes

1. Walter Williams, "Editor's Comments: Special Issue on Implementation," *Policy Analysis*, 1, no. 3 (Summer 1975), 458.
2. Walter Williams, "Implementation Problems in Federally Funded Programs," in Walter Williams and Richard Elmore, eds., *Social Program Implementation* (New York: Academic Press, 1976), p. 31.

66   The Policy Environments

3. Ibid., p. 35.

4. Beryl A. Radin, *Implementation, Change, and the Federal Bureaucracy* (New York: Teachers College Press, Columbia University, 1977), pp. 143-179.

5. Francis E. Rourke, *Bureaucracy, Politics, and Public Policy*, 2nd ed. (Boston: Little, Brown, 1976), p. 42.

6. Philip Selznick, *TVA and the Grass Roots* (New York: Harper Torchbook, 1966).

7. Stephen M. Dorvee, "An Implementation Study of the Tennessee Valley Authority," Dartmouth College, Government 83, 1978.

8. Mitchell Zeller, "Neighborhood Housing Services Program," Dartmouth College, Government 83, 1978.

9. Jeffrey L. Pressman and Aaron B. Wildavsky, *Implementation* (Berkeley: University of California Press, 1973), pp. 1, 82, 4.

10. Stephen R. Munger, "Implementation of Phase II Wage and Price Controls," Dartmouth College, Government 83, 1978.

11. Richard F. Elmore, "Organizational Models of Social Program Implementation," *Public Policy*, 26, no. 2 (Spring 1978), 186-228.

12. Williams, "Implementation Problems in Federally Funded Programs," pp. 16-17.

13. Pressman and Wildavsky, *Implementation*, p. 12.

14. Robert and Rosemary Stevens, *Welfare Medicine in America* (New York: Free Press, 1974), p. 239.

15. Jerome T. Murphy, "Title I of ESEA: The Politics of Implementing Federal Education Reform," *Harvard Educational Review*, 41, no. 1 (February 1971), 53.

16. Max Weber, in H. H. Garth and C. Wright Mills, eds., *From Max Weber: Essays in Sociology* (New York: Oxford University Press, 1946), p. 214.

17. Francis E. Rourke, *Bureaucracy, Politics and Public Policy*, 2nd ed. (Boston: Little, Brown, 1976), p. 13.

18. Donald S. Van Meter and Carl E. Van Horn, "The Policy Implementation Process: A Conceptual Framework," *Administration and Society*, 6, no. 4 (February 1975), 473.

19. Eugene Bardach, *The Implementation Game* (Cambridge, Mass.: M.I.T. Press, 1977), pp. 76-77.

20. John W. Meyer and Brian Rowan, "Institutionalized Organizations: Formal Structure as Myth and Ceremony," *American Journal of Sociology*, 83, no. 2 (1977), 340-363.

21. Martin Rein and Francine F. Rabinovitz, "Implementation: A Theoretical Perspective," in Walter Dean Burnham and Martha W. Weinberg, eds., *American Politics and Public Policy* (Cambridge, Mass.: M.I.T. Press, 1978).

22. Charles Peters and Michael Nelson, *The Culture of Bureaucracy* (New York: Holt, Rinehart and Winston, 1979).

23. Rourke, *Bureaucracy, Politics and Public Policy*, p. 31.

24. Peter Blau and Marshall W. Meyer, *Bureaucracy in Modern Society*, 2nd ed. (New York: Random House, 1971), pp. 50-52.

25. James E. Anderson, *Public Policy-Making* (New York: Praeger, 1975), pp. 108-110.

26. Robert A. Dahl, *Modern Political Analysis*, 3rd ed. (Englewood Cliffs, N.J.: Prentice-Hall, 1976), p. 29.

27. Amitai Etzioni, *Modern Organizations* (Englewood Cliffs, N.J.: Prentice-Hall, 1964), pp. 59-60.

28. Murphy, "Title I of ESEA," p. 57.

29. Stevens, *Welfare Medicine in America*, pp. 21-27, 75-79, 91.

30. George E. Rawson, "Implementation of Public Policy by Third Sector Organizations," paper delivered at the annual meeting of the American Political Science Association, New York, September 1979.

31. Michael J. Yoshii, "The Implementation of Affirmative Action," Dartmouth College, Government 83, 1978.

32. Amitai Etzioni, "Societal Overload," *Political Science Quarterly*, Winter 1977-78, p. 625.

33. Congressional Budget Office, "Federally Assisted Programs Impacting on State and Local Governments" (Washington, D.C., Winter 1978).

34. Pressman and Wildavsky, *Implementation*, pp. 43-45.

Chapter 5

Policy Evaluation (Environment III)

The last two chapters have described the types of political influences at work in the policy formation and implementation environments. At this point a key question arises. Can the actors involved in evaluation examine policy strictly on its "objective" merits, free from considerations of the power and influence of its supporters and detractors? If so, such "objective" or "value-free" evaluation of policies would provide a yardstick with which to measure the performance of policy makers and policy implementers. In short, the evaluation process could be the measure for holding both policy makers and implementers accountable for their actions.

We will approach this question by first examining the different approaches to evaluation taken by various actors in the policy evaluation environment—the policy makers; the policy implementers; and a third set of actors, detached professional evaluators, who view evaluation as a technical exercise.

Before proceeding, we should make clear the scope of the evaluation activities that we will be considering. There are many different criteria that can be used in evaluation, and we will discuss these criteria in more detail in chapter 8. In this chapter, we will focus primarily on a general overview of program evaluation that seeks to answer the broad question of how close a governmental program has come to achieving its stated policy goals. Some evaluation activities pose narrower questions than this. For example, financial audits—conducted by HEW's Audit Office, the General Accounting Office, or other agencies responsible for monitoring the flow of money in governmental agencies—focus on the specific question of whether or not program resources are expended according to legal guidelines. Other evaluative activities, such as preparing program histories, or "case studies," may refrain from making any explicit judgments about programs. Our main concern in this chapter is to assess the role of evaluation in providing a standard for measuring policy programs and the performance of those responsible for the programs.

Evaluation by Political Standards

Evaluation constantly occurs as part of daily life. Everyone makes choices about how to spend time and other resources. In making such choices it is necessary to explicitly or implicitly evaluate the worth of competing claims on these resources. The definition of worth is, of course, dependent on the goals one hopes to achieve with the resources. In this section we will discuss how the first two sets of actors in the policy process—policy makers and policy implementers—approach program evaluation. Since both groups place a high priority on maintaining, or enhancing, their power, they tend to view evaluation in terms of assumptions and procedures that relate to this central goal.

The Policy Maker's Perspective (Monitoring Feedback)

Policy makers occupy their positions of authority in a democratic political system as long as they are able to satisfy their constituents. Their actions can be explained in terms of their desire to maintain or expand their power. As a result, policy makers tend to view program evaluation in constituency terms. They solicit, or anticipate, feedback from the constituency groups on which they depend for support in an effort to gauge those groups' satisfaction with policy programs.

Hence, a key evaluation strategy for policy makers takes the form of monitoring constituency attitudes toward programs. The standard for evaluating a program becomes its popularity, or unpopularity, with those constituents who are most likely to contact policy makers. This perspective assumes that the success or failure of a program can be measured in terms of its acceptance or rejection by those constituents and/or groups who contact policy makers. Since policy makers are anxious to learn how their basic support groups feel, they create opportunities for constituents and others to make their views known and then attempt to monitor the feedback they receive. In this type of monitoring approach the policy makers' roles are relatively passive. Basically, they are available to receive signals and messages. Since the initiative rests with constituents and other interested groups, such an evaluation approach can be politically biased toward the concerns of those who are most likely to contact policy makers, or toward the programs with the most dramatic or proximate effects.

The willingness of constituents and other interested groups to contact policy makers may vary owing to personal considerations (e.g., education, income, share of program benefits or costs, strength of beliefs, membership in organizations interested in policy outcomes, etc.) or because of the visibility of different programs. Those programs which are most immediate in time, or in conferring benefits or costs, are most likely to be evaluated under this approach. Other policies—more remote in time or indirect in their effects—are less likely to be evaluated.

One example of this type of informal monitoring involves the piecemeal appraisal of governmental policy by members of Congress and the claiming of credit for accomplishments realized under governmental programs. As political scientist David Mayhew emphasizes in *Congress: The Electoral Connection,* Congressmen are concerned with keeping their jobs through reelection:

> The electoral goal . . . has to be the *proximate* goal of everyone, the goal that must be achieved over and over if other ends are to be entertained. One former congressman writes, "All members of Congress have a primary interest in getting reelected. Some members have no other interest." [1]

Members of Congress and other elected officials owe their positions to their continued capacity to satisfy the demands that constituents make on them. Because elected officials are usually too busy to systematically assess constituent satisfaction with all the programs under their control, they rely on information brought to them by others as a means of assessing constituency satisfaction. Nelson Polsby describes this process as follows:

> After a bill is enacted, it goes into effect. Presumably this has an impact upon members of the general public, who in turn communicate with their congressman about this and myriad other topics. By monitoring the tides of complaint and appeals for assistance from constituents Congress keeps track of the activity of the entire Federal Government. Congressmen learn quickly enough which agencies are throwing off benefits to their constituents, which cause the people back home grief, which preoccupy them, which they ignore . . . This appraisal process operates day and night on a piecemeal basis and separately from the more formally organized oversight activities of the Congress. [2]

While this "piecemeal" method of appraisal is open to all constituents, it is important to emphasize again that there is a potential bias in the mix of constituents who may take advantage of this opportunity. Such informal appraisal is likely to bring forth the opinions of the more educated, financially better-off, and higher-status occupational groups within a constituency. Constituency feedback may be stimulated and channeled by organized interest groups, and those groups with more resources (information, money, and members), plus those that are most stable and organized. Such groups will carry the greatest weight.[3]

The sources of piecemeal feedback could be expanded to include newspaper and television stories, the complaints of other officials, and rumors. Even the results of social research may "seep" into the policy sphere by such piecemeal channels:

> The policy-maker himself is often unaware of the source of his ideas. He "keeps up with the literature," or is briefed by his aides, or reads state-of-the-art reviews of research in intellectual magazines, or social science stories in the *New York Times,* or the *Washington Post,* or the *Wall Street Journal.* Bits of information seep into his mind, uncatalogued, without citation.[4]

On the basis of such unsystematic feedback, policy makers gain impressions (informal evaluations) about the success or failure of governmental programs and act accordingly.

The Policy Implementer's Perspective (Mobilizing Support)

Since policy implementers' reputations and futures are linked to the success of the programs they manage, they are concerned with maintaining, or expanding, the support of policy makers for their programs.

Hence, once again, their approach to evaluation is designed to accomplish a political objective. The means implementers employ in an effort to influence policy makers are also political. Implementers can attempt to control or shape the information policy makers receive about programs by the following means:

1. Selective release of data and other information that cast the most favorable light on their performance.
2. Mobilizing program supporters to make claims on policy makers.
3. Using program resources to build and expand beneficiary groups and other attentive publics that can be mobilized to provide additional program support.

In these ways implementers attempt to make claims on policy makers. The access provided by policy makers to their constituents, described previously, provides an opportunity for implementers. In an effort to take advantage of this opportunity, implementers often take the initiative in stimulating and organizing constituent feedback to policy makers about program activities.

Since in this type of evaluation approach the test of a program is its capacity to convince policy makers that it is sound, this type of evaluation can be politically biased toward programs that serve organized groups with claims on policy makers, and against programs that confer diffuse benefits or serve dormant populations who do not contact policy makers.

An illustration of the evaluation perspective of policy implementers is provided by Aaron Wildavsky in *The Politics of the Budgetary Process*.[5] The continued financial well-being of programs (and, hence, program implementers) depends on maintaining the good will and support of the congressional appropriations committees. One way in which members of these committees learn about a program is from the clients and others who have had firsthand dealings with it. As a result, agency officials are likely to call upon those with whom they deal—clients and others—for aid in dealing with Congress. As Wildavsky explains,

> Almost everyone claims that his projects are immensely popular and benefit lots of people. But how do officials know? They can only be made aware by hearing from constituents. The agency can do a lot to ensure that its clientele responds by informing them that contacting Congressmen is necessary and by telling them how to go about it if they do not already know. In fact the agency may organize the clientele in the first place. The agency may then offer to fulfill the demand it has helped to generate.[6]

On a more general note,

> Clientele and confidence strategies are desirable in a democratic society. The feedback that clientele give to the participants is essential political information about who wants what programs, at what level, and with what degree of intensity.[7]

Program implementers might also be concerned with additional sources of feedback, including communications to policy makers from other participants in the implementation environment such as state and local officials, interest groups, and other attentive publics.

Hence, both the policy makers and the implementers have heavy political stakes in the evaluation process. As Carol Weiss explains, "Evaluation has always had explicitly political overtones. It is designed to yield conclusions about the worth of programs and, in so doing, is intended to affect the allocation of resources."[8]

Since policy makers and implementers are concerned with the maintenance or enhancement of their power and programs, both tend to hold a defensive perspective toward evaluation. They adopt strategies designed to avoid appraisals critical of their performance. Under the circumstances, neither group can be expected to view evaluation as a nonpolitical, objective activity. If such "objectivity" is to be realized, it must come from the more formal technical evaluators, who presumably have less direct political stakes in the evaluation process.

Technical Evaluation

The third set of actors involved in policy evaluation consists of professional evaluators, people who derive all or part of their income from conducting formal evaluations. They are hired by clients—usually policy makers or implementing agencies—expressly to conduct evaluations that require their special skills and expertise.

As is true with the other actors, the technical evaluators' perspective can be understood in terms of their basic goal, which is to produce scientifically valid findings. If they meet this goal, they may accomplish other, secondary objectives that involve maintaining their professional reputations for competence, increasing their chances of subsequent employment, or possibly influencing the future course of policy.

In order to achieve their goal, however, technical evaluators must satisfy a number of basic requirements that can be imposed on them by policy makers or implementers. Specifically, policy makers and implementers will respond to the work of technical evaluators when they feel that the following basic requirements have been met:

1. Policy maker goals are accurately stated by the technical evaluators.
2. The degree of goal achievement is measured objectively.
3. Conclusions are stated in a manner that relates policy maker goals to program accomplishments.

In order to satisfy these requirements, the programs subjected to technical evaluations must meet a number of basic tests. Specifically, technical evaluation requires that

1. policy goals are stated clearly.
2. these goals are precise enough to be measureable.
3. implementation activities are directed toward achieving these goals.
4. objective measures that relate implementation activities to goals exist or can be created.
5. the data necessary to verify these measures are available.

Hence, technical evaluation is a demanding and systematic task that is designed to objectively assess specific programs. Weiss, in another frequently cited definition of this type of evaluation, explains that

in its research guise, evaluation establishes clear and specific criteria for success. It collects evidence systematically from a representative sample of the units of concern. It usually translates the evidence into quantitative terms (e.g., 23 percent of the audience, grades of 85 or better) and compares it with the criteria that were set. It then draws conclusions about the effectiveness, the merits, the success, of the phenomenon under study.[9]

As the preceding quotation makes clear, whether or not technical evaluators share the same political goals as policy makers and implementers, there is a potential methodological bias in their work due to the fact that technical evaluation focuses on those elements of program performance that are measurable in quantitative terms at the expense of more subjective or suggestive evidence.

If technical evaluators are to produce "objective" findings, they must resolve two potential problems. First, they must be able to develop the methodological capabilities to evaluate programs in measurable, quantitative terms. Second, they must be able to resist political pressure from policy makers and implementers who may attempt to influence their work.

Methodological Obstacles to Technical Evaluation

The hallmark of technical evaluation is that it is based on an "objective" analysis of facts. Technical evaluation is objective insofar as it is based on value choices made by legitimate policy makers rather than on the technical evaluators' own values. Its credibility relies on factual evidence rather than politically motivated opinions to support conclusions.

In theory, questions involving values are resolved by policy makers through the choice of policy goals and the means to carry them out. The factual material for analysis is then produced by policy implementers, who follow the policy makers' directives. In reality, technical evaluators face at least four potential obstacles in their attempts to produce objective evaluations: (1) identifying program goals, (2) characterizing program activities in terms of goals, (3) defining indicators for program performance, and (4) gathering data.

Identifying Program Goals Ideally, policy makers have stated program goals in clear and measurable terms. If technical evaluation is a means-ends analysis, then policy makers are expected to provide analysts with the ends. The first obstacle to objective evaluation is encountered when policy makers fail to define program goals in precise terms.

As explained in chapter 3, the problems policy makers face in dealing with uncertainties, conceptual complexities, and the demands of coalition building differ from those faced by technical evaluators. Thus, it is not always possible for policy makers to produce a policy that is precise enough to be objectively measured by technical evaluators. This problem is described by the Urban Institute's Evaluation Group as follows:

> The vaporous wish is the eloquent but elusive language of goals put forward for most federal programs . . . It is becoming clearer that many federal social programs are simply envelopes for a large federal investment in a program area . . . A program may de deceptive in the sense that it has enough content to allow it to be described in the media, lobbied into existence, and established as a federal effort—and yet the program interventions are not spelled out in any detail. Many program administrators over the last decade have essentially received a program envelope with only vaporous wishes and money inside. Although more detailed definition may not have been necessary in order to spend the money, much more detailed definition is needed to evaluate the process and outcome.[10]

Various writers have postulated that there are a number of different and often conflicting "cues" that technical evaluators can use to determine the intent of policy directives:

1. The "legal imperative" of the policy as written.[11]
2. The "legislative history" of the policy.[12]
3. The "understanding" of a policy held by interest groups and other attentive publics.[13]
4. The goals "developed" by participants during policy implementation.[14]
5. The "translation" of a policy's goals from vague political language to more precise terms by evaluators.[15]
6. The policy goals most consistent with the research requirements of evaluators.[16]
7. Current policy maker understandings of policy goals.

The problem is that these "cues" may produce different definitions of program goals, and none is guaranteed to be acceptable to all policy makers, policy implementers, or members of the attentive public.

Vagueness in stated program goals is an obstacle to technical evaluation in several senses:

1. It forces technical evaluators to compromise their own analytic precision or to "translate" vague goals into more specific terms according to their own interpretations of policy goals.[17]
2. It increases the discretion available to policy implementers and others in the environment of implementation to reinterpret these goals for evaluators.
3. Should technical evaluators choose to focus on a particular goal, the choice itself may be controversial. Others—policy implementers, some policy makers, or interested publics—may contest the choice on the ground that it is not the real goal of a program.[19]

The Housing Act of 1949, for example, stated the general goal of providing a decent home and a suitable living environment for every

American family. Subsequent amendments reformulated that goal in a number of ways—slum clearance, urban renewal, public housing, leased and privately owned housing. Thus, the specific goal to be evaluated was subject to the reinterpretations of several generations of policy makers, and the indicators to be used to measure goal achievement varied correspondingly. In this and other cases the choice of technical evaluators is complicated by uncertainty about what policy makers want to achieve. Hence, the problems posed by general policies—and the technical evaluators' efforts to deal with such vagueness—can compromise the technical evaluators' role and open their findings to political controversy.

Characterizing Program Activities in Terms of Goals

Ideally, from the technical evaluator's perspective, a program is a focused and organized effort devoted to achieving specific goals. However, just as program goals can be vague and imprecise, so program implementation can be diffuse or disorganized. For example:

1. A program's structure for achieving goals may be inappropriate.[20]
2. A program may spread its resources over so many goals that the money appears to be dissipated without effect.[21]
3. A program can deliver goals other than those stated by either its legislation or its own description of purpose.[22]
4. A program can change its structure and goals so often as to create confusion about its overriding purpose.[23]

While other examples exist, the point is clear: Technical evaluators cannot characterize program activities in terms of specific goals under any of the conditions listed.

What appears to be irrational or wasteful from the viewpoint of a technical evaluator may be both politically rational and productive from the viewpoint of policy implementers. A program may broaden its scope to encompass many different goals in order to build client support and thereby prosper politically. In such cases what appears to be technical failure may result in political success. The technical evaluators' difficulties in characterizing program activities in terms of specific goals may stem from the rational political strategies of policy implementers who are dealing with an uncertain world in which incentives are stacked in favor of meeting political demands at the expense of program goals.

Defining Indicators for Program Performance

Ideally, from the technical evaluator's perspective, a program's accomplishments should be measurable in terms of objective indicators. These indicators should encompass measures that have value and credibility for policy makers and policy implementers. The most credible measures are those which can be quantified and counted. The problem is that many of the things that can be counted do not count with policy makers, and many of the things that count with policy makers cannot be counted.

It is at this point that technical evaluation confronts the special problem of devising indicators to measure the worth and efficiency of governmental programs.[24] As the foregoing discussion of policy goals and program activities indicated, controversies or uncertainties often arise over what a program should be producing. Such disagreements can extend to a dispute over how to measure results, because governmental programs may simultaneously produce (or claim to produce) many different things. We now turn to a discussion of the effects of programs and the susceptibility of each to objective measurement.

Outputs, outcomes and impacts   Levy, Meltsner, and Wildavsky distinguish different classes of program effects produced by governmental action in terms of *outputs, outcomes,* and finally, *impacts.* An *output* is the easiest of the three to measure quantitatively, for it is basically a service actually rendered, usually on an immediate or short-term basis. An output of an educational program, for example, can consist of the number of children actually receiving instruction. *Outcomes*—the consequences of programs in human terms—are usually more qualitative and have more long-term implications. An outcome of an educational program might be measured in terms of children's reading scores, but there are many other outcomes from schooling, and not all of these are measurable in the short run. For example, schools may produce such outcomes as changed study habits, improved self-estimates of ability, and so on. Finally, *impacts* may involve even longer-term consequences for society. The impact of schooling may be to produce a literate population and increase the society's economic productivity. Often such impacts are quite remote. Impacts are the most difficult effects to measure because the mechanisms by which impacts are achieved are uncertain and the time involved can be very long.[25]

Technical evaluators, pressed by the need to measure the results of governmental programs, often choose to focus on the most direct and immediate results (i.e., outputs). In turn, they will tend to slight more remote outcomes and often ignore long-range impacts completely. The difficulty is that the more convenient measures do not necessarily evaluate the most important consequences of policies and/or programs.

At best, evaluators can choose to focus on a few "surrogate" output indicators for the broad range of goals promised by any given program.

For example, the Anacostia Community School Project, operating in Washington, D.C., was designed to revamp black urban education through community restructuring of schools. It was evaluated in terms of pupil reading scores.[26] The practical requirements of measuring results led evaluators to use indicators that ignored more diffuse program goals (such as changing family attitudes toward schooling) as well as impacts that were more remote in time (e.g., improving students' life chances).

As a result, technical evaluations tend to focus on those types of performance indicators which are most immediate and most easily quantifiable at the expense of longer-range and more subjective evidence.

Gathering data   One of the strongest arguments in support of the technical evaluation approach is that its conclusions can be verified by reference to specific data. Hence, technical evaluators require access to the data produced by program activities. To the extent that such access is limited, the effectiveness of evaluation is also limited.

The task of gathering data can be difficult when technical evaluators lack the resources to gather their own information or those who have such resources are unwilling to share them. Resources might include personnel, time, access to program clients, records, money, and computer time. Sometimes data may be unavailable as a result of incompetence or a shortage of necessary resources. In addition, those who control the resources (usually policy implementers) may resist sharing their data in order to avoid embarrassment over the disclosure of potential failures.

Program implementers sometimes view the data they control as a political resource to be kept out of the hands of outsiders. Such a view was expressed by President Johnson:

> The President's real problem is with the Congress, not the bureaucracy. It is the Congress that demands numbers from us, insisting that we handle the most people at the least cost. If we went around beating our breasts and admitting difficulties with our programs, then Congress would immediately slash all our funds for next year and then where would we be? Better to send in the reports as they are, even knowing the situation is more complicated than it appears, and then work from within to make things better and correct the problems.[27]

Congress, in this case, was seen as an unsympathetic outsider. The program evaluator is a professional outsider, a neutral whose judgments are to be determined by facts. Not surprisingly, then, implementers sometimes have misgivings about turning over potentially embarrassing data for interpretation by evaluators who are beyond their control.

The task of gathering data can actually put evaluators into direct conflict with policy implementers. Such conflicts can result from differences of opinion over whose priorities are taken as controlling. Key conflicts can involve such issues as the following:

1. The limitations of time—the relative priorities of gathering data versus those of running the program. Here priorities are expressed in terms of whose claims are superior in allocating such scarce resources as money, organizational effort, and beneficiary time and attention.
2. The choice of indicators—differences of opinion over the relative weight to be accorded a few specific and measurable indicators of program performance over other, more suggestive but less definitive measures. This is the conflict over the use of a few output indicators versus a wider focus that encompasses outcomes and impacts.
3. The rights of clients—the rights of clients to privacy versus the needs of evaluators for information. The rights of clients to have their individual needs considered may come into conflict with the preference of evaluators for standardized and comparable treatments.

The process of gathering data can precipitate a series of disputes between technical evaluators and the people whose performance they are evaluating. Such disputes can lead directly to technical failure through inability to get sufficient data to evaluate policies.

Political Obstacles to Technical Evaluation

While technical evaluation aspires to be an objective exercise, the results of such evaluations often have political consequences. Evaluation is, after all, the process of judging the performance of the people who make and implement policy. The ways in which people are judged can affect their reputations and their capacity to command future resources. Anyone involved in conceiving and implementing policy may have a stake in the evaluation process. Policy makers might be faulted for errors of commission (making bad policy choices, setting unrealistic goals, etc.) or omission (e.g., failing to be specific about means and ends). Similarly, policy implementers might be faulted for failing to live up to the legal imperatives of a policy, or to its spirit, or simply for poor administration and management. Others who may have influenced the shaping and implementation of policy—interest groups, state and local authorities, other attentive publics—could be faulted for failure to cooperate, interference, recalcitrance, or indifference.

Hence, technical evaluations have potentially serious political consequences for the political actors in the policy formulation and implementation environments:

Evaluation research assesses the effectiveness of policies (and the programs that derive from them) in meeting the avowed objectives. Even if we change the name and call the effort "the measurement of policy impact," it is rendering a judgment on the merit of policy . . . If results don't come out "right" from their (federal officials', program managers', operating personnel's) standpoint, and if decision-makers pay attention to those results, there may be risk for their agency, their program, and their own reputations, influence, and careers.[28]

Thus, technical evaluations—neutral as they might seem—are ultimately political through their consequences.

The threat posed to program advocates by technical evaluation is actually more fearsome than that posed by other evaluation approaches. This is because, while policy makers and implementers can control their own approaches to evaluation, they have very little control over the indicators used to judge performance under technical evaluation. Hence, technical evaluation makes possible a judgment of failure. This threat often provides a sufficient incentive for those "at risk" to use their political resources in an effort to influence the technical evaluation process. Some may attempt to escape evaluation if they possess sufficient power to block the technical evaluators from appraising their performance. Those who cannot escape, usually program implementers, often use whatever political resources they have to shape the criteria by which they are being evaluated in such a way as to achieve the best "results" for themselves.

The methodological obstacles discussed in the preceding section pose opportunities for policy implementers and others interested in influencing the technical evaluation process. For example:

- The vagueness of program goals can serve as a resource for those who want to contest the technical evaluator's characterization of program goals by calling into question the standard against which a program is being evaluated.
- Program activities that have built political support also give program implementers a resource for opposing technical evaluation. Such activities provide political allies who can be mobilized to influence policy makers and thereby undermine the effectiveness of technical evaluation results.
- Program indicators are also subject to influence or to challenge. Indicators can be called into question as inadequate or misleading or as not being indicative of the "real accomplishments" of a program.
- Policy implementers, and others involved in a program, can resist evaluation by making it difficult for technical evaluators to gather the data essential for their work.

In short, the technical obstacles to evaluation can be compounded by political obstacles.

Program Termination

To summarize, we have seen that at least three distinct perspectives on evaluation may exist simultaneously. Two of these perspectives— monitoring of feedback by policy makers and clientele appraisals by policy implementers—are distinctly political in terms of their goals and means. The third, that of technical evaluators, can be subjected to political influences because of its consequences. While the two explicitly political evaluation approaches of policy makers and implementers have their value, measuring as they do the degree of constituency and clientele support for a program, it is the third that holds the promise of an objective assessment of a program's worth. However, as we have seen, serious technical and political obstacles can stand in the way of this third type of objective evaluation. Paradoxically, technical problems in the form of diffuse policies and the like can provide an opening for political obstacles.

Despite these problems and obstacles, technical evaluation may still have an effect on the policy process. In an effort to gauge this effect, we will consider one way of measuring the impact of such evaluations: their role in terminating programs found to be unsuccessful. This is part of the larger question that this chapter has attempted to answer: What is the role, if any, of technical evaluations in holding policy makers and implementers accountable for their actions?

In an article on "The Politics of Termination," Douglas Bothun and John Comer distinguish between "functional termination" (as the end to a set of program activities) and "structural termination" (as cessation of the institutional arrangements performing these activities).[29] A decision to terminate either a program or an agency, or both, in response to an adverse evaluation constitutes an acid test of the power of technical evaluation to influence behavior—such a decision constitutes an indication of failure on the part of either policy makers or implementers, or perhaps both.

Three important sets of constraints can influence the capacity of technical evaluation to produce termination: (1) the general political context in which such a decision will be made, (2) the requirement that the evaluation be accepted as objectively legitimate on its merits and (3) the development of survival strategies by opponents to termination.

A variety of general political factors make it difficult to terminate governmental programs and the agencies that support those programs. Peter DeLeon, in "Public Policy Terminations: An End and a Beginning," specifies basic sources of difficulty in effecting termination:

At least six obstacles inhibit—if not virtually prohibit—the political act of termination: psychological reluctance; institutional permanence; dynamic conservatism; anti-termination coalitions; legal obstacles; and high start-up costs.[30]

Each of these obstacles can increase the political costs that must be paid by policy makers if they decide to terminate programs. The greater the capacity of a governmental activity to actually raise such costs to policy makers, the less the likelihood that it will be terminated. These obstacles, then, set the general political climate within which evaluation can contribute to termination. Those governmental activities posing the lowest political risks will be most vulnerable to termination. Only within this context can evaluation contribute to termination.

Within these general political constraints, technical evaluators face the more specific methodological constraints discussed earlier. If evaluation results are to be accepted as objectively legitimate, programs must have goals that are specific enough to be measured; implementation activities have to be focused on achieving goals; accurate and objective indicators must be devised; and the data must be available. Failure to deal effectively with any of these requirements makes the technical evaluators' findings vulnerable to attack from those resisting termination.

Hence, both the general climate of resistance to termination and the specific methodological problems involved in justifying such action pose formidable obstacles.

A third constraint working against termination can appear in the form of survival strategies or, in Bothun and Comer's terms, "adaptive and counter strategies employed by agencies and organizations threatened with termination."[31] These strategies can take different forms. The first is to use program resources to build a political base of support against termination. This strategy involves the development of coalitions of supporters, based on specific clients and other attentive publics, in an effort to ensure the legal permanence of the activity.

If this strategy does not work, another survival strategy may be employed—redefining program goals to increase support and/or make the program less vulnerable to evaluation. This can involve the following:

1. Changing program goals and activities as policy makers' cues change (shifting goals to reflect political climate).
2. Adopting goals that will draw more clientele and other supporters to a program; spreading program resources across many items (expanding scope of program).
3. Abandoning unpromising goals or activities in favor of those with greater support (changing domain of program).

4. Resisting measurable activities to avoid being measured on indicators in which failure is possible (reducing effectiveness of evaluation).

These survival strategies are defensive in nature: calculating program activities to generate political support while keeping performance unmeasurable. In effect, they are designed to make full use of the political obstacles discussed in the preceding section as a means for resisting termination. The efforts of technical evaluators to rely on objective measures of success are countered by attempts to mobilize clientele support and by strategies to obscure technical evaluation results.

Not surprisingly, very few evaluations have produced the termination of governmental activities. In a study entitled *Are Government Organizations Immortal?* political scientist Herbert Kaufman found that only 27 organizations in the federal government were terminated between 1924 and 1973, while the number of organizations increased from 175 to 394 during this period.[32] In light of this record it is hardly surprising that Bothun and Comer conclude their analysis by observing that "few programs or policies are terminated; few bureaus, agencies, or departments are eliminated. Indeed, efforts at termination occasionally lead to expansion of resources."[33]

This analysis has indicated some of the obstacles and strategies that make it difficult to produce terminations based on adverse evaluations. The basic limitation is that "objective" or "value-free" evaluations can exist in only a limited number of cases and, in addition, that the application of evaluation results (no matter how objective) ultimately occurs in a political and subjective context. The evaluation environment is very much a part of the politics of policy implementation.

Summary

We began this chapter with the question of whether or not the evaluation environment is the place where policies can be appraised on their merits, free from considerations of power and influence. We focused on the technical approach to program evaluation because this approach holds the best prospects for such an objective assessment. However, we have seen that such evaluations are dependent on a series of methodological requirements that are often absent from the world of governmental policies. Furthermore, the task of conducting such technical evaluations involves its participants in political conflicts because of the possible effects of their work on future program decisions.

The basic limitation on the role of technical evaluators is political. Technical evaluators have no power or constituency of their own, so they must rely on the power and influence of others. Technical evaluators cannot reshape the environments of policy making or policy implementation to meet their technical needs. They must, instead, take the policies and programs as they come from those environments and try to rework them into technically useful material. Furthermore, technical evaluators must depend on the power of policy makers to enact their recommendations. If technical evaluators remain wholly detached—oblivious to the power requirements of those with whom they deal—their work will be exceedingly difficult and their findings inconsequential.

In the final analysis, policy evaluation is subject to many of the same types of political influences and constraints as the first two policy environments. This is so because evaluation is ultimately controlled by the policy makers and policy implementers. As a result, evaluation is not an alternative to political judgments, and it is not a wholly objective means of holding actors in the political system accountable for their actions.

Notes

1. David R. Mayhew, *Congress: The Electoral Connection*, (New Haven, Conn.: Yale University Press, 1974), p. 16.

2. Nelson W. Polsby, "Policy Analysis and Congress," in U.S. Congress, Joint Economic Committee, Subcommittee on Economy in Government, *The Analysis and Evaluation of Public Expenditures* (Washington, D.C.: 1969), 3, 948.

3. See Mayhew, *Congress: The Electoral Connection*, p. 109; and John Kingdon, *Congressmen's Voting Decisions* (New York: Harper & Row, 1973).

4. Carol Weiss, "Research for Policy's Sake," *Policy Analysis* (Fall 1977), p. 534.

5. Aaron Wildavsky, *The Politics of the Budgetary Process* (Boston: Little, Brown, 1964).

6. Ibid., p. 67.

7. Ibid., p. 171.

8. Carol H. Weiss, "The Politicization of Policy Research," in J. Anderson, ed., *Cases in Public Policy-Making* (New York: Praeger, 1976), p. 311.

9. Carol H. Weiss, *Evaluation Research* (Englewood Cliffs, N.J.: Prentice-Hall, 1972), pp. 1–2.

10. P. Horst, J. Nay, J. Scanlon, and J. Wholey, *Program Management and the Federal Evaluator*, Reprint 162-0010-6, (Washington, D.C.: Urban Institute, August 1974), p. 303.

11. Martin Rein and Francine F. Rabinovitz, "Implementation: A Theoretical Perspective," in Walter Dean Burham and Martha W. Weinberg, eds., *American Politics and Public Policy* (Cambridge, Mass.: M.I.T. Press, 1978).

12. Clayton R. Koppes, "Public Water, Private Land Origins of the Acreage Limitation Controversy, 1933–53," *Pacific Historical Review*, 47 (November 1978).

13. Beryl A. Radin, *Implementation, Change, and the Federal Bureaucracy* (New York: Teachers College Press, Columbia University, 1977).

14. Milbrey McLaughlin, "Implementation as Mutual Adaptation," in Walter Williams and Richard Elmore, eds., *Social Program Implementation* (New York: Academic Press, 1976).

15. James Coleman, "Problems of Conceptualization and Measurement in Studying Policy Impacts," in Kenneth Dolbeare, ed., *Public Policy Evaluation* (Beverly Hills, Calif.: Sage, 1975).

16. Donald S. Van Meter and Carl E. Van Horn, "The Policy Implementation Process: A Conceptual Framework," *Administration and Society*, 6, no. 4 (February 1975), 445–483.

17. Coleman, "Problems of Conceptualization and Measurement."

18. Richard Elmore, "Design of the Follow Through Experiment," in A. Rivlin and P. M. Timpane, eds., *Planned Variation in Education* (Washington, D.C.: Brookings, 1975).

19. Carol Weiss, "The Politics of Impact Measurement," *Policy Studies Journal* (Spring 1975), p. 181.

20. Jeffrey L. Pressman and Aaron Wildavsky, *Implementation* (Berkeley: University of California Press, 1973).

21. Robert T. Nakamura and Dianne M. Pinderhughes, "Changing Anacostia: Definition and Implementation," Paper delivered at the American Educational Research Association Meeting, Toronto, March 1978.

22. Jerome T. Murphy, "Title I of ESEA: The Politics of Implementing Federal Education Reform," *Harvard Educational Review*, 41, no. 1 (February 1971); Koppes, "Public Water, Private Land."

23. Radin, *Implementation, Change, and the Federal Bureaucracy.*

24. Mancur Olson, "Evaluating Performance in the Public Sector," in Milton Moss, ed., *The Measurement of Economic and Social Performance* (Washington, D.C.: National Bureau of Economic Research, 1973).

25. F. S. Levy, Arnold J. Meltsner, and Aaron Wildavsky, *Urban Outcomes* (Berkeley: University of California Press, 1974), pp. 4–8.

26. Nakamura and Pinderhughes, "Changing Anacostia."

27. Doris Kearns, *Lyndon Johnson and the American Dream* (New York: Signet, 1976) p. 304.

28. Carol Weiss, "The Politics of Impact Measurement," p. 180.

29. Douglas Bothun and John C. Comer, "The Politics of Termination: Concepts and Process," *Policy Studies Journal*, 7, no. 3 (Spring 1979), 541.

30. Peter DeLeon, "Public Policy Terminations: An End and a Beginning," *Policy Analysis*, (Summer 1978).

31. Bothun and Comer, "The Politics of Termination," p. 545.

32. Herbert Kaufman, *Are Government Organizations Immortal?* (Washington, D.C.: Brookings, 1976).

33. Bothun and Comer, "The Politics of Termination," p. 552.

Chapter Six

The Special
Case of Judicial
Implementation

In the preceding chapters we dealt with the efforts of elected and appointed officials in the three policy environments to formulate, implement, and evaluate policies. This chapter deals with the unique role of the courts in policy formation and implementation. While many court decisions are of interest only to the parties in a case, others have far greater consequences for society. Judicial action has played a significant role in determining and enforcing societal priorities in civil rights, education, criminal procedures, environmental protection, and many other areas. Judges are not politicians in the conventional sense, but they sometimes formulate far-reaching judicial policies. As Glendon Schubert has pointed out, "Judges share with legislators, chief executives, and the heads of major administrative departments the political power and the responsibility to make policy decisions."[1]

Hence, the courts, along with other policy makers, deal with a similar set of implementation challenges, which revolve around the issue of how to use intermediaries to carry out their policy directives.

In order to understand some of the challenges that face courts in dealing with this problem, it is necessary to briefly review their roles in the policy process. The main ways in which the courts can become involved in this process may be summarized as follows:

1. *Policy formation*. Higher courts can use their power to interpret what is required by law or to formulate new policies requiring people to change their behavior in accordance with judicially established priorities. Examples:
   a. The Warren Court in school desegregation.

   b. The California State Supreme Court in the equalization of educational spending.

2. *Policy implementation*. People involved in the implementation environment sometimes use the courts as an arena in which to contest their differences. Courts can play a variety of roles in the implementation of legally enforceable policies:

   a. Deciding whether new policies (set forth in statutes, administrative regulations, or executive orders) are within the constitutional or statutory authority of other policy makers.

   b. Acting as intermediaries between policy formulators and implementers by clarifying what is meant by the policies.

   c. Introducing new considerations or requirements into the relations among implementation actors, such as requiring an administrative agency (e.g., the Selective Service System) to follow the requirements of "due process" in the implementation of the agency's enabling legislation.

   d. Enforcing legal obligations between actors through court orders or other indicated remedies.

3. *Policy evaluation*. The evaluation role of courts is usually limited to assessing, in response to a suit, how well a party has lived up to the *legal* obligations of a legally enforceable policy statement. Thus, for example, courts have evaluated state legislative apportionment plans and school finance plans to see whether they were consistent with higher-court decisions in those areas. Evaluation, in this sense, is confined to deciding whether or or not a party's behavior is consistent with the requirements of law.

Since the role of the judiciary in the policy process can be important, the remainder of this chapter will analyze how the courts formulate and implement judicial policy. At the outset it is important to emphasize that "in the formal, or Constitutional, view there are fifty-one different judicial systems within the American polity: a separate system for each of the states, and a national system." [2] Responsibility for judicial policy in each of these systems is centralized in the United States Supreme Court or in the state supreme courts. However, there are a wide variety of other judicial bodies—appeals courts, district courts, county courts, municipal courts, as well as quasi-judicial administrative bodies—so that the judiciary, taken as a totality, represents a complex mix of federal, state, district, and local authorities.

Judicial Policy Making

Policy formation, as discussed in chapter 3, is the process of making and issuing instructions from policy makers to implementers. Policy is an instrument for changing the behavior of others in the direction favored by policy makers. In this book we have focused primarily on the implementation of social policies that are intended to have widespread effects on the public. Thus, as we have used the term, _policy_ refers to initiatives undertaken to achieve some persistent and systematic change in society.

Within the boundaries of this definition, judicial policy making is in some respects quite similar to but in other respects distinct from policy making in the executive and legislative branches of government.

Similarities

As is the case with executive or legislative policies, the public impact of court decisions can often be significant and widespread. While the technical scope of many court cases may be narrow because the cases are often limited to resolving an immediate controversy between litigants, the long-range ramifications of key court decisions can have very broad and significant impacts on society. For example, a trial court, one that determines questions of fact and law, can decide that a government is obligated to change its behavior with respect to a "class" of citizens, as in decisions involving the determination of welfare eligibility. An appellate court, deciding questions of statutory or constitutional law, can determine that the law requires changes in behavior on the part of certain populations; Supreme Court actions on school integration and prayer are examples of such decisions. It is obvious that these types of "policy decisions . . . reflect certain priorities of values"[3] that extend well beyond the parties immediately involved in the case. In these instances judicial policies can have the same widespread impacts on society as public policies formulated by the other branches of government.

Dissimilarities

The major difference between judicial policy making and policy formulation in the executive and the legislative branches of government involves a set of technical constraints that are imposed by the requirements of "due process." All final decisions of the courts are made in a formal arena defined by the requirements of law. In order to be legitimate, judicial policy must be formulated in accordance with the established rules and procedures that constitute "due process of law."

While judicial policy-making prerogatives are potentially broad, "due process" procedures operate to limit their scope. Specifically, the judicial arena has the following characteristics:[4]

1. Courts are passive institutions—they respond to cases brought to them through the initiative of others (the parties to a case).

2. Courts are limited in the cases they can consider—only those controversies which can be resolved by reference to law, "justiciable issues," are within the jurisdiction of courts.
3. The role of judges is limited to interpreting "rules of law" so as to resolve cases before them. Rules of law originate from a variety of sources: constitutions, statutes, administrative regulations, judicial precedents.
4. Only those people who are before a court can be technically ordered to abide by a decision (although the subsequent legal ramifications of major court decisions can effect large numbers of nonparticipants over time).

The role of the courts, thus, is circumscribed by the formal requirements of the law. Policy is a by-product of the need to resolve cases by means of legal interpretation.

However, while the freedom of judges is limited, they retain considerable discretion to make policy judgments. Although judges have to base their decisions on law, the law is a complex system of rules whose applicability to a particular case is not always certain. Judges can decide which rule of law applies to a case. They can decide which rule should have priority when rules are in conflict. They can interpret what the appropriate rule requires the parties to do in a specific factual situation. Judges can make new legal rules through the accumulation of judicial precedents into a body of common-law principles. In addition, the power of judicial review gives courts the opportunity to decide the validity of policies formulated by other parties by determining whether or not sufficient authority exists for such policies.

Finally, high appellate court judges enjoy wide discretion in deciding which cases they will hear and which they will ignore. And judges have a variety of ways of keeping issues off the agenda. For example, they can conclude that some issues are "not justiciable" or are "political" questions. Hence, they have the power to endorse an existing policy if they refuse to hear a case or define the issue as not among those that may be decided by a court.

Communication Linkages

The first step toward successful implementation of judicial decisions is to communicate policy instructions accurately to those who are responsible for their implementation. In simple cases that involve the resolution of questions of fact between only two litigants, communication and implementation problems are minimal since communication is direct, or one-to-one. The judge tells the parties what the law requires of them; instructions and obligations are usually specific; and there is no question about the capacity of the court to order the parties to comply.

In cases that involve more complex and wide-ranging judicial mandates, however, communication can pose difficult problems. In the 1954 *Brown* decision on school desegregation, for example, the United States Supreme Court said:

> Separate educational facilities are inherently unequal. Therefore, we hold that the plaintiffs and others similarly situated for whom the actions have been brought are, by reason of the segregation complained of, derived of the equal protection of the laws.[5]

The communication challenges in this case arose because the "others similarly situated" were not yet in court. Hence, the *Brown* decision, and other decisions that affect a larger public beyond the parties specifically involved in the court proceedings, must be communicated effectively to larger publics.

Judicial communications, like other policy instructions, can be distorted by being garbled themselves, by being garbled by others, or by a combination of the two. If the meaning of a court decision is ambiguous, it is difficult to interpret such a decision. Other decisions may have relatively clear meanings, but they are garbled in their interpretation by communicators and recipients. The California State Supreme Court decision in *Serrano* v. *Priest*, for example, was precise both in its legal reasoning and about what state authorities were obligated to correct. This decision was, however, misunderstood by President Nixon, the *New York Times*, and legislative leaders in California.[6]

The problems of communicating court decisions to larger publics are numerous. Courts issue their decisions through formal channels—written opinions that are routinely followed by specialists.

All the major written opinions of the United States Supreme Court, for example, are compiled and issued by such organizations as the Lawyers Co-operative Publishing Company, and are later codified in Supreme Court reports so that lawyers and other interested parties can use a formal system to reference these cases (e.g., *Brown* v. *Board of Education of Topeka*, 347 U.S. 483; 98 L. Ed.; 74 Sup. Ct. 1954). Each of the states also has a formal system for codifying its major court decisions.

However, the general public—including those who are indirectly affected by a particular court decision—usually hears about judicial actions through intermediaries: the press, interest groups, or lawyers. These intermediaries are not under the direct control of courts and are free to ignore, partially convey, and otherwise distort court decisions. Courts have no sanctions with which to punish those who misreport a decision.

Courts, perhaps more than other policy makers, have an incentive to make sure that their formal instructions—in the form of written opinions in important cases—are understood. In establishing precedents, the written opinion is the principal device for communicating what a court wants done and why. This is so because courts have relatively few other formal or informal means to clarify what they want except through follow-up cases, which may take months or years to materialize. Congress, for example, can pass vague legislation and then use its legislative oversight powers to further interpret its instructions to bureaucrats. Executives, such as the president, can issue clarifying orders or review and amend administrative regulations to make their meaning clearer. In addition, legislators, executives, bureaucrats, and interest groups all engage in informal negotiations and discussions about what policies mean.

Since formal written messages between the courts and the implementers directly affect the power relationships between these two groups, it is important to analyze these linkages more carefully. We have already noted that such communications are transmitted by written opinions, whose content is often conveyed to affected publics through intermediaries. In this section we will deal with the characteristics of the messages themselves, with other cues given to potential implementers, and with the impact of the beliefs of recipients on their perceptions of court decisions.[7]

Clarity of Decisions

We have stressed the fact that policy instructions that specify goals and means in a precise manner are less likely to be misinterpreted than instructions that are vague. Sometimes, however, judicial policy makers deliberately use ambiguous language, either because they are unclear in their own minds or because they are attempting to minimize the political repercussions of their decisions. For example, the Supreme Court's 1955 implementation order on the *Brown* case stated that desegregation should be carried out "with all deliberate speed." One intent here was to allow state and local school districts, especially in the South, to adjust to the new desegregation policy, but the results led to slowness in compliance.

Just as ambiguous policy instructions from Congress give discretion to bureaucrats, ambiguous court decisions make it possible for lower courts and others to procrastinate, or to reinterpret a case's meaning according to their own values. Ambiguity reduces the amount of control exercised by the court while increasing the power of implementers. Should the implementers disagree with the court, an ambiguous decision permits them to avoid full compliance.

Other Cues

While the specific language of a court decision is the most important part of the message sent to prospective implementers,[8] other cues are often

provided by judges and other judicial decision makers. One such indicator is the political backing for a decision. The size of a Supreme Court
majority, for example, is an important cue regarding the permanence of a
decision. If the court is badly split (e.g., in a 5-4 decision), a change of
court membership might reverse, or limit, the application of a judicial
rule. Similarly, if other influentials—elected officials, legal scholars,
important interest groups—oppose a decision, they may exert sufficient
pressure to change the decision in the future through subsequent litigation, by influencing future appointments to the court, or through support
for constitutional amendments. In the case of court interpretations of
statutes, a hostile reception indicates that the law itself might be rewritten
to modify a court decision.

Since policy is made continuously, rather than once and for all,
prospective implementers assess any directive according to its chances for
persistence. If a court decision appears to be based on a shaky and
transient coalition, people who are not parties to case may decide that the
majority will not persist long enough to force them to act should they
resist. Conversely, if a court majority persists and is repeatedly
assembled—as in the long line of school integration cases—then the
chances increase that it will be taken seriously.

Decisions and Beliefs

A final influence on how effectively judicial messages are communicated and understood is the relationship between the message and the
beliefs of recipients. Court decisions, like other policy instructions, are
sent into a society that holds diverse opinions and beliefs. A court
decision, like any new bit of information, can be interpreted in light of
these preexisting beliefs.[9]

The courts are often called upon to mediate cases and controversies
that may involve ideological issues that deeply divide the society. When
the subject matter of a decision touches on strongly held ideological
beliefs, some degree of distortion is almost inevitable. Supreme Court
decisions banning prayer in public schools, for example, were perceived
by many school administrators as forbidding only those prayers led by the
teacher. In fact, the decisions applied to all prayer, including reserving
time for silent prayer. Social psychologists have pointed out that people
can respond to discrepancies between strongly held beliefs and a contradictory message by distorting the meaning of the message.[10] A court
decision touching on a deeply held belief is a candidate for such distortion.

Hence, with respect to the larger publics affected by wide-ranging
judicial policy, there are a variety of ways in which judicial policies can
be distorted in their communication. Intermediaries can misunderstand,

or otherwise change, the meaning of decisions while transmitting them to larger publics; the decisions themselves may be unclear; other cues can modify the "meaning" a message holds; and the preexisting beliefs of recipients may also exert an influence. These and other sources of communications breakdowns can have an impact on the implementation of judicial policies.

Judicial Policy Implementation

Once judicial decisions have been communicated to relevant parties, the implementation phase of the judicial policy process begins. Like all other policy instructions, judicial decisions consist of sets of instructions that establish the priority of certain goals and the means for achieving them by

1. identifying which actors and arenas are *relevant* to the achievement of policy goals (designating formal implementers by offering incentives and sanctions for particular persons to change their behavior, etc.).
2. defining *relationships* between actors (providers and beneficiaries, superiors and subordinates, buyers and sellers of services, etc.).
3. relating individual behaviors to the purpose of the policy by *organizing* and *coordinating* the parties to achieve policy goals.

   The role of courts in the implementation environment is shaped by the important legal limitations on their powers discussed previously. While courts can make decisions that affect many people beyond those participating in a case, their power to issue direct orders and to assess compliance is limited to those who are before them as parties to a case. Even in this instance the incentives available to courts are usually negative: They are sanctions to be invoked (arrest for contempt, fines, etc.) rather than rewards to be promised. And often the use of such negative sanctions can occur only after procedural requirements—hearings, appeals, and so forth—have consumed considerable time.
   When decisions have widespread effects, implementation grows correspondingly more complex and less subject to control and coordination by the particular court making the initial decision. When, for example, an appellate court interprets the law to resolve a particular case, it is saying what the law requires in all similar factual situations. Lower courts are obligated to accept this interpretation and to apply it when appropriate. And those people who are not yet in court but are behaving in a manner contrary to the newly interpreted legal requirement should also change their behavior to meet the requirements of the law. Thus, the United States Supreme Court's decision in the *Brown* case, which interpreted the Constitution as prohibiting *de jure* racial segregation in

all public schools, affected a massive number of people throughout the United States. Other well-known examples of such widespread decisions include school prayer, defendants' rights, voting rights, and legislative reapportionment.

When court decisions should affect the behavior of large numbers of people who are not direct parties to a case, there still can be uncertainty about which other actors should obey the decision. Since the court's communication with these outside parties is not direct, there are opportunities for these parties to misperceive or selectively perceive their newly formulated legal obligations.

Both communications and compliance difficulties make it necessary for the courts to rely on intermediaries to help implement broadly applicable decisions. Judges do not take the initiative in communicating their decisions to affected publics beyond the parties to a case. At most, they make their decisions available in written form for publication. They do not, for example, send mailings to those whom they believe should know about a decision or issue other directives that identify what those people should do. Thus, if people other than the parties to a case are going to learn about a relevant decision, they have to either monitor court actions—as compiled in case reporters—or rely on others. The intermediaries who communicate court decisions to larger publics are a varied lot, and their activities, as noted previously, may alter or distort the message they convey. The mass media, for example, report major court decisions and usually simplify and dramatize them in the process. Lawyers working for people who could be affected by a decision may tell their clients about it, but they can also interpret the message to require the smallest change in their client's behavior. Interest groups that see a decision as a resource can use it to press claims on affected individuals by telling them that the law requires a change in their behavior in a direction favored by the interest group.

The limited nature of judicial power also makes courts dependent on other intermediaries to help enforce their interpretations of precedents, administrative regulations, and statutory or constitutional law. Since judges cannot take the initiative in bringing people into court, they must rely on others to bring noncompliant parties into court. In some types of cases—for example, those specifying criminal procedures—this does not present too great a problem. It is clear to most of those affected (police departments, district attorneys, etc.) that they will soon be in court and that noncompliant behavior will lead to future losses in criminal prosecutions. As a result, criminal justice authorities have had a good record of voluntarily complying with Supreme Court decisions involving the right to counsel, the requirement that they inform suspects of their rights, and so on.

In other areas intermediaries must play a major role in helping courts enforce decisions on recalcitrant populations. Often these intermediaries are interest groups that see a court decision as an important resource to advance their goals. Thus, for example, the Supreme Court relied on the NAACP's Legal Defense Fund to bring noncompliant segregationist school and voting officials into court, to challenge subterfuges that violated the intent of past decisions, and to organize and coordinate litigation.[11] Other interest groups (ACLU, Jehovah's Witnesses, Lawyers Committee for Civil Rights Under Law, etc.) have played a similar role in making litigation an extension of "pressure group activity." Still other interest groups play a more occasional role, suing to enforce a particular decision as a means of achieving a specific goal (e.g., cases involving Planned Parenthood and state birth control laws).

Another important set of intermediaries consists of the lower courts. When the Supreme Court, or any other appeals court, interprets the law, that decision is binding on all lower courts. But the lower courts have some discretion in deciding just how that precedent should be interpreted. They too can distinguish among factual situations and choose among competing precedents and legal rules to make their decisions. While defiance is rare, the higher courts must rely on the cooperation of lower courts.[12] In short, the implementation problems raised in carrying out judicial policy can be complex. It is not always clear who, beyond the parties to a case, should comply with a new court decision. As a result, several complicating factors can emerge.

First, potential implementers may have substantial discretion over their actions unless they are brought into court. This discretion can reduce compliance when the values of the implementers conflict with those of the court.

Second, courts must rely on intermediaries to communicate their decisions to the larger population. There is a risk that the message will be distorted.

Third, courts must rely on intermediaries to bring noncompliant individuals into court in order to use what power they have to change behavior.

Fourth, the relationships among implementation actors can change during the implementation process: New actors can enter; further litigation can reduce the discretion of some actors; and mechanisms for compliance can change.

Finally, the coordination of implementation activities is a consequence of the separate activities of many different actors: intermediaries communicating decisions to a larger population, people rationally calculating the advantages and disadvantages of voluntary compliance, interest groups using court decisions as a resource to advance their goals, and other courts using subsequent cases as opportunities to reiterate and strengthen the initial decision.

Hence, it is obvious that when the courts deal with complex ideological issues that can affect large segments of society that are not the original parties to the case, the problems of implementation can also become very complex. As a result, it is extremely difficult to generalize about the process of judicial policy implementation. Instead, we will offer some examples of judicial implementation to illustrate the complexity and diversity of this process.

Examples of Judicial Implementation

Three different sets of cases, involving school desegregation, inequalities in educational financing, and criminal procedures, will be described to indicate the diverse nature of judicial policy implementation.

In the desegregation cases, the United States Supreme Court set a broad policy goal of eliminating *de jure* school desegregation in the 1954 *Brown* decision. In a series of later cases it expanded this goal to encompass various facets of *de facto* segregation and school integration. The implementation of the original 1954 *Brown* decision was delegated to the lower federal courts in the 1955 Supreme Court order. Hence, lower federal courts and state and local school authorities were designated as the intermediary implementers responsible for securing compliance under the original *Brown* decision. This is the usual procedure. Only rarely do appellate courts retain jurisdiction to oversee compliance with an order reversed or upheld on appeal.

In the area of educational finance, the California State Supreme Court established a *state* constitutional standard in the 1971 case of *Serrano* v. *Priest* that required "fiscal neutrality" in the financing of schools within the state. The United States Supreme Court rejected this as a national standard in the 1973 case of *Rodriguez* v. *San Antonio School District.* Hence, the California decision was confined to that state, although other state courts have subsequently dealt with school financing decisions within their own boundaries. In the *Serrano* case the California Supreme Court gave discretion to state policy makers (the governor and the state legislature) to devise and institute a plan for compliance.

In the final set of examples, the cases involving defendants' rights, the United States Supreme Court once again devised a national policy, but this time in a more incremental fashion. Policy goals, and the means for achieving these goals, were established over time through the accumulation of a series of different decisions. The intermediary implementers involved in these cases were federal, state, and local criminal justice authorities—the police, the prosecutors, and the courts.

School Desegregation

The Supreme Court's initial policy statements on school desegregation were contained in the *Brown* decision of 1954 and in the court's implementation decision in 1955.

The 1954 decision was based on the Court's interpretation of the "equal protection" clause of the Fourteenth Amendment, which had been added to the Constitution of the United States after the Civil War. Although the Fourteenth Amendment had provided that "no state shall . . . deny to any person within its jurisdiction the equal protection of the laws," the Supreme Court had declared, in the 1896 case of *Plessy* v. *Ferguson*, that "separate but equal" treatment of the races was constitutional. Hence, the 1896 decision had established a constitutional justification for the establishment of a *de jure* segregated school system that was sanctioned by law and was widespread in the South, as well as in a number of northern states.

Following the *Plessy* decision the Court began chipping away at segregationist practices in a number of areas, particularly in state-sponsored graduate education programs, to such an extent that some observers have argued that the 1954 *Brown* case was "not a dramatic shift in doctrine."[12] Nevertheless, the 1954 decision constituted an important watershed, since it involved a complete overruling and repudiation of the earlier *Plessy* doctrine. In the *Brown* case the Court declared that

> separate educational facilities are inherently unequal. Therefore, we hold that the plaintiffs and others similarly situated for whom the actions have been brought are, by reason of the segregation complained of, deprived the equal protection of the laws.[13]

It was immediately obvious that this decision would have very significant and widespread effects throughout the nation. Since it outlawed *de jure* school segregation as a matter of law, it meant that state and local school authorities could no longer finance or maintain schools that were legally segregated on the basis of race. Because of its dramatic ramifications, the Court waited a year before issuing a follow-up decision on *Brown*. The Court was more restrained when it issued this second decision, which instructed the lower federal courts to implement *Brown* "with all deliberate speed."

The major problem the Court faced was that of enforcement. The Supreme Court, acting alone, was incapable of securing compliance in the implementation of the *Brown* decision throughout the nation, but especially in the southern states, since this decision, "although formally binding, was not self-enforcing. Its implementation required the willing cooperation of school districts, or failing that, the continuing imposition of judicial will." [14]

The exact form of this judicial will was specified by the Supreme Court in the second *Brown* case (1955):

> The Supreme Court felt it was incapable of supervising desegregation in every segregated school district in the country. Thus, it gave to the district courts the authority to carry out the principles of Brown with "all deliberate speed." [15]

Thus, the responsibility for monitoring the implementation of the 1954 decision was delegated to lower federal courts by means of the 1955 follow-up decision. The implementation environment in which these courts operated was a difficult one, often characterized by uncooperative state and local officials and also by intransigent judges.

Like many other implementers, the lower federal courts were given considerable discretion in defining policy goals and means. While the Supreme Court set the goal of prohibiting *de jure* segregation, the lower courts exercised substantial discretion in determining both the intent and the effects of laws and other governmental practices that produced discriminatory practices, and in fashioning appropriate means and remedies to deal with those practices.

> Rather than insisting on a uniform remedy, the Court endorsed "practical flexibility" to meet diverse local situations. While desegregation was to occur with "all deliberate speed," Brown II rested primary responsibility on school authorities and left the task of policing and evaluating their efforts to lower federal courts. [16]

Thus, the role of lower federal courts in the implementation of school desegregation policy was potentially very significant. This potential was especially important insofar as local school officials and others attempted to resist compliance with *Brown* and the more precise judicial requirements that followed it.

Despite initial resistance, especially on the part of some school officials, the combination of court actions and the administrative efforts of HEW and other agencies has succeeded in eliminating a great deal of *de jure* school segregation throughout the United States. At the same time that this was occuring, *de facto* segregation of schools, which resulted from residential patterns created by racial discrimination, persisted and even expanded. As a result, the Supreme Court and lower courts extended the meaning of *Brown* through subsequent decisions. In *Green v. Board of Education of New Kent County* (1968), the Supreme Court ruled that the school district was obligated to produce a specific plan to desegregate rather than merely offering the opportunity to desegregate through a policy of open enrollment.

In *Swann* v. *Charlotte-Mecklenburg Board of Education* (1971), the Court sustained a compulsory busing plan ordered by a lower court because it was designed to correct past governmental actions that had created a pattern of segregation. Hence, in *Green* and *Swann* the Court moved beyond a ban on existing *de jure* segregation toward rectifying the *de facto* segregation that may have occurred as a result of prior discriminatory practices. *Keyes* v. *School District No. 1, Denver, Colorado* (1973) extended integration requirements to northern districts whose past practices had intentionally produced a segregated pattern in their schools. Only one limiting case, *Milliken* v. *Bradley* (1974), confined lower-court integration orders to a single school district and rejected the need for metropolitan-wide plans unless there was clear evidence that *de jure* segregation was involved.

As a result of these later decisions, the implementation responsibilities of the courts expanded dramatically. No longer were these courts being asked to deal with *de jure* segregation alone. Now a shift in emphasis has put the courts in the business of correcting *de facto* segregation that had resulted from past *de jure* practices. In essence, this policy shift involved the courts, and many state and local school authorities, in the process of integrating schools so as to achieve a "better racial balance among pupils."

While the *abstract* goal of school integration—and its implicit assumption of an improvement in educational quality—may be widely accepted, the specific remedies for achieving school integration are extremely controversial. Since the lower federal courts must apply these remedies in specific instances, they have borne the brunt of controversy and criticism, with much of this controversy surrounding the issue of compulsory busing.

The controversy over busing has been shaped by the implementation environment facing the lower courts. If an unconstitutional form of *de facto* school segregation is found to exist—using the standards set forth in previous court decisions—lower-court judges are obligated to find a remedy. Most of the causes of such *de facto* segregation are beyond the direct control of the courts:

> Housing segregation is so severe and demographic trends so unfavorable that busing is the only way to achieve integration for the foreseeable future in many communities. Often the only choice is one people most wish to avoid—busing or segregation.[17]

Since judges can only order those before them to comply with their decisions, they must usually work through government officials who are parties to integration suits. And lower courts have only a few available remedies (often limited to variations of busing) with which to direct these governmental officials.

As a result, lower courts have adopted a variety of approaches to busing. We will deal with three such approaches, each taking a different path, in an effort to illustrate the nature of this type of judicial implementation effort.

San Francisco Judge Weigel, in *Johnson* v. *San Francisco Unified School District* (1971), found vestiges of *de jure* segregation to exist as a consequence of past governmental actions (school construction policies, attendance zones, etc.) and inactions (failure to correct resulting patterns).[18] The school board apparently believed in the correctness of the decision and the need to remedy the identified deficiencies. Judge Wiegel set a general requirement that racial imbalance be corrected, but refused to become involved in formulating the details of the plan. Instead, he relied primarily on school authorities to choose among competing plans, so long as the choice corrected the existing racial imbalance. Kirp writes:

> Judge Weigel left implementation in the hands of those formally charged with the responsibility for running the school system; this choice, while not inevitable, conformed to traditional understandings of the demarcation between judicial authority and political and administrative authority.[19]

Kirp continues by noting the disadvantages of this approach:

> In San Francisco, this expression of judicial laissez faire has had significant consequences. The management of desegregation has been a quintessentially political process which, while bounded by the terms of the decree, has been shaped far more by activity outside the courtroom.[20]

Specifically, this political process was shaped by the relatively low priority that many school officials actually placed on achieving integration; by the state of disorganization and turmoil within the school administration; by competing demands for recognition and special educational adjustments from other groups (Chinese- and Spanish-speaking parents, as well as neighborhood associations); and by reduced willingness on the part of the supporters of integration to press aggressively for a comprehensive plan.

As a consequence, school officials "technically" complied with the court's order by preparing an integration plan. In terms of actual, measurable results, however, this plan seemed to satisfy no one: Racial imbalance persisted; no appreciable gains were made in minority student test scores; and no group expressed the opinion that educational quality had improved. Implementation was "successful" in a very narrow sense, since a plan was adopted, but by any more substantive standard very little had changed.

The problem in San Francisco was that the school and political authorities responsible for choosing and implementing the desegregation plan attempted to respond to many diverse demands for special adjustments and exemptions by particular groups of parents.

Boston   Boston school authorities, by contrast to those in San Francisco, were uncooperative from the outset. They challenged the legitimacy of the court to order a change in their behavior and refused to cooperate in producing their own plan or in implementing the plans that were eventually adopted.[21]

Judge Arthur Garrity, in *Morgan* v. *Hennigan* (1974), found unconstitutional segregation in Boston schools and ordered desegregation. Instead of cooperating in the implementation of this order, key school officials refused to devise an acceptable desegregation plan. Thus, Judge Garrity increasingly relied on people other than Boston school authorities—the staff of the State Department of Education, and then court-appointed "masters"—to devise desegregation plans, and the judge participated extensively in working out the details of those plans.

Since Boston school authorities failed to staff desegregation activities adequately and often adopted a public posture of defiance, Judge Garrity ordered the creation of a Department of Implementation, which, while formally a part of the Boston schools, was in fact responsible to him. In effect, Judge Garrity and his appointees became both the desegregation policy makers and the implementers for the Boston schools.[22] Robert B. Richards argued in a seminar paper that the Boston public schools were put in virtual "receivership" by the judge, who limited or suspended the discretion of school and political authorities in important respects.

Because of the size and visibility of Judge Garrity's role, his actions were blamed for everything that went wrong with desegregation in Boston: violence in the schools, antibusing demonstrations, an increase in racial tension throughout the city, white flight to the suburbs. Boston city authorities were faced with the consequences of the plan—particularly increased police costs due to the violence that resulted—yet they did not have a significant voice in the shaping of court orders. Mayor White complained about Judge Garrity's role as follows:

> Blacks and Whites are going through major changes in this city but apparently the judiciary isn't . . . What the hell does he think? He's bigger than the mayor of this city? What does he think? We're a bunch of clerks?[23]

The Boston example has some similarities with the San Francisco case, but there are also major differences. In both cases plans were formulated and implemented in a complex, and often hostile, political environment. The major distinction, however, is found in the fact that Judge Weigel chose to define broad legal requirements and left the further formulation of plans and their implementation to local authorities sensitive to the multitude of political demands outside the concern of the court. The advantage of Weigel's approach was that local authorities cooperated through compliance with the "letter" of Weigel's orders despite losses in substance. Judge Garrity did not expect this modicum of cooperation from school authorities. Therefore, he chose the active and controversial role of intervening personally in the actual formulation and implementation of desegregation plans. Hence, he was accused of political insensitivity and alienated local officials in his efforts to directly push his own substantive solutions.

Wiegel's approach might be characterized as a "political" solution since he set a limited judicial standard and turned over responsibility for implementation to actors in the political arena. Garrity's approach was a "receivership" solution in that he suspended the normal political process and substituted a judicially imposed effort in its stead.

Corpus Christi   The final busing example, discussed in seminar work by David R. Joyce, involves the use of "technical" solution, which relied on a computer-generated plan. This solution was implemented in an environment that falls somewhere between the San Francisco and Boston situations. While Corpus Christi authorities could not produce a plan acceptable to the court, they were willing to comply with a plan once it had been devised.

In *Cirneros* v. *Corpus Christi Independent School District* (1970), the federal district court found *de jure* segregation against Mexican-American and black students.[24] Between 1970 and 1975 ten plans devised by Corpus Christi school authorities were rejected by the court because they "failed to integrate the schools or hold out a promise of doing so." It appeared to the court that Corpus Christi school authorities were either unable or unwilling to make progress toward integrating their schools. The "political" solution having failed to produce an acceptable plan, the court turned to a "technical" solution in 1975 with the adoption of a plan devised by computer experts.

The plan was formulated by Joseph Rupp, a local education activist opposed to busing, and by two court-appointed computer experts. This committee programed a computer to devise a school attendance plan designed to meet three major criteria: achieving a desired integration ratio in each school; whenever possible, assigning students to schools within two miles (walking distance) of their homes; and minimizing the distances students were to be bused when busing was necessary. To devise the plan that came closest to meeting these criteria, the court-appointed committee produced a program with 655 equations and 17,000 unknowns in each equation!

As might be expected, the resulting plan was a complex one. The district was divided into 452 grids, each containing 40 students, and each grid was assigned to a particular school to achieve the desired balance. To minimize busing, a lottery system was devised that would keep students in their "neighborhood" schools for the bulk of their education through a system of rotating transfers on a temporary basis.

Corpus Christi school authorities implemented the plan, with mixed results. The program worked with respect to its main criteria: The degree of integration approximated the desired ratios; a number of children were able to continue walking to school; the rotating-transfer policy preserved neighborhood schools to some extent; and busing distances were minimized. There were, however, many shortcomings in fulfilling even these criteria: The integration ratios fell short because some parents—opposed to putting their children in schools where they would be in the minority—kept their children home or put them in private schools or moved out of the district. Another problem involved the measurement of walking distance—the computer was programed to measure distance as the crow flies—and some students were forced to walk much greater distances, so that "forced busing" was replaced with "forced walking."

Other difficulties materialized because of the limited criteria employed by the computer program itself. While the rotation criterion achieved the goal of preserving neighborhood schools, it did so at the cost of educational discontinuity for the transferred students. Other psychological costs—the belief that being transferred was akin to "serving time" outside of a neighborhood, as well as broken friendships—were also paid by the transient students. The problems faced by bilingual students, now scattered throughout the system, were exacerbated by the limited number of bilingual teachers and the inexperience of other teachers in dealing with integrated classes.

Hence, the results of judicial implementation of desegregation policy are mixed in each of the cases examined. In each instance different actors went to court in an effort to implement policies that would improve the quality of education for minority students. The goal of improving the quality of education, however, extends well beyond the authority of the judiciary. The courts—operating within the constraints of "due process" and established procedures—dealt with determinations of fact (Did *de jure* segregation exist?) and with the selection of remedies intended to achieve the requisite degree of integration or racial balance. While the courts were capable of determining facts, their formulation of remedies rarely satisfied the diverse expectations of participants.

The degree of failure in each approach is attributable to the limitations the courts faced in devising implementation solutions: "political" failure in San Francisco owing to the relatively low priority political officials assigned to the goal of achieving racial balance; "political" hostility and noncooperation and a high level of community conflict in Boston; and "technical" failures in Corpus Christi that resulted from the limited capacity of technical solutions to consider and reconcile complex educational and political problems.

School Finance

As the preceding examples have indicated, school desegregation represents a very difficult implementation problem for the courts. The definition of policy goals is ambiguous; the means are controversial; and the intermediaries are numerous and often either uncooperative or politically incapable of reconciling the conflicting demands made upon them. Judicial implementation of desegregation is akin to trench warfare: slow progress made at great expense. The school finance issue is a different type of situation: a more clear-cut goal, with the choice of means left to a set of readily identifiable and apparently cooperative political authorities. In the eyes of the court the goal was to be achieved with limited, but effective, use of judical intervention. The promise in the California school finance case was one of major reforms with a minimum of judicial effort.

In the 1971 case of *Serrano* v. *Priest*, the California State Supreme Court determined that the state school finance system could not make the amount spent on local education solely a function of the wealth of local school districts.[25] While the issues involved are complex, the problem can be described in simple terms. Local districts are the units that run the public schools by raising and spending money. Money comes from a variety of sources, primarily local property taxes and state and federal aid. The amounts of money spent by local districts differ largely because the amount of taxable property in different local communities varies widely. There are rich districts and poor districts, measured by the amount of taxable property each has available to fulfill its obligations to schoolchildren.

The system of relying heavily on local property taxes to finance schools was challenged in a class action by parents in a lower-spending school district. The California Supreme Court determined that the system violated *state* constitutional requirements. Specifically, the system was found to have classified people in terms of (district) wealth and, hence, made the right to education (protected by the state constitution) a function of local wealth.[26]

The California State Supreme Court was quite precise about what the law prohibited: educational spending inequalities based solely on district wealth. While it was clear that the state school finance system would have to be changed, the court granted substantial discretion to state policy makers—the legislature and the governor—regarding how to comply. The court did not mandate any specific form of compliance (e.g., abolition of the property tax), nor did it prohibit unequal educational spending in any but the specified instance. The very important questions of how and when the judicial goal was to be achieved were left to state authorities.

As a result, state authorities were free, within the boundaries specified by the court, to alter their school finance system. The elected policy makers were responsible for determining which tax sources should be used to pay for equalization (sales, income, statewide property taxes, or whatever). And interest groups were free to press for their own goals (e.g., urban factors providing extra money for cities, as well as similar bonuses for disadvantaged students, and transportation adjustments for rural districts, etc.). The only constraint placed by the court on the policy makers was that their solution meet the state constitutional standard that is now called fiscal neutrality.

The court appears to have adopted this limited role for three different reasons. First, some analysts believed that the existing school finance system was not popular and that a court decision would "break the logjam of the status quo" and free the state to establish a more fiscally equitable system.[26] Many state officials—the superintendent of public instruction, the controller, the speaker of the Assembly, the chairmen of legislative education committees—welcomed the decision. Thus, the court may have believed that these intermediary implementers would comply without specific coercion because many shared the court's goals. Second, the court may have been hesitant to require more specific actions because it lacked the special competence and power to assess alternatives. The complexity of the existing school finance system, and its delicate balance of many competing interests, posed high information costs that could be paid more readily by the legislature than by the court. Finally, it was a legislative prerogative to raise any additional money needed to pay for equalization.[27]

The approach taken in *Serrano* is one that recognizes the advantages and disadvantages of courts as policy-implementing institutions:[28]

1. The court avoided the difficult "political" question of precisely defining educational quality (its measurement and means for insuring it) and

focused instead on prohibiting one pattern of school resource allocation and substituting in its stead a guideline of "fiscal neutrality."
2. The burden of compliance—defining both the means and the specific level to be achieved—was left to state lawmakers.

While compliance with *Serrano* and similar state court decisions has yielded mixed results in other states (reform is being enacted or has been enacted in Minnesota, Kansas, Michigan, and California, with slower progress in New Jersey), the limited goal of fiscal neutrality has been achieved in a number of instances.

Defendants' Rights

Unlike the first two examples, our third set of cases did not take shape in a single watershed decision. In the area of defendants' rights, the United States Supreme Court—in a series of decisions spanning several decades—has incrementally developed a body of law that puts a positive obligation on state and local criminal authorities to insure the rights of individuals in criminal proceedings. Court decisions that have addressed such issues as the right to adequate counsel and the application of "due process" protections to those accused of crimes have involved a variety of different Supreme Court cases, including *Betts* v. *Brady* (1942), *Mallory* v. *United States* (1957), *Rogers* v. *Richmond* (1961), *Gideon* v. *Wainwright* (1963), *Miranda* v. *State of Arizona* (1966).

A second major distinction between implementation of defendants' rights and the desegregation and educational financing cases is that the final set of cases have all been confined primarily to a group of actors who operate within the judicial arena. Whereas the desegregation cases involved a complex set of interactions between the courts, state and local school authorities, high-intensity interest groups, and the like, and the educational cases involved interaction between the courts and the executive and legislative branches of government, the key actors in the defendants' rights cases have been other judicial actors such as court prosecutors, police, and corrections officials.

As a consequence, compliance by these intermediary implementers has been, for the most part, voluntary. State and local criminal justice authorities have changed their practices to conform to judicial standards. While these cases have resulted in some friction between the Supreme Court and outside political authorities—for example, the "law and order" campaign of Richard Nixon in 1972 and changes in federal criminal statutes to modify some decisions—outright refusals to comply have been minimal.

Two different explanations can be advanced to explain the court's success in implementing its policy goals in the case of defendants' rights: (1) the incremental way in which the policies were formulated and (2) the characteristics of the population of intermediary implementers.

Whether or not the Supreme Court used incrementalism as an explicit policy formulation and implementation strategy is unimportant. It is clear that the policy did develop incrementally and that the pace and character of the individual decisions did aid in securing compliance on a gradual basis, ultimately producing a transformed criminal justice system. The incrementalism took several forms. Some new judicial rules—such as an absolute right to counsel in serious criminal prosecutions—were tried in limited arenas (such as federal prosecutions) before being applied to a wider arena (state actions). The workability of a rule was tested prior to its application to other situations. The rules themselves were gradually expanded to cover more factual situations. So, for example, the standards for determining whether or not a defendant had a "fair trial" were redefined over many cases. A "special circumstances" rule entitling specific indigents to lawyers started with a narrow set of circumstances and gradually encompassed more types of trials and defendants. By the time the "special circumstances" rule was replaced with a form of absolute right to counsel, the remaining circumstances were relatively small.[29] Such a selective development of cases segmented the problem of compliance into many specific adjustments. Thus, criminal justice authorities were not faced with a broad rule requiring many changes. Instead, they found themselves marginally adjusting specific practices in response to new judicial standards. The advantage for the Court was that it could see how well or how poorly a new limited rule had been complied with prior to moving further in its development and implementation.

The second explanation for the relative success of policy implementation in this area involves the characteristics of the environment in which the policies were implemented. As explained earlier, the key formal actors were drawn from the judicial arena. While criminal justice authorities are numerous and decentralized, they are particularly vulnerable to the judicial sanctions that can be imposed for failure to comply. These authorities want to convict those whom they charge with crimes. Failure to follow court decisions means that defendants—who have an incentive to use past decisions as a resource—have a ground for appeal that can make their convictions doubtful. Defendants and their lawyers are an additional set of intermediaries whose incentive to press for compliance remains strong. Finally, prosecutors—who play a central role in this system—may feel an obligation to obey the law stemming from their professional role. Thus, the implementation environment of the criminal justice system is such that both the value orientation of actors and the incentives employed encourage voluntary compliance.

Summary

In this chapter we have described the unique policy formation and implementation environments faced by the courts. The policy formulation role of courts is governed by strict procedural requirements and is limited in its goals to resolving controversies by reference to what the law requires. When judicial decisions have consequences beyond the parties to a case, there are often serious difficulties in communicating new legal requirements to populations that are not yet within the jurisdiction of courts.

The difficulties in the judicial implementation environment reflect the unique role of the courts in the policy system. Courts are most effective in the implementation environment insofar as they pursue compliance with specific judicial requirements through intermediaries who are direct parties to a case. Even here, as our school desegregation examples indicate, there are problems posed by the limited nature of judicial power. When, however, the courts must rely on a complex mix of political implementers drawn from a wide variety of different arenas to deal with highly controversial issues, their role in implementation is much more susceptible to serious breakdowns.

Notes

1. Glendon Schubert, *Judicial Policy-Making: The Political Role of the Courts* (Glenview, Ill.: Scott, Foresman, 1965), p. 1.

2. Ibid., p. 21.

3. Ibid., p. 1.

4. Denis G. Sullivan, Robert T. Nakamura, and Richard F. Winters, *How America Is Ruled* (New York: Wiley, 1980), chaps. 23–24.

5. *Brown v. Board of Education of Topeka*, 347 U.S. 483, 1954.

6. Arnold J. Meltsner, Gregory W. Kast, John Kramer, and Robert T. Nakamura, *Political Feasibility of School Finance Reform in California* (New York: Praeger, 1972), pp. 228–232.

7. Some of these categories are adapted from Stephen Wasby, *The Impact of the United States Supreme Court: Some Perspectives* (Homewood, Ill.: Dorsey Press, 1970).

8. This argument parallels Erving Goffman's distinction between an "expression given" (a message sent with an expressed intention of making a particular impression) and an "expression given-off" (other messages from the sender that are taken to reveal the true nature of what is occurring). See Erving Goffman, *The Presentation of Self in Everyday Life* (Garden City, N.Y.: Doubleday, 1959), chap. 1.

9. See Aaron B. Wildavsky, "The Analysis of Issue Contexts in the Study of Decision-Making," *Journal of Politics*, November 1962.

10. The cognitive dissonance model is explained by Robert Lane and David Sears, *Public Opinion* (Englewood Cliffs, N.J. Prentice-Hall, 1964). For an application to a court decision, see William K. Muir, *Prayer in the Schools: Law and Attitude Change* (Chicago: University of Chicago Press, 1967).

11. Clement Vose, "Litigation as a Form of Pressure Group Activity," in Raymond Wolfinger, ed., *Readings in American Political Behavior* (Englewood Cliffs, N.J.: Prentice-Hall, 1966).

12. Anthony Champagne and Stuart Nagel, "Civil Rights Policies: Minimizing Discrimination Based on Race and Sex," in Theodore Lowi and Alan Stone, eds., *Nationalizing Government: Public Policies in America* (Beverly Hills, Calif.: Sage Publications, 1978), pp. 301–339.

13. *Brown* v. *Board of Education* (1954). For an extensive listing of cases see Gary Orfield, *Must We Bus: Segregated Schools and National Policy* (Washington, D.C.: Brookings, 1978), pp. 20–22.

14. David L. Kirp, "Race, Politics, and the Courts: School Desegregation in San Francisco," *Harvard Educational Review*, November, 1976, p. 583.

15. Champagne and Nagel, "Civil Rights Policies," p. 303.

16. Kirp, "Race, Politics, and the Courts," p. 583.

17. Orfield, *Must We Bus*, p. 118.

18. Kirp, "Race, Politics, and the Courts," p. 598.

19. Ibid., p. 598.

20. Ibid.

21. Orfield, *Must We Bus*, pp. 144–146.

22. Orfield, *Must We Bus*, and Robert B. Richards, "Formulation and Implementation of Desegregation Policy in Boston," seminar paper, Dartmouth College, March 8, 1979.

23. Quoted in Alan Lupo, *Liberty's Chosen Home* (Boston: Little, Brown, 1977), p. 286.

24. The material for this section is drawn from David R. Joyce, "Formulation and Implementation of School Desegregation Policy in Corpus Christi, Texas," seminar paper, Dartmouth College, Government 83, March 8, 1979. Joyce relied primarily on material from *School Desegregation in Corpus Christi, Texas*, report of the Texas State Advisory Commission on Civil Rights, May 1977.

25. Arnold Meltsner and Robert T. Nakamura, "Political Implications of Serrano," in John Pincus, ed., *School Finance in Transition*, RAND School Finance Series (Boston: Ballinger, 1973); David L. Kirp, "Judicial Policy-Making: Inequitable Public School Financing and the *Serrano* Case (1971)," in Allan P. Sindler, ed., *Policy and Politics in America* (Boston: Little, Brown, 1973).

26. John E. Coons, William H. Clune, and Stephen D. Sugarman, *Private Wealth and Public Education* (Cambridge, Mass.: Belknap Press, 1970). For a discussion of the effects of *Serrano*, see Gerald C. Hayward, "*Serrano* and School Finance Reform in California," in J. Alan Thomas and Robert K. Wimpelberg, eds., *Dilemmas in School Finance* (Chicago: Midwestern Administration Center, 1978).

27. Robert T. Nakamura, "Information and the Policy Process: Experts and the Formulation of School Finance Reform in California," unpublished Ph.D. dissertation, University of California, Berkeley, 1974).

28. This analysis has been summarized from David L. Kirp, "Law, Politics, and Equal Educational Opportunity: The Limits of Judicial Involvement," *Harvard Educational Review*, May 1977, pp. 117–137.

29. See Anthony Lewis, *Gideon's Trumpet* (New York: Vintage, 1964).

PART 3

Linkages

Chapter Seven

Implementation Linkages: Policy Makers and Implementers

At the outset of this study we viewed the policy process as a series of three functional environments—policy formation, policy implementation, and policy evaluation—that are interconnected by a circular system of communications and compliance linkages. Now that we have examined each of these environments, it is important to analyze the different types of linkages that can tie the policy system together.

The "classical" model described in chapter 1 was based on the assumption that these linkages are hierarchical, with policy makers at the top ordering subordinate implementers to carry out their commands in a tight, technical, nonpolitical fashion. Our analysis, however, has indicated that there are a variety of political forces at work in all three of the policy environments. As a result, there appear to be many situations in which implementers possess a considerable degree of independent discretion and authority to exercise their own political judgments in order to influence and shape the policy process.

Political scientists Laurence I. Radway and Arthur A. Maass have pointed out three different types of discretionary powers that administrators may be able to exercise in the course of their daily operations:

1. Technical discretion (the policy mandate is clear and the administrator plays the role of the technical expert in fulfilling it).
2. Discretion in the reconciliation of interests (the policy mandate is in dispute, and the administrator acquires certain discretion to mediate and facilitate negotiations).

3. Discretion in social planning (the policy mandate is vague, and the administrator is authorized to work out definite rules for action and to plan goals for governmental activities).[1]

If we view these discretionary options in terms of different types of linkages that can exist between policy makers and implementers, it becomes apparent that each involves a successive shift of power away from the formal policy makers and toward the implementers. The first type, technical discretion, fits most closely into the "classical" concept, in which the policy makers dominate and control the policy process. In the third type, social planning discretion, the implementers possess the power to plan policy goals.

In order to clarify the significance of this shift of power, this chapter will describe five different types of linkages that can exist between policy makers and implementers. These linkages are outlined in table 7-1. Each of the scenarios in the table is characterized by a shift of power from policy makers to implementers. As a result, policy makers and implementers in the later scenarios must wrestle with the difficult task of negotiating political agreement on policy goals and the means that will be employed to carry out these goals. This increases the complexity of the policy process and the possibility of implementation breakdowns because, in addition to dealing with potential *technical* breakdowns, the actors may have to resolve the *political* breakdowns that can occur if negotiations between policy makers and implementers are unsuccessful.

Before examining the different scenarios in more detail, it is important to stress that each is designed to indicate the general types of linkages that can exist between policy makers and implementers. They should not be viewed as mutually exclusive, self-contained approaches, since the implementation process may involve a mix of different linkages at the same time. Instead, they indicate that the political nature of policy implementation can vary and that implementation breakdowns can also vary, depending on which scenario is employed to carry out different policies.

A more detailed analysis of each of the five approaches will illustrate this point more clearly. Once we have described these different types of linkages between policy makers and implementers, we can consider (in the next chapter) how evaluators are linked into the policy process.

"Classical" Technocrats

The basic assumptions that underlie the first set of linkages between policy makers and implementers are the following:

1. Policy makers delineate clear goals and implementers support these goals.
2. Policy makers establish a hierarchical command structure and delegate *technical* authority to specific implementers to carry out their goals.
3. Implementers possess the technical capabilities to achieve the goals.

This first scenario describes the tightest of all the linkages in terms of the policy makers' control over the implementation process. Implementers possess some technical discretion, but their power is restricted to such an extent that this first type of linkage most closely resembles the "classical" model described in chapter 1. It is basically a hierarchical approach, in which policy makers control the policy process and implementers act as their technical designees.

If there are implementation breakdowns in this first scenario, they occur because implementers lack the technical knowledge necessary to carry out policies, rather than because of their political opposition of these policies. We will look at a successful example of policy implementation using this approach before considering the kinds of technical mishaps that can take place.

After John F. Kennedy was elected president in 1960, he announced a new goal for the nation: placing a man on the moon before the end of the decade. Although the underlying rationale for this policy may have been diffuse (competition with the Russians, restoration of a sense of national pride, etc.), the goal was delineated with a high degree of precision in terms of both specific objective and chronological timetable. In this particular case all the basic assumptions of the "classical" technocratic approach to implementation were met. A policy objective was defined precisely. There was a high degree of consensus among the president, Congress, and implementers in the scientific community on the desirability of achieving this policy goal. A new implementation command structure in the form of NASA was created, with a strong base of political and financial support, to devise the technical means to realize the goal. These implementers were able to take the technical actions necessary to achieve the goal. As a result, astronauts Neil Armstrong and Edwin Aldrin set foot on the lunar surface on July 20, 1969. Mission accomplished.

The NASA example might indicate that technical implementation is noncontroversial and easy, but this is not always the case. Another example will illustrate some of the difficulties that can plague this first type of technical scenario.

In 1954 the Atomic Energy Act was amended to permit the licensing of private and public utilities to construct nuclear power plants and to use fissionable materials in order to generate and distribute electrical power. Once again the basic assumptions of the "classical" implementation approach were met. The policy goal of encouraging and realizing the

Table 7-1   ALTERNATE IMPLEMENTATION LINKAGES

Policy Makers (Environment I)	Policy Implementers (Environment II)	Potential Breakdowns
1. "Classical" Technocracy		
a. Policy makers[a] formulate specific goals. b. *Policy makers delegate technical authority* to implementers to achieve goals.	a. Implementers support policy makers' goals and devise technical means to achieve these goals.	a. Technical failure of means
2. Instructed Delegation		
a. Policy makers formulate specific goals. b. *Policy makers delegate administrative authority* to implementers to devise the means to achieve goals.	a. Implementers support policy makers' goals and negotiate administrative means among themselves to achieve goals.	a. Technical failure of means b. Negotiation failures (complexity, stalemate)
3. Bargaining		
a. Policy makers formulate goals. b. *Policy makers bargain with implementers* over both goals and/or means to achieve goals.	a. *Implementers bargain with policy makers* over goals and/or means to achieve goals.	a. Technical failure of means b. Bargaining failures (stalemate, non-implementation) c. Cooptation or "cheating"

4. Discretionary Experimentation

a. Policy makers support abstract (undefined) goals.
b. Policy makers delegate broad discretionary authority to implementers to refine goals and means.

   a. *Implementers refine goals and means* for policy makers.

     a. Technical failure of means
     b. Ambiguity
     c. Cooptation
     d. Unaccountability

5. Bureaucratic Entrepreneurship

a. Policy makers support goals and means formulated by implementers.

   a. *Implementers formulate policy goals and means* to carry out goals and means and persuade policy makers to accept their goals.

     a. Technical failure of means
     b. Cooptation
     c. Unaccountability
     d. Policy preemption

[a] In all five cases the term *policy makers* refers to those individuals in Environment I who possess the formal authority and legitimacy to formulate policies. This definitional distinction holds true even though implementers can become policy makers (scenario 5), and vice versa, in the everyday work of public policy formation.

development and utilization of nuclear power to generate electrical energy was clearly delineated. The Atomic Energy Commission was designated to implement the policy, and it possessed powerful resources in the form of information resources, scientific expertise, financial support, and other incentives. There was strong consensus among all the key actors that this was a desirable goal at the time the policy was conceived.[2]

In 1955 the Atomic Energy Commission announced its first Power Demonstration Reactor Program, which provided a series of subsidies to encourage private industry and the utilities to get into the nuclear power-generating business. It would be inaccurate to argue that no progress has been made in implementing this program during the past quarter-century. By 1979 there were 70 operating nuclear reactors in the United States, which provided 12 percent of the nation's total electrical power, and another 92 plants had construction permits.[3] Yet the nuclear power program can hardly be cited as a classic success story. The program was launched in a wave of enthusiasm and high expectations. Today the situation looks somewhat different.

The initial problems grew out of a complex series of technical difficulties. Some of these problems involved engineering considerations: how to build fail-safe backup systems to deal with potential accidents; how to safely dispose of radioactive wastes; how to minimize thermal pollution and other adverse environmental effects. A different set of technical problems related to issues of legal liability and the provision of insurance to cover the financial costs of possible accidents. A third set of economic problems involved cost overruns that resulted from on-line systems failures and/or the spiraling effects of inflation.

This combination of technical difficulties led to program delays, and to a growing sense of unease among the public as these delays created skepticism and increased visibility for the program. By the early 1970s, this growing unease led to protests, pickets, canceled projects, further delays, and increasing reluctance on the part of many utilities to become involved. By the late 1970s, the controversy had escalated to a point at which one observer was moved to comment,

> An awesome struggle is brewing between the proponents and the opponents of nuclear power. Before it ends it may well prove to be one of the most divisive and bitterly contested American issues of the late twentieth century.[4]

This prediction took on ominous overtones on Wednesday, March 28, 1979, when an accident occurred at the Three Mile Island nuclear plant in Pennsylvania. During the ensuing week the public was deluged with confusing reports involving "meltdowns," the "China syndrome," and hydrogen bubbles. It was obvious that the technical difficulties involved in the development of nuclear power are more difficult than either the policy makers or the implementers had originally envisioned. At present the future course of nuclear power development is unclear. The "man-on-the-moon" program had also been plagued with technical breakdowns, including a fire that cost the lives of some of the astronauts, but it was able to overcome these problems. It is difficult to predict whether this will also be possible in the case of nuclear power development.

However, one fact is already obvious. The nuclear power program has become increasingly more politicized during the past twenty-five years, largely owing to technical failures that have eroded public confidence in the program. As a result, new agencies and actors have entered this arena at an escalating rate, so that today the different groups involved in implementation include the following:

1. A growing number of federal agencies, including the Nuclear Regulatory Commission, the Department of Energy, the Interstate Commerce Commission, the Department of the Interior, and the like.
2. The congressional committees responsible for energy policy.
3. The intermediary implementers—utility companies, financial institutions, and other industrial and commerical interests responsible for carrying out various aspects of the program.
4. State governments, where legislatures and voters acting through the referendum process can decide whether to permit nuclear power plants within state borders (e.g., California's Proposition 15, Oregon's Ballot Measure Nine, Vermont's legislative site approval requirement, etc.).
5. Various congressional and executive investigating groups, including the "blue ribbon" Kemeny Commission appointed by President Carter following the Three Mile Island incident.
6. The courts, and other arms of the judicial branch of government (police, etc.), which have intervened to resolve disputes along the lines described in chapter 6.
7. Last, but far from least, a host of interest groups, which have actively attempted to influence the implementation (and even achieve the nonimplementation) of the program.

As a result of this proliferation of actors, one of the key assumptions behind the "classical" implementation model has broken down. The nuclear power program is no longer a tightly centralized, hierarchical implementation scenario. Instead, it has become very loose and is characterized by multiple access points where different actors can intervene in an attempt to influence implementation decision making.

The political consequences of this development are very significant. As political scientist Peter Woll has observed,

> The nature of the administrative structure . . . has an important impact on the way in which pressure groups operate. If a variety of separate agencies have . . . authority, this will increase the number of access points for pressure groups and consequently their influence upon the policy process.[5]

Hence, as the nuclear power example indicates, even the "classical" technocratic scenario can become politically complicated if the implementers are not able to effectively make technical adjustments that are necessary to carry out policy goals. Yet—and this is a major point—this "classical" type of linkage represents the *least complex* approach to policy implementation in terms of its political ramifications and its potential political breakdowns. If the basic assumptions of this model are met, policy goals will be stated precisely; political control will be centralized in a hierarchical command structure; and there will be political consensus between policy makers and implementers on the desirability of achieving policy goals.

When policy makers express their goals more diffusely and multiple groups of different implementers disagree over these goals and/or the means to achieve them, the implementation of policies becomes increasingly more complicated. In addition to dealing with potential technical breakdowns, the actors in these other scenarios may have to resolve difficult political differences that can plague the implementation process.

Instructed Delegates

Under the second set of linkages implementers begin to exercise a higher degree of political discretion because policy makers are willing to delegate to them general authority to make rules and regulations and to take other administrative actions to carry out policy goals.

This second scenario follows the "classical" model in that policy makers still delineate precise goals and implementers still support those goals. However, implementers now enjoy more latitude in determining the administrative means that will be employed to carry out the goals, and if several groups of implementers are involved, they are expected to negotiate agreements on those means. Hence, the basic assumptions in this model are as follows:

1. Policy makers delineate clear goals and implementers agree on the desirability of those goals.
2. Policy makers instruct one or more groups of implementers to achieve the goals, and delegate discretionary *administrative* authority to those implementers.
3. Implementers possess the technical, administrative, and negotiating capabilities to achieve the goals.

Although policy makers still exercise control over policy formation in this scenario, the implementers now possess more power to determine the means that will be employed to achieve the policy makers' goals. As a result, the possibility of different types of breakdowns increases. First, once again (as is true in all the scenarios) technical breakdowns can occur if the implementers lack the expertise and skill to carry out their tasks. Second, since several groups of implementers may be employed, they can disagree over the means that should be used to accomplish the policy makers' goals. If negotiations over means between different groups of implementers are unsuccessful, this can lead to political breakdowns in the implementation process. Finally, the basic assumption behind this approach is that policy makers issue clear and precise instructions to implementers. If those instructions are ambiguous and garbled, this increases the possibility of political infighting between implementers over what the policy makers want and what means should be employed to achieve their goals.

A student seminar paper written by Laurie Laidlaw on U.S. immigration policy illustrates the kinds of political difficulties that can occur under this second type of implementation linkage. Laidlaw's paper provides an example of a situation in which policy makers have established very precise goals but difficulties have arisen owing to political disagreements in the implementation environment. Although immigration policy involves a host of complex variables and value judgments relating to civil liberties, the basic statute that governs this policy (the Immigration and Nationality Act of 1952 as amended in 1965 and again in 1976) specifies very precisely (by means of numerical ceilings and limitations) the number of aliens to be admitted to the United States for permanent residence each year. This statute also spells out regulations to control visas that are issued to temporary foreign visitors. Despite the precision of these numerical goals and regulations, the implementation of immigration policy is breaking down. At present approximately 400,000 immigrants are legally admitted to the United States each year, and an unknown number are entering illegally. "An independent study commissioned by the Immigration and Naturalization Service estimates that there are 8 million illegal aliens in the United States, and that these illegal aliens are continuing to enter the country at a rate of about 1 million per year."[6]

One of the major problems with immigration policy grows out of the fact that implementation responsibilities are split between a number of different federal agencies, including the Immigration and Naturalization Service (INS) of the Department of Justice (responsible for entry inspections and enforcement); the Department of State (responsible for issuing temporary visas to foreign visitors); the Department of Labor (responsible for issuing temporary employment certificates to foreign workers in designated areas, such as migrant farm workers); and the Social Security Administration of the Department of Health, Education and Welfare (responsible for assigning social security certificates to temporary visitors and/or workers). These agencies can create difficult political problems because they may interpret their administrative roles in quite different ways. INS, for example, focuses its major energies on the strict "legal mandate" of maintaining immigration quotas, and its key thrust is to block the entry of illegal immigrants by means of border patrols and other tough enforcement measures. The State Department, on the other hand, is concerned with the "consensual imperative" of maintaining a favorable national image abroad, and hence it is quite liberal in granting temporary visas to foreign visitors. Once these visitors have entered the United States, however, it is quite possible for them to go underground and remain in the country as illegal aliens. Hence, both the INS and the State Department exercise discretion in discharging their delegated administrative authority to carry out immigration policy, but their efforts can produce quite different policy results.

Another case that illustrates the difficulties implementers can encounter when more than one agency exercises delegated administrative powers is found in Pressman and Wildavsky's book on the efforts of the Economic Development Administration (EDA) to create jobs for the hard-core unemployed under the Public Works and Economic Development Act of 1965. Although the policy goals set forth in this act were not as precise as the immigration quotas, the legislation did specify a fairly concise set of guidelines. Titles I–VI of the act provided for assistance to "redevelopment areas" (cities or counties of 250,000 or more) where both unemployment and underemployment rates had been persistently greater than those for the nation as a whole (at the time, 6 percent or more). The act instructed the implementers to select sites that met this criterion, and it delegated authority to use a flexible variety of administrative remedies, including direct grants; long-term, low-interest loans; and technical assistance for planning to achieve the policy goal of providing jobs for the unemployed. The EDA administrators decided to focus their efforts on Oakland, California, for a variety of reasons: its very high unemployment rate (then 8.4 percent); time constraints that prevented them from launching a more diversified program in different cities; and political factors in Oakland that they felt would give their program a high degree of visibility.

The initial problem the EDA faced was a technical one: It did not know how to create jobs for the hard-core unemployed. After wrestling with this problem the EDA staff adopted a strategy of awarding grants to private firms for new construction projects and then negotiating with those firms to provide jobs for the unemployed.

Under its first major award the EDA agreed to provide $10.5 million in federal grants and loans to the Port of Oakland for the construction of a new airport hangar that would be leased to World Airways. As part of this lease arrangement World Airways agreed to formulate an employment plan to provide jobs for the hard-core unemployed, who would be trained at government expense. While this leasing arrangement was complex, the job training program added a further complication, since a number of different governmental agencies were involved in implementing federal job training programs.

In order to activate the World Airways training program, it was necessary for the EDA to negotiate agreements with other federal agencies that were responsible for different aspects of unemployment training. In October 1966 World Airways had actually prepared an employment training plan under the Manpower Development and Training Act (MDTA), which was administered by the Department of Labor. The local MDTA advisory council in Oakland had approved this plan, in which World Airways had agreed to train 510 aircraft maintenance personnel. The subsequent difficulties and delays took place because the EDA and other federal implementing agencies could not reach agreement on the World Airways plan:

> When the training proposal finally reached Washington, it proved impossible for the EDA, Labor and HEW to agree jointly to support it. The EDA was worried about costs per trainee; HEW felt it would be too much of a financial opportunity for World . . .
> Although federal officials vary somewhat in their interpretations of how the training proposal was killed, by 1968 it was clear that the three federal agencies could not get together to approve the project. Finally, World Airways withdrew its proposal. A key part of the EDA Oakland project had been dismantled . . . Given divergent organizational objectives, the building of agreement—which was necessary for the furtherance of the program— became a difficult task.[7]

The entire EDA–Oakland experience is full of examples of break-downs that resulted from failures in negotiations between different implementing agencies. One of the major themes of Pressman and Wildavsky's book is the "complexity of joint action" that can result from multiple decision and clearance points involving diverse implementing bodies. Their case study illustrates the types of difficulties that can occur under the second type of implementation linkage, especially if several agencies are delegated administrative powers to carry out policy goals. There were technical breakdowns based on the implementers' inadequate conceptual theories as to how to create jobs for the unemployed in Oakland. There were also disagreements between different implementing agencies about how to exercise their delegated powers. Finally, there were political failures that resulted from unsatisfactory negotiations between the different implementing groups. Although implementers may support policy makers' goals under the "instructed-delegation" scenario, this type of linkage is characterized by a degree of complexity, and a potential for political conflict, that extends considerably beyond the confines of the technocratic model.

Bargainers

The third set of linkages between policy makers and implementers represents a major departure from the first two approaches. In the first two scenarios both policy makers and implementers agreed on the desirability of policy goals. In this third case, no such consensus necessarily exists, either with respect to goals or with respect to the means that should be employed to accomplish these goals.

The assumptions at work here are as follows:

1. Formal policy makers delineate policy goals.
2. Policy makers and implementers do not necessarily agree between (or among) themselves on the desirability of those goals.
3. Implementers bargain with policy makers, and with each other, over both goals and means.

Since implementers do not necessarily share the same goals as policy makers, their power position vis-à-vis the policy makers can increase dramatically because they can exercise considerable clout through threats of noncompliance and nonimplementation. As a result, there are a variety of potential breakdowns in the bargaining scenario. First, there can be the same technical failure of means that characterizes the other scenarios. Second, breakdowns can result, once again, from failures in negotiations, which can lead to inertia, stalemate, or nonimplementation on the part of disgruntled implementers. Finally, since the implementers do not necessarily agree with the policy makers on goals, they can circumvent policies, and coopt resources, to serve their own ends. In other words, they can pay lip service to a policy goal while actually "cheating" in order to take the money and use it to serve their own policy objectives.

The final outcome of bargaining between policy makers and implementers is determined by the distribution of relative power resources (actual or perceived) among the two groups. If the policy makers monopolize power resources, they can usually coerce implementers to carry out their policies even if the implementers do not like those policies. If the power resources are distributed relatively evenly between the two sides, implementation can take place through bargaining compromises. However, if the implementers monopolize power resources and do not want to bargain at all, policies will not be implemented.

Three different examples will illustrate these variations in bargaining. In the first, policy makers were able to marshal sufficient power resources to impose their will on implementers. In the second, a more equitable distribution of power resulted in implementation by means of bargaining compromises. In the final case, the implementers possessed so much power that they refused to carry out a policy.

1. Policy Maker Power

On Tuesday, April 10, 1962, Roger I. Blough, chairman of the board of the United States Steel Corporation, visited the White House to advise John F. Kennedy, president of the United States of America, that his company was announcing an increase in the price of steel. Kennedy's initial reaction was one of disbelief. Since the previous autumn he had pushed for a policy agreement between labor and the steel industry that was designed to achieve a noninflationary wage and price settlement. Only a few days prior to Blough's visit, the labor unions had agreed to such a settlement and signed a contract that involved only a modest wage increase on the understanding that the steel companies would hold the line on prices. Now Roger Blough, the chairman of the largest steel company in the nation, was informing the president that the bargain no longer held.

Kennedy was furious:

> The President, who usually keeps his temper under rein, let go. He felt he had been double-crossed—deliberately. The office of the President had been affronted. The national interest had been flouted.
>
> Bitterly, he recalled that "My father always told me that all businessmen were sons-of-bitches but I never believed it till now!"
>
> It was clear that the Administration would fight. No one know exactly what could be done, but from that moment the awesome power of the Federal Government began to move.[8]

In addition to feeling that he had been betrayed, President Kennedy felt that the policy stakes involved in this issue were very high:

> Nothing in the range of domestic economic policy had brought forth a greater effort by the Administration than the restraint it sought to impose on steel prices and wages . . .

A price increase or an inflationary wage settlement, it argued, would set off a new wage–price spiral that would stunt economic growth, keep unemployment high, cut into export sales, weaken the dollar and further aggravate the outflow of gold.[9]

The President, as the chief policy maker, now decided that he would become the chief enforcer. He marshaled an awesome array of power resources that were designed to force U.S. Steel to implement a policy agreement that he assumed it had previously accepted as part of a good-faith bargaining effort:

During the next seventy-two hours, four antitrust investigations of the steel industry were conceived, a bill to roll back the price increases was seriously considered, legislation to impose price and wage controls on the steel industry was discussed, agents of the Federal Bureau of Investigation questioned newspapermen by the dawn's early light, and the Department of Defense—biggest buyer in the nation—began to divert purchases away from United States Steel.[10]

Obviously, this type of counterattack placed extremely heavy pressure on U.S. Steel. The key to this particular power struggle was to be found in a critical weakness in the company's bargaining position. Although U.S. Steel was the largest producer in the country, it was not the only producer. Once U.S. Steel had announced its price increase, a number of the other steel companies—Bethlehem, Republic, Jones and Laughlin, Youngstown, and Wheeling—fell into line and announced similar increases of their own. But there were a few holdouts. Inland, Kaiser, Lukens, and Colorado Fuel & Iron, among others, indicated that they would study the situation before considering price increases. These companies accounted for about 16 percent of the nation's steel production capacity.

As a result, the administration adopted a fourfold strategy:

First, the rallying of public opinion behind the President and against the companies. Second, a divide-and-conquer operation within the steel industry. Third, antitrust pressure from the Justice Department, the Federal Trade Commission, the Senate and the House. Fourth, the mobilization of friendly forces within the business world to put additional pressure on the companies.[11]

The situation finally broke open on Friday, April 13, when the divide-and-conquer strategy began to produce results. In the morning, the chairman of one of the holdout companies, Inland Steel, announced that he did not feel that an increase in steel prices at this time would be in the national interest. Later the same morning, the administration followed up on this opening:

> At 11:45 Secretary McNamara said at his news conference that the Defense Department had ordered defense contractors to shift steel purchases to companies that had not raised prices. Later in the day the department awarded to the Lukens Steel Company, which had not raised prices, a special armor plate contract for Polaris-missile submarines.[12]

At 3:20 in the afternoon another large producer, Bethlehem Steel, announced that it had decided to rescind its proposed price increase. From then on it was simply a waiting game. At 5:28 the same afternoon U.S. Steel also announced that it had decided to rescind its price increase.

This case illustrates a situation in which a bargaining agreement was implemented because the key policy makers (President Kennedy and the apparatus of the federal government under his control) were able to assemble sufficient power resources to enforce that agreement. In addition, it indicates a disagreement over policy goals. Roger Blough and his colleagues at U.S. Steel believed that a price increase was necessary to meet rising costs. John F. Kennedy and his colleagues in the U.S. government were concerned with the inflationary consequences of such a price increase. Because Kennedy felt that U.S. Steel's proposed price increase represented a violation of trust and an affront to the presidency, he was not interested in quarreling over compromises. Instead, he used the power of the presidency to force the implementation of policy. In the end, U.S. Steel had no choice but to carry out Kennedy's orders.

2. Balanced Power Resources

In an article on "Policy Implementation Through Bargaining," Helen Ingram analyzes the relationships between the federal government and the states under the Water Resources Planning Act of 1965 Title III federal grants-in-aid program. On the basis of her analysis Ingram concludes that

> rather than buying compliance by offering a grant, the federal government achieved only the opportunity to bargain with the states. A bargaining framework fits more accurately than a superior–subordinate model the complex intergovernmental relations involved in grants-in-aid. Instead of a federal master dangling a carrot in front of a state donkey, the more apt image reveals a rich merchant haggling on equal terms with a sly, bargain-hunting consumer.[13]

The key concept in Ingram's observation is that bargaining occurs on equal terms. As she points out, both the federal government and the states could bring considerable leverage to the bargaining table. In the case of the federal government, money and professional expertise constituted powerful incentives. The states, on the other hand, had potential strength in numbers; they were able to gain access to federal policy-making machinery through their congressional delegations; and they controlled essential information for monitoring the effects of grants.

The Title III planning program illustrates a balanced bargaining scenario in which resources were relatively equitably allocated between two groups, both of which had a long-range interest in reaching an acceptable compromise agreement. In terms self-interest, the federal agencies were anxious to maximize their control over state plans and the states were interested in obtaining the greatest possible leeway to pursue their own goals with federal money. "The result is a process of implementation that is a complex succession of bids and counterbids between the state and federal levels during which the initial aims of each are substantially modified." [14]

Hence, the Title III example provides a case of bargaining in which power resources were distributed relatively evenly. The compromises reached by policy makers and implementers resemble the "mutual adaptation" approach proposed by Milbrey McLaughlin, which was described in chapter 1. [15]

3. Implementer Power

In October 1965 the Coordinating Council of Community Organizations in Chicago complained to the Office of Education that the Chicago School District was diverting federal education funds to segregated schools in violation of Title VI of the Civil Rights Act of 1964. Upon receipt of the complaint, Francis Keppel, the commissioner of education, decided to defer payment of federal funds to Chicago school authorities until an investigation had determined whether these charges were true. The amount of federal money involved was approximately $25 million. The mayor of Chicago, the Honorable Richard J. Daley, was furious at Keppel's decision.

Although all the details are not clear, Daley took decisive action. He met with President Johnson in order to indicate his views on this matter:

> The story goes that Daley and Lyndon Johnson met in New York during the official welcome for the Pope. In conversation that day, Daley threatened to pull Congressional votes from Lady Bird Johnson's [highway] beautification program if the termination of education monies from Chicago was not rescinded. [16]

Johnson's reaction to Daley was somewhat different from Kennedy's reaction to Blough. The issue was not Mrs. Johnson's beautification program. It was Daley's power. Daley was a power broker as well as a president maker. He was not only the "boss" of one of the nation's largest cities but also a formidable figure in national Democratic party politics. When Daley spoke, Johnson listened. When Daley wanted action, Johnson acted:

> When Johnson returned to Washington, he gave the "fix-it" assignment to White House aide Douglas Cater, who worked directly through Wilbur Cohen, the Undersecretary of HEW, to wiggle the Office of Education out of the situation.
>
> It took less than a week for the full cycle to develop: press and public reaction in Chicago, Congressional pressure in Washington, Daley's meeting with Johnson, the White House directive to HEW, a quick trip to Chicago by Undersecretary Cohen, and official release of the funds and HEW withdrawal of its investigation.[17]

This was a bargaining scenario in which no bargaining took place. The power resources were distributed too unevenly. Daley was not interested in implementing federal desegregation policy in Chicago's schools, and there was no way the policy makers could force him to carry out this task. Once President Johnson had issued the "fix-it" order, the Office of Education didn't stand a chance. Daley simply blew Commissioner Keppel out of the water.

The "Chicago massacre" was a classic case of a breakdown in the bargaining scenario in which Mayor Daley was able to exercise enough political leverage to ignore the implementation of federal civil rights desegregation policy while coopting the federal money and spending it as he saw fit. The result was nonimplementation and "cheating."

These three examples indicate that bargaining linkages between policy makers and implementers can produce varied results depending on the power resources available to these two groups of policy actors.

Discretionary Experimenters

A "discretionary experimental" linkage is employed when policy makers are unable to master the detailed formulation of policy and hence are willing to delegate broad discretionary authority to implementers. The underlying assumptions are threefold:

1. Formal policy makers support abstract general goals but are unable to articulate them clearly owing to lack of knowledge and/or other uncertainties.
2. The policy makers delegate/broad discretionary powers to implementers to refine the goals and to develop the means to accomplish them.
3. Implementers are willing (and able) to perform these tasks.

This fourth approach involves a dramatic delegation of power away from policy makers and toward implementers. This delegation takes place as a result of conditions of uncertainty that were discussed in chapter 3: Policy makers are usually busy people who are active in many areas but are specialists in none. Thus they labor under uncertainties created by their own technical limitations as well as the difficulties inherent in defining and posing solutions for complex social problems. In addition, policy makers must assemble coalitions from among people with different definitions of both the problem and diverse preferences about solutions. Not surprisingly, then, policies are often vague about the problem to be solved and the means for solving it. Vagueness in policy statements means that the responsibility for more specific definition is shifted from policy makers to implementers.

Although the policy makers may be plagued by uncertainty, they are still willing to delegate authority to implementers for two basic reasons. The first is to create an appearance of responsiveness to political pressures. Constituents may demand that they "do something!" (e.g., about the riots), and this experimental approach enables the policy makers to indicate that they have responded to these demands (e.g., "I voted to appropriate funds for the Riot Control Commission"). Second, there may be general areas of social concern that policy makers feel are important enough to warrant the commitment of venture capital to a search for technically feasible solutions. As chapter 3 indicated, this is basically a variation of what Lindblom calls incrementalism—a decision-making strategy to cope with shortages of information in which action is undertaken because it is simultaneously a step toward a solution and a way of gathering better information for the next step.

Hence, this fourth type of linkage involves a discretionary, experimental approach to implementation. Policy makers are willing to delegate broad powers to implementers, either in response to demands for action or as an attempt to gather information through a rolling process of implementation in which policy goals are continually readjusted on the basis of new knowledge that is generated from learning by doing.

A common example of this experimental approach is seen in governmental research and development programs in areas such as the health sciences. Venture funds are allocated to the National Institutes of Health, or to university medical schools, to conduct research on cancer, stroke, heart disease, and other illnesses.

A recent case of a breakdown in health care policy under this experimental scenario is described in a study of *The Swine Flu Affair* by Richard Neustadt and Harvey Fineberg,[19] which analyzes the steps that led the Ford administration to initiate a massive and costly influenza immunization program in 1976. According to a *New York Times* commentary on the book,

> The blunders of the swine flu program could have been minimized had the political world shown a bit more sophistication. Dr. David J. Sencer, then head of the Center for Disease Control, was able to rush his superiors into embarking on this large-scale immunization program by conjuring up fears of a repetition of the deadly 1918 flu pandemic. Then the Assistant Secretary of Health, Theodore Cooper, a cardiac surgeon, deferred to Dr. Sencer's presumed expertise. As laymen, David Matthews, Secretary of Health, Education and Welfare, and President Ford felt constrained to accept the experts' opinion once a group of consultant specialists endorsed the Sencer–Cooper program.
>
> But, as so often happens, the specialists were captured by their speciality . . . Their outlook was narrow. They did not weigh the potential benefits against the high costs of being wrong. As it turned out, the whole idea of preventive medicine suffered a blow when the costly vaccinations were shown to have serious side effects in some cases—while swine flu itself was conspicuous primarily by its absence. . . .
>
> The Federal Government's 1976 immunization fiasco . . . demonstrates the consequences of the imperfect teamwork between Washington's two cultures, one composed mainly of politicians and lawyers and the other of scientists and engineers.[20]

An even more celebrated case of "discretionary experimentation" involved the community action component of the War on Poverty, which grew out of the Economic Opportunity Act of 1964. While the Office of Economic Opportunity •enjoyed some areas of program success, its Community Action Program experienced considerable difficulty, in large measure because of its very ambiguous experimental mandate. As Lawrence M. Friedman points out, "The central instruments of legislation were basically vague, lacking in specificity and even in policy. This means they were, or could be, almost all things to all people."[21]

Nowhere was this more apparent than in the celebrated language of Section 206(b) of the law that established the Community Action Agencies (CAAs) and designated them to implement "a comprehensive attack on poverty . . . which is developed and conducted with the maximum feasible participation of the residents of the areas and the members of the groups served."

In essence, the CAAs represented a new type of implementation experiment through which participants would both formulate policy goals and carry out those goals in an effort to alleviate social problems. By the end of January 1966 more than 900 federal grants had been made for the planning of community action programs in some 1,000 counties, and CAAs had been established in the nation's 50 largest cities.

The community action agencies ran into difficult problems from the very beginning. The most passive agencies were captured by local government officials, who viewed them as a source of new federal funds, and the most militant were decimated by other local officials, who viewed them as a threat to their established power base:

> At the risk of oversimplification, it might be said that the CAAs most closely controlled by City Hall were disappointing and the most antagonistic were destroyed.
>
> For the most militant agencies, something like a four-stage sequence seems to have been followed. First, a period of organizing with much publicity and great expectations. Second, the beginning of operations, with the onset of conflict between the agency and local government institutions. Third, a period of counter-attack from local government . . . Fourth, a victory for established institutions, or at best, stalemate, accompanied by bitterness and charges of betrayal.[22]

In addition to using this fourth scenario for purposes of social experimentation, policy makers occasionally grant broad discretionary powers to administrators in an attempt to avoid facing up to controversial policy issues. In this way they pass the burden of resolving political conflicts to the implementers. An example of this type of "passing the buck" discretionary implementation is seen in Title IX of the Education Act Amendments of 1972, which provided that

> no person in the United States shall, on the basis of sex, be excluded from participation in, be denied the benefits of, or be subject to discrimination under any education program or activity receiving Federal financial assistance.[23]

This legislation was written in such a manner that it left open a host of questions that Congress decided to sidestep in order to leave their political resolution to the implementing agency, HEW.

In a seminar paper Maja Wessels points out the difficulties involved in relating this policy to the field of men's and women's athletic programs, especially at the college and university level. One extremely controversial issue was whether or not intercollegiate revenue-producing sports such as football and basketball should be covered by the law. The congressional sponsors of the bill provided conflicting political "cues" on this issue. Senator Birch Bayh, who had introduced the bill in the upper chamber, generally favored a tough implementation stance that would cover a wide variety of athletic activities. However, one of the cosponsors in the House, Representative Edith Green, was equally clear in holding that the legislation should not apply to revenue-producing sports:

> When funds for athletic departments come out of tuition, fees, or tax dollars, women students are to have equal opportunity with men. But intercollegiate sports financed by gate receipts is an entirely different matter, and was not covered by Title IX.[24]

HEW was faced with the challenge of interpreting the political intent of this vague Title IX policy. As a result, it adopted a delaying strategy. Instead of issuing administrative rules, it held hearings and put out feelers in an effort to determine how different groups felt about the policy. As Wessels points out in her paper, this meant that the implementing agency "took on the legislators' burden" in an effort to resolve the political conflicts that had not been taken care of by the policy makers. As a result, Title IX policy was "up for grabs,"[25] to use Eugene Bardach's terminology, as different pressure groups attempted to persuade HEW to see things their way. The National Collegiate Athletic Association (NCAA), which represented men's sports, pushed for a lenient interpretation of Title IX instructions, while various women's and civil rights groups pushed for a broad interpretation that would cover as wide a range of athletic activities as possible.

HEW procrastinated for three years before finally issuing its initial regulations in 1975. These regulations were actually designed to buy more time, since they provided for a three-year grace period during which colleges and universities were directed to examine their athletic programs and practices and to take appropriate remedial steps to eliminate the effects of discrimination. Finally, in December 1978, HEW Secretary Joseph A. Califano, Jr., announced a second set of draft regulations that provided that there must be equal expenditure of money per person for those involved in intercollegiate athletics. A major political uproar ensued over how these regulations related to the big revenue-producing sports, especially men's intercollegiate football. The department's signals on this were not clear:

> HEW's proposed policy interpretation stated that the department "recognizes that certain sports that produce revenue, such as football and basketball, may require greater expenditures without having a discriminatory effect." But HEW officials emphasized that football is "not exempt" from these guidelines just because of that recognition.[26]

HEW issued still a third set of Title IX regulations in December 1979 after Patricia R. Harris had replaced Secretary Califano. These regulations specified that "colleges must give the same proportion of athletic scholarship aid to women that they give to men." Secretary Harris added that colleges did not have to spend the same amount of the total athletic budget on each woman that they spent on each man: "If 70 percent of a college's athletes are men and 30 percent are women, the women must receive 30 percent of the financial aid for athletes. How to achieve that we have left to the maximum discretion of the institution itself." [27]

In retrospect one thing is certain: HEW's implementation difficulties with Title IX policy resulted from the fact that Congress shifted the burden of resolving political conflicts into the implementation environment by failing to provide clear instructions on its own policy goals. In a perceptive article on Title IX policy, Anne N. Costain argues that policy makers are placing increasing reliance on "symbolic" responses to constituency demands while pushing the burden of unresolved conflicts onto implementing agencies:

> An increasingly common way for the federal government to handle the demands generated by disadvantaged groups is for the U.S. Congress to pass legislation responding to the grievances of the group, then for the bureaucracy to delay implementation of this legislation for prolonged periods of time . . .
> Congress has relatively little to lose in this process. It is on record as supporting the group's demands. Bureaucratic intransigence can be blamed for any subsequent failures in policy implementation. [28]

It would be misleading and inaccurate to imply that all implementation efforts that rely on the discretionary, experimental type of linkage are undesirable or doomed to failure. In instances in which serious policy problems exist but information and knowledge is limited, the experimental approach to implementation may represent the only feasible opportunity to address these problems.

This point was made quite eloquently by Frances Fox Piven in a critique of Moynihan's criticisms of community action initiatives. In this critique Piven commented on

> the fundamental political nature of social-welfare measures—spawned in the first place to maintain a political leadership, and then continuously adapted to a changing political environment. In that process of adaptation, public goals are a political resource more than a set of first principles guiding action . . .
> Through this process, government action may become unintelligible to the critic who looks at goals and programs to discover a paradigm for rational action. But the motivating force in government action, the force which shapes public goals and the programs and structures created in their

name reflects another sort of rationalism—the adaptive rationalism through which a political system and its member parts are maintained.[29]

In his own introduction to the paperback edition of his own book, Moynihan admits that Piven has offered a valid observation: "This seems to me to be an accurate and useful point. *Government programs rarely begin with anything like as clear a purpose as the system presupposes*"[30] (italics added).

While this fourth type of "discretionary experimentation" linkage between policy makers and implementers can at times produce good results, it is susceptible to a variety of potential breakdowns. These can include one or more of the following: (1) technical failures due to insufficient implementer expertise and knowledge, (2) confusion that can result from ambiguous policies, (3) "cheating" and cooptation by the implementers, and (4) both implementer and policy maker unaccountability as a result of the diffusion of responsibility that can occur under this scenario.

Although this type of linkage can be very risky, it is also the most innovative approach to implementation, especially in areas of uncertainty. Despite its potential difficulties, the experimental scenario is sometimes the only possible way to deal with unusually complex policy issue areas if anything at all is to be done in these areas.

Bureaucratic Entrepreneurs

The fifth type of linkage that can exist between policy makers and implementers differs most markedly from the "classical" approach. In this fifth, "bureaucratic entrepreneurial" scenario, the implementers seize power from the policy makers and gain control of the policy process. The underlying assumptions at work here are the following:

1. Implementers formulate their own policy goals and marshal sufficient power to convince the formal policy makers to adopt those goals.
2. Implementers negotiate with policy makers to secure the means necessary to achieve their own policy goals.
3. Implementers are willing (and able) to carry out their policy goals.

This shift in power from policy makers to implementers can result from a number of developments. First, some implementers are able to dominate the policy process through their ability to generate and control the information necessary to formulate policies. Second, the stability and continuity inherent in the administrative bureaucracy can enable implementers to simply outlast and wear down policy makers. Finally, individual implementers can exercise entrepreneurial and political skills that enable them to dominate policy formation. These entrepreneurial initiatives can be based on a variety of different talents. Since this final scenario represents such a turnaround from the more traditional "classical" approach, it is worthwhile to examine each of these different strategies in some depth in order to clarify how the implementers can come to dominate the policy-making process.

The Power of Information (Nixon's Family Assistance Plan)

A clear example of how implementers can use their control of information resources to promote their own policy objectives is provided in Martin Anderson's book on *Welfare*. Anderson had served as research director for Richard Nixon's 1968 presidential campaign before he joined the White House domestic staff following the election. According to Anderson, President Nixon, who placed a high priority on cleaning up "the welfare mess," was open to new policy solutions:

> President Nixon was willing to consider any and all proposals for welfare reform . . . His staff had naively assumed that we would simply review whatever issue was a problem, identify the major areas of difficulty, consult leading experts, and with their help craft a solution . . .
> If didn't quite work that way for a number of reasons. First was the magnitude and complexity of the task itself. When President Eisenhower left office in early 1961, there were somewhere around forty major domestic programs. When Nixon took office there were 400 . . . It was difficult to find out exactly what was going on in the existing programs . . . The domestic side of the federal government had gotten so big that it was literally impossible to grasp it, intellectually, in its entirety.
> The result is that you must depend on the bureaucracy that is already there when you arrive. The bureaucrats are always more than happy to oblige.[31]

Anderson goes on to describe how Daniel Moynihan, the Democrat whom Nixon had named to direct his Urban Affairs Council ("the domestic cabinet of the new Administration"), was able to draw upon the federal bureaucracy to produce a welfare policy that Nixon eventually accepted as his own family assistance plan:

> Moynihan was one of the very few people on the White House staff who had operated in the Washington bureaucracy. He had an extensive network of contacts throughout HEW and OEO . . . who flooded him with research data and other information . . .

When Nixon made clear his intent to push welfare reform, Moynihan was quickly provided with a detailed plan by fellow Democrats in the federal bureaucracy . . . Nixon was delighted to get a detailed welfare reform plan on such short notice . . .

It was a classic example of the power of research in the making of national policy.[32]

In another article on the family assistance plan, Theodore Marmor and Martin Rein also note the dependence of the policy makers in the Nixon administration on the HEW bureaucracy:

The Nixon Administration did not have an entourage of new appointees within HEW . . . Instead, HEW Secretary Robert Finch relied on economists he inherited from the Johnson Administration, and they trotted out their favorite negative income tax ideas.[33]

Although the family assistance plan was never enacted into law, and hence never implemented, there is no doubt that the implementing agencies—particularly HEW—were able to use their control over information to shape Nixon's welfare policy goals.

The Power of Bureaucratic Resistance (a "Straight Arrow" Quits the Pentagon)

In the summer of 1978 Defense Secretary Harold Brown appointed Stanley B. Resor as his under secretary for policy. This appointment was part of President Carter's attempts to gain more control over Defense Department policy and "do something about rampant bureaucracy in the Pentagon." After nine months on the job Under Secretary Resor announced that he was resigning in frustration. A *New York Times* account explained the reasons behind Resor's resignation as follows:

The Carter Administration, like previous ones, accurately diagnosed the Pentagon disease but failed to impose a cure. It is generally agreed that competing power clusters have defied rational civilian control—one result being that the development of weapons dictates defense policy, rather than the other way around.

Mr. Resor, a former Secretary of the Army, had been expected to change that. How, exactly, was not clear. Although he was the third-ranking Defense official, his aides numbered a handful vs. about 20,000 Pentagon employees. . . .

Some observers called Mr. Resor a "straight-arrow" public servant who simply got "frozen out" by a bureaucracy whose power games he had no taste for. Others faulted Mr. Brown, a science-and-hardware Secretary, for not getting more involved in reorganization. Most agreed the idea was doomed regardless.[34]

The administrative bureaucracy gives stability and continuity to the policy process, but this enables the implementing agencies to outlast and wear down all but the most durable policy makers. As a result, these agencies can end up controlling the policy makers who theoretically possess the authority to control them.

The Power of Entrepreneurial Initiatives

The third way implementers can gain leverage over policy making is through the exercise of entrepreneurial skills, which can take a variety of different forms.

1. Managing Public Opinion   J. Edgar Hoover, who directed the Justice Department's Federal Bureau of Investigation (FBI) from 1924 until his death in 1972, illustrates one such approach.

Hoover originally joined the Justice Department in 1917. In 1924, after helping Attorney General Palmer conduct the "red raids" against suspected communists following World War I, he was appointed director of the Bureau of Investigation at the age of 29. He immediately began to streamline his administrative authority, recruit and train agents, and institute new, scientific techniques of crime detection. By the early 1930s he was running a tight ship. His only problem was that the ship had nowhere to go, since it had only limited authority to take on significant duties once the "red scare" had subsided. By 1932 newspaper accounts from Washington indicated that the FBI was about to be abolished and that Hoover would be out of a job.

A series of dramatic events opened the way for Hoover to change all this. On March 1, 1932, Charles A. Lindbergh, Jr., the infant son of the nation's air hero, was kidnaped. Congress responded by passing the so-called "Lindbergh law," and Hoover swung his bureau into the business of tracking down kidnapers. On June 17, 1933, a group of gangsters gunned down five Bureau agents and local police officers who were escorting a convicted mail robber into Kansas City's Union Station. The killing took place in broad daylight, and the press quickly headlined the incident as the "Kansas City massacre." The nation was stunned. Hoover seized this opening: "He determined to go public, to build a reputation for the Bureau and to construct what came to be a cult around himself."[35]

The public embraced this new cult with enthusiasm:

> J. Edgar Hoover, only a few years before a man worried about losing his job, was transformed almost overnight into the champion of the nation, the knight on a white charger riding down the forces of evil.[36]

Both President Roosevelt and Congress recognized the public opinion groundswell behind Hoover. In a single day—May 19, 1934—Congress passed six laws, cultivated by Hoover, that provided the bureau with tremendous new authority:

> These laws put a whole host of new crimes under federal jurisdiction for the first time: the robbing of a national bank, the flight of a defendant or witness across state lines, the transmission of threats against federal officials, racketeering by businessmen engaged in interstate commerce, transporting stolen property across a state line, resisting a federal officer. All these new headline-catching crimes fell under the purview of just one federal agency, the Bureau of Investigation.[37]

Once the FBI had gained this authority, Hoover began to make skillful use of a public relations campaign to glorify the bureau's accomplishments. In the 1930s, the focus was on gunning down gangsters—"Pretty Boy" Floyd, "Machine Gun" Kelly, "Baby Face" Nelson, "Ma" Barker and her son Fred. In the 1940s, it was "the FBI in war and peace" as the emphasis shifted to rounding up aliens, conducting security checks, and launching counterespionage operations. In the 1950s, suspected communists once again showed up on the FBI's "most wanted" lists. By the time John F. Kennedy was elected president in 1960, Hoover had manipulated public opinion to a point that he was untouchable:

> It was no secret that Kennedy wanted to replace J. Edgar Hoover. Nor was it a secret that, after considering the strength of Hoover's support—in Congress, the press and the general public—Kennedy decided to live with Hoover, rather than paying the cost of ousting him.[38]

Hoover served as director of the FBI under eight presidents, outliving seven of them. During his long reign he had continuously consolidated and expanded his power. In the end he dominated the field of law enforcement as the nation's chief policy maker/implementer par excellence.

2. "The Best Bill Drafter in Albany" Not all of the memorable bureaucratic entrepreneurs have been confined to the federal government, and perhaps the shrewdest and most skillful of the lot—at least in terms of technical ability to manipulate the policy-making process—was a state official, New York's Robert Moses, who serves as the fascinating focus of Robert Caro's Pulitzer Prize-winning book, *The Power Broker*.

During his lengthy career Moses perfected a fourfold strategy that enabled him to amass tremendous power. This strategy consisted of (1) dramatizing the need for new policies; (2) creating the bureaucratic agencies necessary to implement those policies; (3) writing laws so that he could control those implementing agencies; and (4) rewriting the laws so that he could exercise his powers with complete autonomy, subject to no outside constraints of any kind.

Moses began his rise to power by means of two seemingly innocuous bills that he drafted for the New York State legislature in 1924, when he was serving as a member of Governor Al Smith's staff. The first bill created the Long Island State Park Commission, and the second established the State Council of Parks. At Moses's request, the bills were introduced by F. Trubee Davison, a freshman legislator from the North Shore of Long Island, who was only 22 years old and one year out of Yale University. The bills came to the floor on the last day of the 1924 legislative session, and both the Assembly and the Senate passed them unanimously without debate.

Once the bills had passed, Governor Smith appointed Moses president of the Long Island State Park Commission, a post that gave him automatic membership on the State Council of Parks, of which he was elected chairman. The legislation that Moses had drafted gave him tremendous power in these new positions.

> Almost every clause . . . contained a sleeper . . .
>
> Section eight said the commission had the right to operate parks. But section nine said that "the term . . . parks as used in this act—shall be deemed to include . . . parkways, boulevards and also entrances and approaches thereto, docks and piers, and bridges . . . *and such other appurtenances as the . . . commission shall utilize . . .*"
>
> Section eight said the commission had the right to "acquire . . . real estate." But section ten said that "the term real estate as used in this act shall be construed to embrace all uplands, lands under water . . . and all real estate heretofore or hereafter acquired or used for railroad, street railroad, telephone, telegraph *or other public purposes.*"[39]

Moses, the master builder, had written a blank check, which the policy makers had signed. By the mid-1930s he was confident enough in his growing reputation as the implementer who got things done to run for governor of New York State. It was a mistake. After a disastrous campaign, his 35 percent share of the vote was the smallest polled by a gubernatorial candidate of any major party in the 157-year history of the state. Moses vowed that he would never again depend on the fickle whims of the public or its elected representatives to frustrate his ambitions. He set out once again to secure his power base. The "best bill drafter in Albany" jumped back into the policy-making environment and drafted amendments to the various legislative acts that had placed restrictions on his authorities.

The key vehicles Moses used to enhance his power were the revenue bonds issued by his authorities. These bonds not only produced the capital to construct new bridges, parkways, and parks but also generated massive amounts of new revenue to finance these projects. Moses buried a clause deep in his proposed amendments that permitted his authorities to recall these revenue bonds *before* they had expired, and to reissue new bonds in their stead that could be used to finance a wide range of new projects. Once the legislators had approved this provision, Moses was beyond their control:

> A bond was a legal agreement between its seller and its buyer. A legal agreement was, by definition, a contract. Under the Constitution of the United States, a contract was sacred. No state—and no creature of a state such as a city—could impair its obligations. No one—not Governor, not Mayor, not State Legislature, not City Board of Estimate—could interfere with its provisions . . . The elected representatives of the state and city may have given Robert Moses these powers. But the elected representatives of the state and city could never take them back.[40]

Moses had devised a system under which he could implement his own policies in perpetuity. He could issue 40-year bonds, recall them at the end of 39 years, and issue another series of bonds for 40 more years.

From 1924 to 1968 Robert Moses pursued an astonishingly active career, serving at one time or another (and often simultaneously) as chairman of the Long Island State Park Commission, chairman of the State Council of Parks, chairman of the New York State Power Authority, chairman of the Triboro Bridge and Tunnel Authority, and New York City's park commissioner. For almost a half-century he operated virtually independently of successive governors, mayors, legislators, or other elected policy makers who had inadvertently granted him authority to operate beyond their control. Finally, in 1968, Governor Nelson Rockefeller eased him out of office. Moses was then 80 years old. By the end of his public career, he had formulated and implemented his own transportation policies, which literally reshaped the landscape of the nation's most populous metropolitan area.

3. **Divide and Conquer**   In the early 1950s Harold L. Ickes, who had completed a lengthy stint as Franklin D. Roosevelt's secretary of the interior, issued a harsh post-mortem appraisal of the federal agency that had constituted his bitterest rival in the field of flood control and reclamation policy:

One way to describe the Corps of Army Engineers would be to say that it is the most powerful and the most pervasive lobby in Washington. The aristocrats who constitute it are our highest ruling class. They are not only the political elite of the army, they are the perfect flower of bureaucracy. Within the fields which they have elected to occupy, they are the law—and therefore above the law.[41]

In 1979, almost two decades after Ickes made his stinging rebuke, a high official in the Carter administration bemoaned the Corps's role in the "Tenn-Tom" project, a controversial new $1.7 billion dollar barge canal in Mississippi and Alabama: "The Corps is a good construction agency and that's what they should be doing. Let someone else make policy."[42]

The Army Corps of Engineers is almost as old as the nation:

The Corps is both a civil and military engineering and construction agency, responsible since the early 1800s for national internal improvement programs and public works for harbors and navigable rivers. After the Mississippi for flood-prevention programs on that river. The Flood Control Act of 1936 formally extended its civilian work to all of the United States.[43]

The Corps has developed its power base through an ingenious "divide-and-conquer strategy." Although technically part of the executive branch of the government, the Corps has long developed close working relations with Congress and local interests:

The benefits which its program brought local areas have resulted in strong Congressional, local government, civic and business support for its activities. Since 1901, these interests have been organized as the National Rivers and Harbors Congress, working closely with the Corps in identifying and assigning priorities to appropriate policies.[44]

Hence, the first phase of the Corps's strategy was to drive a wedge between the executive and legislative branches of government. The second phase was to divide the policy makers within Congress by developing powerful allies among individual members. The Corps has built up the allegiance of selected senators and representatives through a series of "pork barrel" projects that benefit individual districts and constituencies. Thus, when the Corps comes under attack it can turn to its congressional allies to defend and protect its policy initiatives.

The Carter administration learned this lesson firsthand when it considered halting the controversial Mississippi–Alabama barge canal project:

When President Carter threatened in 1977 to cut off funds for Tenn-Tom, Senator John Stennis (D-Miss.), its most influential backer, asked the White

House to hold a hearing in Mississippi. More than 2,000 persons jammed the session, nearly all of them supporting Tenn-Tom. Carter, whose election was clinched by Mississippi's electoral votes, let the work continue. The Corps of Engineers, though under attack across the country, still can count on help in Congress if the President tries to trim its powers.[45]

A recently published study by Daniel Mazmanian and Jeanne Nienaber has indicated that the Corps of Engineers has become more responsive during recent years to environmental interests as represented in the National Environmental Policy Act. According to their study, "Contrary to what its critics expected, the agency seemed to be making a conscious and serious effort to accommodate itself to the spirit of the environmental movement as well as the letter of the law."[48]

While this is an encouraging analysis, the study also indicates that such responsiveness stems from the entrepreneurial ability of the Corps, which it has used to develop new environmental constituency groups. As Mazmanian and Nienaber conclude, "The Army Corps of Engineers has once again proved to be a most politically astute organization."[49]

Although the foregoing examples illustrate the use of different entrepreneurial strategies, they have a common denominator: The implementers are able to amass sufficient power to bend the policy process to their own ends. In terms of producing results and getting things done, the "bureaucratic entrepreneur" approach is one of the most efficient of all the implementation scenarios. Because implementers are pursuing their own policy goals, they can often compile impressive records of accomplishment—combating crime, constructing bridges, building dams, and what have you. At its worst, however, this approach can lead to an unchecked accumulation of power that produces a degree of bureaucratic unaccountability and irresponsibility that is difficult to reconcile with the tenets of democratic theory.

In a book on the FBI, Sanford Ungar concludes that

> J. Edgar Hoover had a degree of authority and prerogative seldom seen in democratic governments. The longer he stayed in power, the greater these prerogatives became and the more inconceivable it became that he might ever be removed. The phenomenon seemed at times to grow out of the medieval notion of the divine right of kings . . . Such bizarre fantasies conjure up the image of a man who regarded himself as infallible and godlike, and who exercised arbitrary and sometimes inexplicable control over thousands of lives.[50]

Robert Caro provides a similar appraisal when he observes that Robert Moses was an implementer who could get things done, but that "his methods of getting things done were dictatorial, preemptory, arbitrary, arrogant—authoritarian."[51] In sum, the bureaucratic entrepreneur scenario can constitute one of the most productive—but also one of the most dangerous—of all the approaches to policy implementation.

Summary

In this chapter we have described and illustrated five different types of linkages that can exist between policy makers and implementers. Within these different scenarios implementers can serve as (1) "classical" technocrats, (2) instructed delegates, (3) bargainers, (4) discretionary experimenters, and (5) bureaucratic entrepreneurs.

Under each of these diverse linkages power to control the policy process shifts further from the formal policy makers and closer to the implementers. Hence, in terms of the conceptual overview outlined in chapter 2, these scenarios indicate how the "principle of circularity" described by Rein and Rabinovitz can be used to characterize the shifting relationships between the actors who occupy the policy formation and policy implementation environments. As the next chapter will indicate, these different circular relationships also influence the manner in which evaluators are ultimately linked into the policy process.

Notes

1. Laurence I. Radway and Arthur A. Maass, "Gauging Administrative Responsibility," *Public Administration Review*, 9, no. 3 (Summer 1949), 183.

2. Official government support for nuclear power was very strong at this point, as witnessed by President Eisenhower's "Atoms for Peace" address to the United Nations in 1953 and the Joint Committee on Atomic Energy's pressure to move the AEC aggressively into the nuclear generating program. See Frank Smallwood, "The JCAE: Congressional 'Watchdog' of the Atom?" American Political Science Association Annual Meeting, New York, September 1960.

3. *New York Times*, March 3, 1979, p. 12.

4. Roger M. Williams, "Massing at the Grass Roots," in Peter Woll, *American Government Readings and Cases*, 6th ed., (Boston: Little, Brown, 1978), p. 331.

5. Peter Woll, *American Government Readings and Cases*, 6th ed. (Boston: Little, Brown, 1978), pp. 337–338.

6. Laurie J. Laidlaw, "U.S. Immigration Policy: A Case Study in the Politics of Implementation," Dartmouth College, Government 83, March 1979.

7. Jeffrey L. Pressman and Aaron B. Wildavsky, *Implementation* (Berkeley: University of California Press, 1973), p. 30.

8. Wallace Carroll, "The Steel Price Crisis of 1962," in Raymond E. Wolfinger, ed., *Readings in American Political Behavior* (Englewood Cliffs, N.J.: Prentice-Hall, 1970), pp. 150–151. See also Grant McConnell, *Steel and the Presidency* (New York: W. W. Norton, 1963).

9. Carroll, "The Steel Price Crisis of 1962," pp. 148-149.

10. Ibid.

11. Ibid., p. 157.

12. Ibid., p. 161.

13. Helen Ingram, "Policy Implementation Through Bargaining," *Public Policy*, 25, no. 4 (Fall 1977), 499-501.

14. Ibid., p. 502.

15. Milbrey McLaughlin, "Implementation as Mutual Adaptation: Change in Classroom Organization," in Walter Williams and Richard F. Elmore, eds., *Social Program Implementation* (New York: Academic Press, 1976), pp. 167-180.

16. Beryl A. Radin, *Implementation, Change and the Federal Bureaucracy* (New York: Teachers College Press, Columbia University, 1977), p. 62.

17. Ibid., p. 67.

18. Charles E. Lindblom, *The Policy-Making Process* (Englewood Cliffs, N.J.: Prentice-Hall, 1968), p. 13.

19. Richard E. Neustadt and Harvey E. Fineberg, *The Swine Flu Affair* (Washington, D.C.: U.S. Government Printing Office, 1978).

20. "Lessons of Swine Flu" (editorial), *New York Times*, November 11, 1978.

21. Lawrence M. Friedman, "The Social and Political Context of the War on Poverty: An Overview," in Robert H. Haveman, ed., *A Decade of Federal Antipoverty Programs* (New York: Academic Press, 1977), p. 40.

22. Daniel P. Moynihan, *Maximum Feasible Misunderstanding* (New York: Free Press, 1970), p. 131.

23. Maja Wessels, "HEW and Title IX Implementation," Dartmouth College, Government 83, March 1979, p. 4.

24. Ibid., p. 6.

25. Eugene Bardach, *The Implementation Game* (Cambridge, Mass.: M.I.T. Press, 1977), pp. 90-95.

26. Gordon S. White, Jr., "Colleges Mystified by Title IX Fund Rules," *New York Times*, December 15, 1978, p. A27.

27. Gordon S. White, Jr., "Mrs. Harris Strengthens Title IX Policies," *New York Times*, December 5, 1979, p. B11; UPI Washington, "Title IX: Balance Sports Scholarships," *Rutland* (Vt.) *Herald*, December 5, 1979.

28. Anne N. Costain, "Eliminating Sex Discrimination in Education: Lobbying for Implementation of Title IX," *Policy Studies Journal*, 7, no. 2 (Winter 1979), 189-195.

29. Frances Fox Piven, "Federal Intervention in the Cities: The New Urban Programs as a Political Strategy," quoted in Moynihan, *Maximum Feasible Misunderstanding*, pp. iv-xvi.

30. Moynihan, *Maximum Feasible Misunderstanding*, p. xvi.

31. Martin Anderson, *Welfare* (Stanford, Calif.: Hoover Institution, 1978), pp. 5-7.

32. Ibid., pp. 6-8.

33. Theodore Marmor and Martin Rein, "Reforming 'The Welfare Mess': The Fate of the Family Assistance Program," in Alan P. Sindler, ed., *Policy and Politics in America* (Boston: Little, Brown, 1973), pp. 12-13.

34. "A 'Straight Arrow' Quits the Pentagon," *New York Times*, March 11, 1979.

35. Stanley J. Ungar, "The King: J. Edgar Hoover," in Peter Woll, ed., *Behind the Scenes in American Government* (Boston: Little, Brown, 1977), pp. 273-274.

36. F. J. Cook, *The FBI Nobody Knows* (New York: Macmillan, 1964), p. 155. See also H. and B. Overstreet, *The FBI in Our Open Society* (New York: Norton, 1969), pp. 76-77.

37. Ibid., pp. 155-156.

38. M. A. Krasner, S. G. Chaberski, and D. K. Jones, *American Government Structure and Process* (New York: Macmillan, 1977), p. 185.

39. Robert A. Caro, *The Power Broker* (New York: Vintage Books, 1975), p. 175.

40. Ibid., p. 624.

41. Harold L. Ickes, "Foreword," in Arthur A. Maass, *Muddy Waters* (Cambridge, Mass.: Harvard University Press, 1951), p. ix.

42. *U.S. News & World Report*, "Behind the Furor over Tenn-Tom," February 19, 1979, p. 65.

43. Emmette S. Redford, David B. Truman, Andrew Hacker, Alan F. Westin, and Robert C. Wood, *Politics and Government in the United States* (New York: Harcourt Brace Jovanovich, 1965), p. 702.

44. Ibid., p. 702.

45. *U. S. News & World Report,* "Behind the Furor over Tenn-Tom," p. 65.

48. Daniel A. Mazmanian and Jeanne Nienaber, *Can Organizations Change?* (Washington, D.C.: Brookings, 1979), p. 3.

49. Ibid., p. 194.

50. Ungar, "The King," pp. 267–268.

51. Caro, *The Power Broker,* p. 632.

Chapter Eight

Evaluation Linkages: Assessing Implementation Scenarios

Our analysis of the policy evaluation environment in chapter 5 indicated that evaluation is vulnerable to political influences because it can ultimately affect both policy makers and implementers. In this chapter we will consider the ways in which evaluators are integrated into the policy process.

As the preceding discussion of the different implementation scenarios has indicated, policy makers and implementers can be linked together through a shifting series of circular power relationships. Since evaluators rarely occupy a strong political base, it is virtually impossible for them to engage in direct power confrontations with the other policy actors. Instead, the work of evaluators is integrated into the policy process by means of the different criteria they can employ to appraise the performance of policy makers and implementers under the different implementation scenarios.

Political judgments are extremely significant here because many diverse criteria can be used to measure the "success" or "failure" of policy implementation efforts. As psychologist John P. Campbell has observed in discussing the evaluation of organizational effectiveness,

> To ask the global question about whether an organization is "effective" or "ineffective" is virtually useless. An organization can be effective or ineffective on a number of different facets that may be relatively independent of one another.[1]

Campbell's observation highlights the need to clarify the different criteria that can be used to evaluate performance under the five different implementation scenarios described in chapter 7.

Evaluation Criteria

In a thoughtful discussion of "Types and Categories of Evaluation," public health sociologist Edward A. Suchman has proposed five interrelated criteria to evaluate "success or failure" of health programs. These are

1. Effort (the quantity and quality of the activity which takes place . . . An assessment of input or energy regardless of output).
2. Performance (the results of effort rather than the effort itself).
3. Adequacy (the degree to which total performance is adequate to the total amount of need).
4. Efficiency (evaluation of alternative paths or methods in terms of cost).
5. Process (how and why a program works or doesn't work).[2]

While Suchman's criteria are explicitly designed to evaluate health care, his classification reinforces Campbell's observation that effectiveness can be measured in different ways depending on the types of evaluation criteria employed. On the basis of the analysis already presented in this study, it is possible to identify a somewhat modified set of criteria that can be used to evaluate implementation effectiveness in carrying out different kinds of public policies.

As was explained in chapter 5, public policies can be evaluated in terms of short-term quantifiable *outputs* (e.g., number of people served, miles of roads built, etc.), longer-term, subjective *outcomes* (e.g., changes in student reading skills based on test scores, etc.), or very long-term *impacts* (e.g., changes in basic attitudes and behavior).

The first criterion to be described here places a high premium on the quantitative measurement of more immediate outputs, while the later criteria tend to emphasize longer-term outcomes and impacts.

Criterion 1—Policy Goal Attainment

The most prevalent way to evaluate implementation efforts involves an attempt to measure whether or not the tangible *results* of these efforts achieve the goals set forth in policy directives. This usually takes the form of a quantitative approach to evaluation that attempts to measure specific outputs against policy goals.

This goal attainment approach is grounded in the assumption that policies are designed to produce measurable and tangible results. Consequently, the primary objective of this type of evaluation is to determine whether or not the implementers have attained the results set forth in policy mandates.

There is a large and growing body of literature that stresses this type of goal attainment evaluation. This approach is certainly implicit in Pressman and Wildavsky's statement that implementation "means just what Webster and Roget say it does: to carry out, accomplish, fulfill, produce, complete."[3] The same basic orientation is emphasized by many organization theorists, such as Richard M. Steers, who asserts that

> central to any discussion of organizational effectiveness is the notion of goals. In fact most definitions of organizational effectiveness ultimately rest on the question of how successful an organization has been in attaining its stated objectives.[4]

The standard of measuring outputs against specific goals has, for some, become synonymous with both good policy and good management. As Joseph S. Wholey and associates put it,

> We define management as the purposeful application of resources to tasks in order to achieve specified objectives . . . In order to allow a program to be managed to achieve objectives . . . measurable objectives have (to be) specified.[5]

Key executive leaders—presidents, governors, and mayors—often press for the clarification of policy goals as a means of controlling governmental management, as in Johnson's efforts to develop planning, programming, and budgeting systems (PPBS), Nixon's management by objectives (MBO) and Carter's zero-based budgeting. Such a means–ends analysis has an attractive sensibility to it.

At present this approach is the dominant focus of much evaluation research, and major efforts are being made to develop more sophisticated and refined techniques that can be used to count specific outputs as the basis of evaluation measurement (e.g., miles of roads built, number of school graduates, etc.). The hope is that this will produce objective, "value-free" findings.

The reason that outputs are emphasized so heavily in this first evaluation criterion is because there are time constraints and methodological limitations. As indicated in chapter 5, both outcomes and impacts involve longer-range payoffs. In addition, since they deal with more subjective changes in skills and/or attitudes, both are often very difficult to measure objectively. Outputs, on the other hand, are more readily quantifiable and immediate.

In order to be used for evaluation purposes, however, results must be measured against specific objectives that are spelled out in policy directives. Hence, this first evaluation criterion fits most closely with the more technically oriented implementation scenarios, specifically, the "classical" technocratic and instructed-delegate types of linkages.

Criterion 2—Efficiency

A second way to evaluate policy implementation is by means of efficiency criteria. While goal attainment places heavy emphasis on results and outputs, efficiency criteria attempt to evaluate *quality of performance*, usually in relation to cost. This is sometimes referred to as *effort* evaluation.

This second approach uses much of the same methodology as the goal attainment approach in an attempt to measure efficiency indicators in cases in which there are no clear-cut policy outputs to be evaluated such as when public policies have been developed to deal with broad or amorphous areas of concern. Such policies are encountered, for example, in relation to the government's provision of what are called collective goods. Anthony Downs points out that such goods—national defense, foreign relations, public safety, etc.—are often quite remote in time and space, and the technology for delivering them is uncertain.[6] Mancur Olson argues that the contribution of any single provider—such as a governmental agency or employee—toward the production of collective goods cannot be separately measured.[7] Thus, the evaluation of policies providing collective goods is often conducted in terms other than measuring policy outputs and results. Instead, the focus falls on surrogate indicators as indirect means to measure efficiency in relation to cost.

An example at the federal level is found in the area of national defense. How does one evaluate the effectiveness of an organization such as the Strategic Air Command (SAC), which is designed to prevent war through the development of a creditable nuclear deterrence strategy? It might be argued that SAC should be evaluated as a success if war is avoided, but certainly there are a host of other factors, in addition to nuclear deterrence, that could lead to this result. Similarly, it would be ludicrous to evaluate the SAC's effectiveness in terms of its accuracy in dropping bombs on foreign targets, since its policy objective is not to use its nuclear capability. In the absence of specific output indicators, other measurements must be devised to evaluate implementation effectiveness.

In the case of an organization such as the SAC, these measures very often take the form of efficiency criteria that are designed to appraise various aspects of organizational performance. In terms of internal evaluation, for example, SAC leaders must presumably rely on different types of tests and simulations to monitor such performance capabilities as readiness and response time. External evaluation (to the extent that it takes place at all) focuses on cost trends and other expenditure data in an attempt to determine whether implementation is being carried out in an economical and efficient manner. This is where the phrase "more bang for the buck" becomes relevant.

A second example of the use of efficiency criteria, this time at the state level, grows out of the experience of one of the authors of this book, who has served for the past six years as chairman of the Vermont Higher Education Planning Commission. This group is designed to coordinate a diverse mix of public and independent colleges, universities, community colleges, vocational training programs, and student financial assistance programs that are scattered throughout the state. Since the commission is constantly faced with the challenge of evaluating the effectiveness of this system, we have developed a number of very broad policy goals (such as equality of access to diverse educational opportunities beyond high school), and we attempt to measure some policy outputs (such as the number of students receiving degrees each year). Since these goals and outputs are quite diffuse, however, we spend most of our time developing efficiency criteria that focus on such questions as How much does it cost to educate students in different institutions? How do per capita expenditures for higher education in Vermont compare with those of other states? How much program duplication and overlap exists within the system?

Although the key thrust of efficiency criteria is to focus on the quality of performance rather than on the realization of specific policy outputs, its methodology is quite close to the goal attainment approach in that it relies heavily on quantitative indicators for measurement purposes. Its basic orientation is to determine the most efficient means to carry out general goals. Hence, because its primary focus is on means rather than ends, it fits quite closely with the second implementation scenario, instructed delegation.

Criterion 3—Constituency Satisfaction

The next two approaches to policy evaluation involve a fundamentally different perspective in terms of both focus and methodological orientation. Instead of attempting to use quantitative indicators to measure specific outputs or to appraise efficient performance, the third and fourth criteria evaluate effectiveness in terms of the *satisfaction* levels of different external groups. Here the indicators used to evaluate implementation effectiveness are shifted. While the measure is satisfaction, the mechanism by which a policy "satisfies" is not examined explicitly. Instead, the measure of policy effectiveness is delegated to a relevant population. As we noted in chapter 5, policy makers emphasize this type of evaluation when they monitor the feedback of constituents, and implementers use a similar approach when they evaluate the responses of their consumer and clientele groups.

Under the third criterion, evaluators follow the lead of the policy makers and appraise *constituency* satisfaction as the relevant indicator of successful performance. This third approach to evaluation does not focus on adherence to precise policy objectives but on the modification and compromise of goals in an effort to reconcile conflicts and accommodate the concerns of those constituency groups, whose goals may shift over time. The ultimate measure of success under this approach is whether policy makers have been able to maintain a broad base of constituency support for the policies they are sponsoring.

Instead of emphasizing quantitative and technical measurement, this approach relies on the subjective and qualitative feedback monitoring discussed in chapter 5. Since this approach places a high premium on compromise and accommodation, it fits most closely into the more political scenarios, specifically, the "bargaining" model of policy implementation.

Criterion 4—Clientele Responsiveness

While the third evaluation criterion emphasizes constituency satisfaction as a measure of success, the fourth criterion is oriented toward *consumer* and *clientele satisfaction*. Its basic focus is on those specific groups who are being serviced by policies and how responsive these policies (and those responsible for implementing them) are to clients' perceived needs.

Sociologist Charles Perrow discusses this type of evaluation emphasis as an example of "revelatory analysis":

> Revelatory analysis asks "who is getting what" from the organization, or "effectiveness for whom?" The question . . . sees organizations as intentional human constructions but not necessarily rational systems guided by official goals . . .
> If we define organizations as intentional human constructions wherein people and groups within and without the organization compete for outputs of interest to them under conditions of unequal power, we have posed the issue of effectiveness quite differently.[8]

It is significant to note that Perrow goes on to discuss this type of evaluation approach in relation to "human service organizations, such as hospitals, prisons, social agencies, welfare departments, public schools and so on." Perrow is talking about a more political type of evaluation, and his focus on human service organizations indicates that the clientele responsiveness criterion fits closely with the experimental approach to policy implementation, which places a high premium on program adaptability, flexibility, and accommodation in its attempts to meet consumer and clientele needs and demands.

Criterion 5—System Maintenance

As noted in the preceding chapter, Frances Fox Piven argues that

> the motivating force in government action, the force which shapes public goals and the programs and the structures created in their name reflects . . . the adaptive rationalism through which a political system and its member parts are maintained.[10]

Piven is describing a fifth type of evaluation criterion, system maintenance. Here the key standard of measurement is a policy's effectiveness in holding together social institutions so that the political system can continue to exist as a viable entity. This concept represents a very important criterion for evaluating the effectiveness of policy implementation on both the macro scale (e.g., the stability of a national or international political system) and the micro scale (e.g., the ongoing viability of individual implementing agencies).

The organization theorists classify this as a "natural systems" perspective of evaluation:

> The natural systems view makes the assumption that if an organization is of any size at all, the demands placed on it are so dynamic and complex that it is not possible to define a finite number of organizational goals in any meaningful way. Rather the organization adopts the overall goal of maintaining its viability, or existence, through time without depleting the environment or otherwise fouling its nest.
>
> Thus, to assess an organization's effectiveness, one should try to find out whether an organization is internally consistent, whether its resources are being judiciously distributed over a wide variety of coping mechanisms, whether it is using up its resources faster than it should, and so forth.[11]

In many respects this system maintenance criterion is the broadest one of all, and it incorporates elements drawn from each of the other criteria, such as efficiency, responsiveness, and adaptability. When applied on a micro scale it certainly has relevance to the bureaucratic implementation scenario, but its ultimate reach extends beyond this one type of implementation approach.

Evaluating Implementation Scenarios

As the preceding discussion has indicated, different criteria can be used to evaluate the effectiveness of policy implementation efforts. These criteria correspond quite closely to the implementation scenarios described in the preceding chapter. Table 8-1 outlines the nature of the basic relationships between the different criteria and the five scenarios.

Thus far our discussion has focused on the use of evaluation criteria *after* a policy has been implemented. However, it is clear that the existence of these different criteria can have an influence *during* the implementation process. If those responsible for policy implementation know that they are being evaluated according to a specific criterion or set of criteria, their behavior during implementation can be influenced by this knowledge. Thus, depending on which scenario we are discussing, the prospect that certain evaluation criteria will be stressed can help shape the implementation process.

In scenarios 1 and 2, for example, "classical" technocrats and instructed delegates may have strong incentives to faithfully follow their policy directives because they presume that they will be evaluated according to the criteria of goal attainment and efficiency. In scenarios 3 and 4, the relationship of policy makers and implementers to their constituency and clientele groups will be important. On a larger scale, the evaluation criterion most relevant to scenario 5—system maintenance—forces close attention to those groups and individuals who can threaten the existance of an organization.

In these senses, although the evaluation criteria are not intended to be mutually exclusive, each has a "complementary fit" with a different implementation scenario. Hence, to the extent that the criteria provide a linkage between the evaluation environment and the other policy environments, they constitute incentives for policy makers and implementers to follow the assumptions of the different scenarios in order to satisfy the requirements of the different evaluation criteria.

The fact that these linkages exist poses a number of extremely difficult conceptual problems that require the exercise of an astute degree of political judgment.

1. How to avoid using inappropriate criteria to evaluate alternate implementation scenarios.
2. How to weigh different criteria if they produce cross-cutting and contradictory findings.
3. How to compare the evaluation of a given scenario with the "hypothetical unknowns" of a different scenario that is not used.

Table 8-1 *EVALUATION CRITERIA: DIFFERENT IMPLEMENTATION SCENARIOS*

Evaluation Criterion	Focus	Key Characteristic	Major Methodology	Most Relevant Scenarios
1. Goal attainment	results (achieving ends)	goal precision: output indicators	technical: quantitative	classical technocratic and instructed delegation
2. Efficiency	performance (maximizing means)	productivity costs	technical: quantitative	instructed delegation and classical technocratic
3. Constituency satisfaction	political accommodation (constituents)	compromise and goal adjustment	qualitative feedback	bargaining
4. Clientele responsiveness	political accommodation (consumers)	program adaptability and flexibility	qualitative feedback	experimental
5. System maintenance	institutional viability	stability and continuity	mixed	bureaucratic

Each of these potential problems can be illustrated by reference to some specific case studies.

Evaluating Scenarios: Methodological Obstacles

One of the best documented examples of an evaluation of a governmental social experiment involves the 1968–1969 Westinghouse study of Project Head Start, a program for children of preschool age administered by the Office of Economic Opportunity (OEO).

In June 1968, three years after Head Start had been launched, the director of OEO contracted with Westinghouse Learning Corporation to conduct a study to determine whether Head Start had improved children's cognitive development (intellectual readiness) and affective development (attitudes, motivation, and self-concept).

Although the Westinghouse study was conducted relatively quietly, hints of possible negative findings began to leak out early in 1969 as it neared completion. According to a seminar paper by Robert Schpoont, previous internal monitoring by OEO staff had indicated that participation in Head Start "was responsible for large IQ jumps; some children's IQs, after one year in the program, had increased 10 to 30 points." [12] The Westinghouse study, however, which involved ex post facto tests of former Head Start children who had been out of the program up to three years, concluded that "Head Start children cannot be said to be appreciably different from their peers in the elementary grades who did not attend Head Start in most aspects of cognitive and affective development." [13]

As soon as these findings were made public, a furor broke out over the methodological validity of the study. Groups of critics both inside and outside OEO argued that the evaluation had been premature. A bitter methodological controversy erupted over whether an ex post facto study could produce reliable results or whether Westinghouse should have conducted a longitudinal study, which would have examined the impact of Head Start on a given group of children over time.

Despite its controversial nature, the Westinghouse study generated political repercussions at the very highest levels. "In his message to Congress on Economic Opportunity on February 19, 1969, President Nixon referred to the study, noting that 'the preliminary reports . . . confirm what many have feared: The long term effect of Head Start appears to be extremely weak.'" [14]

Since the program enjoyed a fairly broad base of popular support, it was not killed (although in 1970 it was transfered from OEO to HEW). There is little doubt, however, that the Westinghouse evaluation had an effect on Head Start, and possibly on other Great Society programs as well. According to Martin Rein and Sheldon White,

It was an important factor, among others, leading to the *containment* of the program. Immediately after the Westinghouse evaluation and in a fairly explicit response to it, Head Start began and completed the phasing out of its summer programs . . . And for some years after the Westinghouse study, the budget allocated to Head Start remained steady . . . [despite] support [which] would normally have caused some enlargement.[15]

A decade after the Westinghouse study was released, another group of investigators pooled the results of a series of longitudinal studies (studies over time) which they had conducted in an effort to evaluate the long-term outcomes and impacts of the Head Start program.

The findings of this group, which called itself The Consortium for Longitudinal Studies, were published in 1979 by HEW, and summarized in an article by Professor Irving Lazar of Cornell University.[16] These findings indicate that the Head Start program provided significant long-lasting educational (as well as social) benefits to participants. For example, children who had been in the program were less likely to require placement in special remedial classes, and less likely to be retained in grade (i.e. "left back") or to become high school dropouts. The publicity which greeted this second set of findings was very different from that following the original Westinghouse study in 1969. *Newsweek* ran a story entitled "A High Grade for Head Start," and a *New York Times* editorial lauded the program as "A Triumph of Social Engineering"![17]

These startlingly different findings indicate how the use of different methodological approaches can influence the evaluation of performance under the different implementation scenarios. Although Head Start represented an experimental type-4 scenario, the 1969 Westinghouse study attempted to evaluate the effectiveness of this program by measuring short-term outputs. The 1979 Consortium study, on the other hand, focused on long-range outcomes and impacts. The findings of the two studies were markedly different because the two groups had employed different methodological approaches to evaluate the effectiveness of the Head Start program.[18]

Evaluating Scenarios: Multiple Goals and
Cross-Cutting Findings

A second evaluation problem arises when attempts are made to measure the "success" of implementation efforts which involve diffuse or shifting policy goals along the lines described at the end of chapter 5. The problem can encompass the evaluation of diffuse goals which evolve and shift over time, or the evaluation of multiple goals which may be designed to achieve different ends.

A seminar paper by Peter Monahan provides an illustration of diffuse and evolving goals. Monahan attempts to evaluate policy implementation under programs sponsored by the National Endowment for the Arts (NEA). At the very beginning of his paper he asks, "How does one determine if the Endowment is an example of 'successful' policy implementation? It is difficult to determine what the goals of the policy are, since the policy area, art, is virtually impossible to quantify and measure."[19]

Despite these difficulties, Monahan uncovers some indicators that he interprets as signs of success. When Congress established the Endowment in 1965, the law included a matching grant requirement:

> No more than 50 percent of any program's funding may come from federal or state sources. In other words, all funds must be matched on at least a 1:1 ratio. The obvious implication of this is that the recipient must generate some kind of local support, or no grant can be made. It was hoped that public funds would be likely to generate a 3:1 match from private sources.[20]

The actual results of this matching requirement have been better than expected. In 1965

> corporate support for the arts in the United States was only about $22 million, according to the Business Committee for the Arts. By 1976 it had grown to $221 million and in 1977 reached an estimated $235 million. By way of comparison, corporations give about two-and-a-half times as much money to the arts as the National Endowment for the Arts.[21]

This is, of course, exactly what the Endowment had hoped to achieve. According to Monahan's analysis, NEA estimates that private funding is currently being generated by the matching grants program in an amount close to five times that contributed by NEA.

In addition to successfully eliciting financial support, NEA has adopted other techniques that have enhanced its effectiveness:

> Rather than having full-time permanent staff members selecting and rejecting applications, the Endowment uses noted, experienced artists from all the areas receiving grants. These artists form a panel of peers to review and select all applications to be funded. Although the Endowment is not bound by this peer selection, it generally recognizes the better ability of peers to judge merit, and also attempts to remove the "heavy hand of government" by isolating the selection process from the bureaucracy as much as possible.[22]

There are a number of other indicators that Monahan cites in his report, including heavy involvement by state arts councils and the like.

The basic point is that he deems NEA to be a success because there is considerable evidence that it is very *responsive to the consumers and the clientele* it is designed to serve.[23]

Monahan's appraisal, however, constitutes only one person's assessment of NEA, and it is certainly possible that other evaluation criteria could produce less positive results. A report released in May 1979 following a nine-month investigation by a House Appropriations Committee staff was consistently critical of NEA:

> In the report's summary, it states that NEA is deficient in its management policy and practices . . . that its panel review system is too expensive . . . and that the Endowment relies too heavily on "a closed circle of advisors" from the arts community for its peer review system which, it charges, is often utilized by the recipient for his own professional pursuits.[24]

Hence, it is obvious that different evaluation criteria can produce diverse findings. Whereas Monahan viewed NEA as a discretionary experimental scenario and judged it to be responsive in terms of the fourth criterion of consumer and clientele satisfaction, the House committee staff emphasized the second criterion, management efficiency. Who is right? Representative Sidney R. Yates, the congressman who requested the Appropriations Committee investigation, expressed frustration with the committee's report:

> I don't think the report achieved the purposes I'd hoped for. I wanted to see how the Endowment worked to assist this committee in under standing what it is funding. But I found nothing instructional or beneficial about the Endowment's work commented upon. It isn't what I intended.[25]

The role of political judgment in reconciling these kinds of contradictions is illustrated in an address delivered by Luther Gulick at the twenty-fifth anniversary dinner of the American Society for Public Administration. Gulick recalled that in the late 1930s he had served as a member of President Roosevelt's Commission on Administrative Management of the federal government. After a long and arduous study the commission's technical support team reached the conclusion that the system of employee contributions that had been instituted under the recently initiated social security program was inefficient and highly wasteful. According to the study, the costs involved in setting up and processing millions of individual employee accounts exceeded the amount of money that the employees contributed to these accounts. As a result of this negative "efficiency" evaluation, the commission recommended that the employee contributions should be dropped entirely and that social security should be financed exclusively on employer contributions.

When Gulick presented this recommendation to President Roosevelt, the president rejected the idea. To quote from Gulick's recollection of the incident,

> The President . . . had me up to his room where he had breakfast in bed. He asked me to restate the proposition, and then said: "I don't see any hole in the argument, but the conclusion is dead wrong. The purpose of the accounts for Tom, Dick, and Harry is not to figure out what we collect or pay. It is to make it impossible when I am gone for the * * * Republicans to abolish the system. They would never dare wipe out the personal savings of millions. You can't do that in America!"[26]

In other words, the commission had evaluated this implementation scheme in terms of the "efficiency" criterion, while President Roosevelt used the criterion of "system maintenance." Gulick later admitted that the president was right:

> The error we technical management and accounting experts almost fell into was the inadequate definition of the system we were analyzing. We did a good job on the law, on the bookkeeping, the administrative mechanics, and the fiscal and cost analysis. But we missed two dimensions of the problem, the political and the psychological, and we overlooked the problem of strategy which was always so important in the mind of the President.[27]

As Gulick's example makes clear, it is impossible to ignore the role of political judgment in analyzing, and reconciling, the distinctions between different evaluation criteria.

Evaluating Scenarios: The Problem of "Hypothetical Unknowns"

A third type of evaluation problem grows out of the difficulty of comparing findings about an implementation scenario that is actually used against the "hypothetical unknowns" of another scenario that is not used. Whenever we are evaluating implementation performance, we are subconsciously appraising findings about "what is" compared to speculations about "what might have been" if we had used a different approach.

In a criticism of wage and price controls, tax surcharges, and other governmental interventions in the national economy, Mark Willes, president of the Minneapolis Federal Reserve Bank, argues that "controlling the economy with macroeconomic policy is a tricky business, to say the least." Then he asks, "But how do we know that things wouldn't have been worse without these policies?"

A tough question. He provides a partial response when he observes that

> To answer this question, an experiment, a controlled comparison of the actual policies and some alternative policies, needs to be set up. For such an experiment, one needs a model of the economy that can predict the effects of different policies without bias, and unfortunately such a model does not exist.[28]

This is an area in which some of the newer research methodologies—computer simulation, modeling complex systems, and the like—may be able to make a powerful contribution to policy research and evaluation. However, many policy situations encompass a host of complicated variables, and it will not be easy to devise any simple solutions.

Summary

The preceding discussion has attempted to clarify some of the conceptual complexities that are involved in linking diverse evaluation criteria to the different implementation scenarios. The fact that these problems exist does not mean that evaluation is unnecessary or undesirable. To the contrary, the development and refinement of more accurate evaluation methodologies is crucially important to the policy process.

No matter how sophisticated our methodologies, we still face the political task of reconciling multiple and sometimes contradictory evaluation criteria when we assess the implementation of public policies.

Notes

1. John P. Campbell, "On the Nature of Organizational Effectiveness," in Paul S. Goodman and Johannes M. Pennings, eds. *New Perspectives on Organizational Effectiveness* (San Francisco: Jossey-Bass, 1977), p. 18.

2. Edward A. Suchman, *Evaluation Research* (New York: Russell Sage, 1967), pp. 61-68. A number of interesting evaluation studies have been done in the health fields; see: Herbert C. Schulberg et al., eds., *Program Evaluation in the Health Fields* (New York: Behavioral Publications, 1969), esp. discussion of goal attainment models (pp. 17-19, etc.); Harold S. Luft, "Benefit-Cost Analysis and Public Policy Implementation," *Public Policy*, 24, no. 4 (Fall 1976), 437-462; N. P. Roos, "Contrasting Social Experimentation with Retrospective Evaluation: A Health Care Perspective," *Public Policy*, 23, no. 2 (Spring 1975), 241-257.

3. Jeffrey L. Pressman and Aaron B. Wildavsky, *Implementation* (Berkeley: University of California Press, 1973), p. xiii.

4. Richard M. Steers, *Organizational Effectiveness: A Behavioral View* (Pacific Palisades, Calif.: Goodyear, 1977), p. 17.

5. Joseph S. Wholey et al., "If You Don't Care Where You Go To, Then It Doesn't Matter Which Way You Go," in Clark C. Abt, ed., *The Evaluation of Social Programs* (Beverly Hills, Calif.: Sage Publications, 1976), p. 97.

6. Anthony Downs, "Why the Government Budget Is Too Small in a Democracy," *World Politics*, 12, no. 4 (July 1960), 544–563.

7. Mancur Olson, *The Logic of Collective Action* (Cambridge, Mass.: Harvard University Press, 1971).

8. Charles Perrow, "Three Types of Effectiveness Studies," in Goodman and Pennings, *New Perspectives on Organizational Effectiveness*, p. 101.

9. For a discussion of six governmental social experiments conducted by OEO, HEW, and HUD, see John O. Wilson, "Social Experimentation and Public Policy Analysis," *Public Policy*, 22, no. 1 (Winter 1974). Some of the difficulties encountered by such an experimental view in educational evaluation are discussed by P. Michael Timpane, "Educational Experimentation in National Social Policy," *Harvard Educational Review*, (November 1970), and David Cohen and Michael S. Garet, "Reforming Educational Policy with Applied Social Research," *Harvard Educational Review*, (February 1975).

10. Frances Fox Piven, "Federal Intervention in the Cities: The New Urban Programs as a Political Strategy," quoted in Daniel P. Moynihan, *Maximum Feasible Misunderstanding* (New York: Free Press, 1970), pp. xv–xvi.

11. Campbell, "On the Nature of Organizational Effectiveness," p. 20.

12. Robert Schpoont, "The Politics of Education: Project Head Start," Dartmouth College, Government 83, March 1979, p. 7.

13. Walter Williams and John Evans, "The Politics of Evaluation: The Case of Head Start," *Annals of the American Academy of Political Science*, (July 1969), 13.

14. Schpoont, "The Politics of Education," p. 9.

15. Martin Rein and Sheldon H. White, "Can Policy Research Help Policy?" in Thomas D. Cook et al., eds., *Evaluation Studies Review Annual* (Beverly Hills, Calif.: Sage Publications, 1978), p. 30.

16. *Lasting Effects After Preschool* (Washington, D.C.: U.S. Government Printing Office, 1979); Irving Lazar, "Invest Early for Later Dividends," *The Interstate Compact* (Fall 1979). .

17. Gil Sewall, "A High Grade for Head Start," *Newsweek* (October 8, 1979), 102; "A Triumph of Social Engineering," *New York Times* (November 3, 1979), editorial.

18. For a very comprehensive analysis of the Head Start Westinghouse evaluation see: Lois-ellin Datta, "The Impact of the Westinghouse/Ohio Evaluation on the Development of Project Head Start," in Apt, *The Evaluation of Social Programs*. pp. 129–191.

19. Peter J. Monahan, "The National Endowment for the Arts: A Study in Policy Implementation," Dartmouth College, Government 83, March 1979.

20. Ibid., p. 12.

21. Lee Rosenbaum, "Money and Culture," *Horizon* (May 1978), 24.

22. Monahan, p. 12.

23. Ibid., p. 16.

24. Ruth Dean, "Yates Critical of Arts Report," *Washington Star*, May 4, 1979, p. E-10.

25. Ibid.

26. Luther Gulick, "Twenty-Fifth Anniversary of the American Society for Public Administration," *Public Administration Review*, 25, no. 1 (March 1965), 3.

27. Ibid., pp. 3–4.

28. Mark Willes, "The Rational Expectations Model," *Wall Street Journal*, April 2, 1979, p. 26.

PART 4

Leadership

Chapter Nine

Policy Implementation and Leadership Styles

Throughout this book we have characterized the policy process as a series of circular linkages between the three environments of policy formation, implementation, and evaluation. The challenge of forging these linkages into a coherent whole falls upon the political actors who occupy leadership positions, particularly the policy makers, who must coordinate activities in all three environments if they are to achieve their goals.

Now that we have examined the different environments and the diverse types of linkages that can be used to hold them together, it is appropriate to return to Harry Truman's premonition about the Eisenhower presidency, which was cited in the foreword to this study. "Poor Ike," Truman had mused, "He'll sit here and he'll say 'Do this! Do that!' and nothing will happen . . . He'll find it very frustrating."[1]

Was Truman's prediction overly pessimistic? Do all presidents—and other key public policy makers—inevitably face the frustrations of inaction and inertia in trying to get their policies implemented, or was Truman's observation uniquely related to Eisenhower's style of presidential leadership?

To answer this question, it is necessary to look at Eisenhower's approach to policy implementation before comparing his performance with the leadership styles of some other, more recent policy makers.

Policy Implementation: The Eisenhower Presidency

Because of his military background President Eisenhower was steeped in the hierarchical approach to implementation, in which superiors (generals) instructed subordinates to carry out orders under the threat of heavy sanctions. Therefore, it is hardly surprising that when he assumed the presidency he emphasized the "classical" and instructed-delegate approaches to policy implementation.

"Classical" Technocracy

President Eisenhower's major policy achievements, as well as his command staff organization, were very closely related to the "classical" implementation scenario. A key example is to be found in what many observers have cited as Eisenhower's greatest policy initiative. The National Defense and Interstate Highway Program of 1956 met all of the key assumptions of this first approach to policy implementation:

1. Policy goals were stated in precise terms (41,000 miles of interstate highways to be completed by 1972).
2. Policy makers and implementers shared these goals (the president, Congress, the Bureau of Public Roads, the state highway departments, the highway lobby, and the general public all supported this policy).
3. Power to control the implementation process was centralized in a hierarchical fashion (the federal government possessed very strong compliance incentives to dominate the implementation process through a 90 percent federal funding formula, and Congress provided the Bureau of Public Roads with statutory authority to determine the final routes of the interstate system in cases of controversy).
4. The implementers (state highway departments, engineering professionals, construction companies, etc.) were granted the *technical* authority and possessed the technical competence for carrying out the policy goals.

The results of this particular policy can literally be measured in miles of concrete. By the 1970s over 40,000 miles of highways had been constructed (although not all were completed in time to meet the original 1972 deadline). There have been some unanticipated "spillover" effects (e.g., environmental impacts, potential contribution to the decline of some central cities, etc.), but in terms of achieving its specific policy goals this program must be considered a "classical" success story.

Instructed Delegation

Eisenhower relied very heavily on an instructed-delegation approach to his centralized staff organization within the executive branch. He established a cabinet system of staff administration in which he delegated major authority to key department secretaries on the assumption that they would carry out his orders and get things done for the good of his administration. According to Louis Koenig's study, "Eisenhower's key tactic was to delegate duties . . . 'The marks of a good executive,' he advised his department heads, 'are courage in delegating work to subordinates and his own skill in coordinating and directing their effort.'"[2]

Once again, Eisenhower used the instructed-delegate staff model because it fit closely with his military background. As Koenig observes, "The Eisenhower managerial method was a product of his military experience."

Bargaining

President Eisenhower did not feel comfortable with the bargaining scenario, and there is little evidence that he made much use of this approach to policy implementation. Early in his first term, for example, he announced that one of his central policy goals was to decentralize the growing concentration of federal power to state and local governments. In March 1953 he sent a message to Congress that called for the creation of a special commission on Intergovernmental Relations to devise "a sounder relationship between federal, state, and local governments."[3] This, in turn, led to the establishment of a Joint Federal–State Action Committee, which consisted of three cabinet members, the director of the Bureau of the Budget, and ten state governors.

The Action Committee was designed to negotiate agreements under which federal programs would be reallocated to states and localities. In 1957, after two years of bargaining, the committee could agree only on the transfer of two relatively modest federal programs—vocational education and waste treatment—to state and local authorities. Although Eisenhower expressed strong philosophical support for a decentralization policy, he did not provide aggressive leadership in following up on the implementation of this policy. When the committee's negotiations failed to produce results, he did not intervene in an effort to work out compromises or to bargain with federal and state officials to achieve his policy goals.

As a result, no substantial decentralization of federal programs to state and local governments took place during the Eisenhower presidency. Instead, the federal government continued to grow in power and authority while Eisenhower was in the White House.

Discretionary Experimentation

Eisenhower made very little use of the experimental approach to implement policies. It is impossible to provide specific examples of Eisenhower's use of the experimental scenario because he did not advocate social innovations or encourage major initiatives in such areas as welfare policy, unemployment, urban revitalization, or civil rights.

Since Eisenhower viewed his role as one of upholding the basic principles of government, he was willing to *enforce* the implementation of social policies, but only after they had been formulated by others. Thus, in 1957, when Governor Orvil Faubus of Arkansas refused to comply with a Supreme Court order to desegregate schools in Little Rock (which grew out of the Court's 1954 *Brown* decision), Eisenhower ordered contingents of the 101st Airborne Division to Little Rock to carry out this order.[4] The use of military troops, however, can hardly be cited as an example of a discretionary experimental approach to policy implementation. As a result of his hesitant posture toward social experimentation, many of Eisenhower's critics have charged that he failed to break new ground in addressing the nation's deep-seated domestic problems.

Bureaucratic Entrepreneurs

The Eisenhower administration's reliance on "cabinet government" did provide some entrepreneurial opportunities for his chief departmental secretaries. Again quoting from Koenig's study,

> In adapting the military staff system to the Presidency, Eisenhower viewed his Cabinet secretaries essentially as field commanders. Like field generals, the several secretaries were invested with broad initiative and responsibility for their allotted sectors of operation.[5]

Under this staff system, Eisenhower's special assistant, Sherman Adams, and key cabinet officers such as Secretary of State John Foster Dulles and Secretary of the Treasury George M. Humphrey were able to exercise considerable entrepreneurial power, since the president often entered policy making "at a fairly late point in decision-making, when his area of choice had been narrowed considerably and his dependence upon his staff had become too great."[6] However, these officials were originally brought into the public sector at the formal policy-making level, and they were not part of the ongoing bureaucratic establishment.

Since Eisenhower's administration launched a relatively limited number of new policy initiatives, his presidency was not overly conducive to exploitation by bureaucratic entrepreneurs other than the top cabinet officers. There were occasions when Eisenhower responded to technical proposals from the bureaucracy, as in his promotion of the "Atoms for Peace" program. In addition, like all of his presidential contemporaries, Eisenhower deferred to powerful establishment figures such as J. Edgar Hoover. However, he did little to encourage the permanent bureaucracy to develop new approaches to policy problems, and few new programs emerged during his tenure in the White House.

Comparative Leadership Styles

In an analysis of political leadership styles, Douglas Yates classifies the Eisenhower presidency as a "managerial" approach "characterized by pragmatism, problem solving and a desire to increase administrative efficiency". According to Yates, this type of political leader "shares with the business manager certain basic premises about the way the world works." Among these is the belief that "successful policy depends on rationally structured and efficient organization" with heavy reliance on "strategies of administrative reorganization and improved management techniques." [7]

Yates's description of this kind of managerial leadership fits very closely with Eisenhower's reliance on the least political implementation scenarios, particularly the "classical" and instructed-delegate approaches. Lyndon Johnson, on the other hand, followed a dramatically different style by placing heavy emphasis on the experimental, negotiating, and bargaining approaches to policy implementation. The reasons for these differing implementation styles are to be found in the contrasting political ideologies of the two men. Eisenhower, who presented himself as "above politics," tended to stress technical and managerial rationality in his approach to policy implementation. Since his leadership was relatively cautious, restrained, and formal, he was basically a scenarios 1 and 2 ("classical" and instructed-delegate) president. Johnson, who was very political, adopted a much more flamboyant implementation style. As a result, he was more comfortable with scenarios 3 and 4 (bargaining and experimental).

None of the other recent presidents falls so neatly at one end of the implementation scale or the other. One of the most intriguing—and perplexing—presidents in terms of policy implementation is Jimmy Carter. Carter's military and engineering backgrounds have led him, like Eisenhower, to approach many policy issues in a "classical," technical, managerial manner. As a result, political scientists Aaron Wildavsky and Jack Knott predicted that much of Carter's leadership would focus on the procedural, rather than the substantive, aspects of the policy process in an effort to achieve "simplicity, uniformity, predictability, hierarchy, and comprehensiveness." [8] Such an approach is certainly obvious in some of Carter's key domestic initiatives, such as civil service reform and his proposals to reorganize the federal bureaucracy.

Yet there is a streak of unpredictability in Carter that makes it impossible to classify him exclusively as a technical rationalist. In the field of international policy his dramatic approach to the Middle East negotiations, beginning with the Camp David summit and culminating with his trips to Egypt and Israel, demonstrated a flair for bargaining and experimentation that was analogous to Lyndon Johnson's most daring domestic initiatives. As columnist David S. Broder commented,

> It is as obvious as anything can be that the tactics which Carter used in the Middle East . . . were in total contradiction to all the engineering analogies in which he has nominally built his approach to leadership. Careful preparation, strong institutional support, fail-safe mechanisms—none of these was possible in this daring venture.[9]

In one very basic respect, however, Carter's initial leadership style appears to have closely paralleled Eisenhower's. This may be seen in Carter's use of a "cabinet government" managerial model that involved heavy reliance upon instructed delegation to departmental secretaries. As James Fallows, one of Carter's former speechwriters, has noted,

> Like no other President since Eisenhower, Carter seemed to think that organizations would run in practice as they did on paper: people would perform their assigned functions and seek no others; orders, once given, would be carried out; when people were asked to direct specific bureaus or departments, their loyalties would still lie with the larger interests of the Administration . . . With Watergate over and Nixon deposed, "Cabinet Government" became a good-government rallying cry. Carter took up the cry, eagerly accepting a naive book by Stephen Hess which proposed that the secret to efficient management was to give Cabinet secretaries free reign.[10]

In another commentary on the Carter presidency, Rochelle Jones and Peter Woll also note this predilection toward "cabinet government." According to their observations, "President Carter has promised to give his Cabinet officials unprecedented autonomy in running their departments. He has repeatedly said his Cabinet secretaries will not be dictated by White House staff." As a result of this observation, Jones and Woll offer the ominous warning that "a lot of people who thought . . . that a vote for Carter was a vote to clean up the mess in Washington are in for a disappointment."[11]

The reason for this disappointment is explained by Fallows, who points out the difficulties that can occur under this implementation approach when the instructed delegates tend to follow their own political and bureaucratic instincts and interests rather than the orders that emanate from the president:

> If a President wants to allow Cabinet secretaries full day-to-day control, he must make special, almost daily, efforts to find out how that control is being used. Otherwise, when a President declares hands off the departments, a depressingly predictable sequence will begin. The White House staff will

defer to the departments—until the first big calamity happens. A secretary might play to the department's constituents rather than the President's . . . A big scandal might arise . . . A secretary might appear to be building his own empire . . . Deception, inefficiency, a dozen other ills infecting the various government departments will make a President angry . . . If he cares about his policies, and his political future, he will feel compelled to act.[12]

In the final analysis, Carter did feel compelled to act, although his unprecedented "mass resignation" cabinet reshuffle of July 1979 may have come too late to save his presidency. At a minimum, however, Carter's experience with the cabinet government implementation approach indicates the crucial role that personality and personal preferences can play in influencing leadership style.

Leadership Style: The Personal Component

As the preceding discussion has indicated, the key to effective leadership involves the personalities of the policy makers themselves and the attitudes they bring to bear on the policy process.

If leaders are rigid, inflexible, and unimaginative in adjusting their preferred styles to the political challenges they face, they have very seriously limited their chances of implementing their policy options. Hence, the final—and most crucial—ingredient in effective policy implementation involves the personal component of leadership.

During the past quarter-century a growing number of studies have attempted to analyze political leadership in sterms of basic personality patterns that grow out of deep-seated character traits. One of the most ambitious of these studies is *The Presidential Character,* by political scientist James David Barber. According to Barber's analysis, a president's personality is patterned by a series of influences, and this patterning is "a matter of tendencies":

It is not that one President "has" some basic characteristic that another President does not "have." That old way of treating a trait as a possession, like a rock in a basket, ignores the universality of aggressiveness, compliancy, detachment, and other human drives. We all have all of them, but in different amounts and in different combinations.

Barber asserts that three basic personality factors constitute the core of this patterning:

1. Style (the president's habitual way of performing his three political roles: rhetoric, personal relations, and homework . . . Style is his way of acting).

2. World view (the President's primary, politically relevant beliefs, particularly his conceptions of social causality, human nature, and the central moral conflicts of the time . . . World view is his way of seeing).
3. Character (the way the President orients himself toward life—not for the moment, but enduringly . . . At the core of character, a man confronts himself . . . Character is his way of judging himself and his own self-esteem).

This last personality factor is the most deep-seated. According to Barber, "character has its main development in childhood, world view in adolescence, style in early adulthood."[13]

Different patterns, or mixes, of style, world view, and character have produced quite diverse leadership types, which political scientists have attempted to categorize at all governmental levels. In the federal sector, for example, Yates has classified presidents, and presidential candidates, as

1. Aristocrats (characterized by high estimates of self-esteem in terms of their personal skill and capacity to govern—Franklin D. Roosevelt, John F. Kennedy, Nelson Rockefeller).
2. Moralists (characterized by an issue-oriented emphasis on ideal, rules and principles—e.g., Woodrow Wilson, Adlai Stevenson, Eugene McCarthy).
3. Managers (characterized by a more pragmatic and less ideological emphasis on administrative style, rational structure, efficient organization, setting objectives, "getting things done"—e.g., Dwight Eisenhower, Richard Nixon, Gerald Ford).
4. Populists (characterized by a concern for "the people"; emphasis on political solutions over abstract principles—the "rough and tumble, sweaty process of persuasion and bargaining"—e.g., Harry Truman, Lyndon Baines Johnson).
5. Hybrids (mixtures of the above).[14]

At the state level, Barber has analyzed members of the Connecticut legislature in terms of level of political activity and long-range political aspirations. He perceived two low-level activity groups: spectators (modest achievers who view legislative service in terms of its excitement and entertainment value as an end in itself) and reluctants (another modest-achievement group who view service as a matter of civic duty and public responsibility). Barber also uncovered two highly active groups of legislators, whom he classified as advertisers and lawmakers. Advertisers are self-seekers who attempt to use legislative service as a steppingstone to advancement in other careers. Lawmakers, in contrast, are individuals who view legislative service as a worthwhile investment, both in terms of their own long-range public service ambitions and the satisfaction they gain from shaping public policy.[15]

Finally, at the local level John Kotter and Paul Lawrence have used still another typology to classify the behavior of mayors in twenty medium-sized cities that they studied during the 1960s. On the basis of how the mayors approached their duties of agenda setting, network building, and task accomplishment, Kotter and Lawrence classified them into five categories: "ceremonial types, caretakers, personality/individualists, executives, and program entrepreneurs."[16]

Whatever typologies are used to classify political leaders, their attributes and attitudes are important to the policy process because they influence their conception of, and attitudes toward, implementation. Policy makers rarely have sufficient time or resources to implement their policy objectives by themselves. President Eisenhower's intervention in the Little Rock desegregation controversy and President Carter's role in the Middle East peace negotiations are exceptions to the rule. In both cases these presidents decided that the stakes were so high that their direct participation in the implementation process was required. In most instances, however, policy makers must depend on other implementers to carry out their policy objectives for them. As a result of this dependency relationship, the leadership styles and attitudes that policy makers bring to the implementation process can dramatically affect this process in at least two important ways.

The Constraints of Overextension

Policy makers can be constrained in achieving their goals because their ambitions may exceed the competence of their implementers. As Francis E. Rourke points out, the choices available to policy makers are very directly related to the ability of their implementing agencies to carry out these choices:

> In the end, the President is heavily dependent upon the ability of bureaucratic organizations for his own success. Indeed, as President Johnson discovered in the case of Vietnam, a president's orders may be disastrous for him if their execution is beyond the capabilities of his bureaucracy.[17]

In retrospect, President Johnson not only attempted to push his implementers beyond their capabilities in Vietnam, but he may also have suffered from this problem at home with respect to many of his Great Society programs. The faulty implementation of these initiatives was not necessarily due to the fact that any single goal was intrinsically unsound or that governmental implementers are incapable of performing their tasks with a minimal degree of competence. Instead, Johnson overloaded the implementation agenda beyond his capacity to ensure that the programs were implemented effectively. This problem grew out of his own leadership attitudes and personal style. Many of his policy initiatives were formulated in a casual, impulsive, almost haphazard fashion, and as the agenda became weighed down with escalating demands (Vietnam and domestic), both policy makers and implementers simply had insufficient time and energy to ensure any meaningful degree of comprehensive follow-through on the implementation of these programs.

A perfect case in point involves Martha Derthick's analysis of the New Towns In-Town program, which was designed to provide housing for the poor and to upgrade the nation's decaying urban areas:

> The program was President Johnson's idea. One morning in August 1967, as he was sitting in his bedroom at the White House and talking to Special Assistant Joseph A. Califano, Jr., it occurred to the President that federally owned land in the cities could be used for housing. Within hours, his staff had assembled a working group from the executive departments to figure out how this could be done.
>
> Housing for the poor had been much on the President's mind. No public need seemed more urgent. Riots spreading through the nation's cities seemed to be the slum-dweller's protest against the conditions of the slum. To build new housing was one way to improve those conditions . . .
>
> The President hoped to increase housing construction in a dramatic way . . . The President wanted to start the new program in the District of Columbia. As the federal government's own city, it would be relatively responsive to his initiative. Action there would be highly visible and thus effective as a demonstration to other cities and to members of Congress of what could be done.[18]

It may be exciting for the president to sit in his bedroom (where Roosevelt met with Luther Gulick when evaluating social security!) and formulate new policies, but the price implementers may have to pay for this type of adventurousness can be very high. In this particular case the Department of Housing and Urban Development (HUD) was designated to pick up the pieces. It reformulated its own programmatic approach, which led to a number of serious breakdowns:

> HUD officials soon came to regard the program as a way of demonstrating the newest ideas in city planning and the newest techniques in development. In their hands it became a model-communities program. The more they thought of it this way, the better they liked it . . . As HUD shaped the program to its own purposes and developed its own administration . . . slowly this presidential program became also a departmental program.
>
> Along the way, HUD met a number of problems. One was confusion over objectives. It soon became clear that their program would not satisfy either the President's original purpose—to build quickly a large amount of

new housing for the poor—or HUD's purpose—to create relatively large, semi-autonomous model urban developments within metropolitan areas. In addition to all the other problems it was encountering, such as lack of local interest . . . HUD had to explain to the White House staff why it was not making more progress toward the President's objectives . . .

A second problem was defining relations with other federal executive agencies. HUD needed to establish control over the program yet retain the cooperation of the other agencies. . . .

A third problem was internal conflict. The program could create difficulties of resource allocation for HUD's operating units, and it could put a heavy administrative burden on the regional offices. If the program were to succeed, officials at the top of the department and in the surplus lands project office needed the cooperation of these agencies.

A fourth problem . . . was relations with Congress. If Congress had participated in creating the program, presumably HUD would have been more careful to inform it about administration, but the White House had decided to avoid Congress at the outset.[19]

The New Towns In-Town program provides a clear illustration of how the personal component of leadership style can influence the implementation process. Johnson's impulsive approach to policy formation, coupled with inadequate follow-up once this new experimental implementation scenario was launched, produced dismal results. "Four years after the start of the . . . program, only 120 units of housing had been built."[20]

Unfortunately for the Great Society, this type of flamboyant leadership style also affected a variety of other programs. As Bernard J. Frieden and Marshall Kaplan note in *The Politics of Neglect,*

The design of the Model Cities Program . . . meant that the White House would have to give it continuing, if intermittent, attention in order to bring the various federal agencies in line behind it. This requirement was a less familiar demand on the Johnson White House, which was not normally attuned to the management of operating programs. Johnson's assistant, Harry McPherson, had other messages to draft; the President had a war in Vietnam that demanded his attention; and the support for Great Society social programs was evaporating rapidly. As McPherson saw it from his perspective as a speech writer, promises of social reform drew a rapidly diminishing response.[21]

The Constraints of Undue Caution

As the preceding examples illustrate, the first major constraint on the attainment of policy goals can occur if policy makers attempt to push their implementers (and themselves) too hard and then fail to follow up on the political consequences of their actions. In addition, a second, and more subtle set of constraints that policy makers can place upon themselves and their subordinates grows out of their own preconceptions about the nature of the implementation process. In this second case overly cautious policy makers may simply fail to even consider diffuse and innovative initiatives because they have made the prejudgment that such policies cannot be implemented in a rational, precise, and tightly organized manner. As a result of these inhibitions, such policy makers are reluctant to exercise their own power because of preconceived fears of potential implementation failures. Under the first set of attitudes, the policy makers may engage in the sin of commission because they ask their implementers to do more than they are capable of doing. In the second case, the problem is closer to a sin of omission because the policy makers fail to use the diverse range of implementation options available to them.

While the first problem, attempting to push implementers beyond their capabilities, characterized the Johnson presidency, the second problem, undue caution, appears to characterize Eisenhower's conceptions of implementation leadership. To the extent that Eisenhower failed to carry out policies, it was not because he said "Do this! Do that!" and nothing happened, as Harry Truman had predicted. Instead, he was hesitant to say "Do much of anything adventuresome," especially in the more diffuse social policy areas, because he failed to see how experimental policy initiatives could be implemented in a tight, logical, and efficient fashion consistant with his managerial style. James Fallows indicates that a similar emphasis on managerial rationality may have affected the Carter presidency. He writes:

> Run like a bureaucracy, the White House took on the spirit of a bureaucracy . . . By choosing stability, harmony, and order as his internal goals, by offering few rewards for ingenuity and few penalties for dullness or failure, Jimmy Carter created an administration in which . . . the result was to evade many of the issues Carter had been elected to deal with, to switch on the automatic pilot and forget that a new crew had been chosen because of the need to change course.[22]

This is not to argue that Johnson's more flamboyant style is automatically more desirable or productive than Eisenhower and Carter's more cautionary managerial posture. Both approaches have their strengths and weaknesses. Johnson may have overextended himself and his resources by attempting to accomplish too much. Eisenhower and Carter, on the other hand, may have underextended themselves by sacrificing innovation to managerial efficiency. As political scientists Peter Bachrach and Morton

Baratz have explained, "Power may be, and often is, exercised by confining the scope of decision-making to relatively safe issues." [23] This appears to have been the case with the Eisenhower presidency. Carter, on the other hand, has been willing to open up some major issues—energy policy, SALT II, and the like—but his managerial style has inhibited their effective resolution.

While rational analysis is obviously desirable in the policy process, it is equally clear that not all policies can be implemented exclusively through the kind of tightly structured managerial rationality found in the "classical" model. After observing a variety of development projects financed by the World Bank in countries where information sources were uncertain and organizational capabilities minimal, political economist Albert O. Hirschman was moved to argue that

> the only way in which we can bring our creative resources fully into play is by misjudging the nature of the task, by presenting it to ourselves as more routine, simple, undemanding of genuine creativity than it will turn out to be. Or, put differently: since we necessarily underestimate our creativity, it is desirable that we underestimate to a roughly similar extent the difficulties of the tasks we face. [24]

Hirschman goes on to warn that this approach is very susceptible to dangers and failures, and that its primary utility is as a transitional device "in inducing risk-averters to commit themselves to risk-taking behavior" so that they will learn in the process of doing. A remarkably similar theme has been enunciated by political scientist Alfred de Grazia, who has maintained that involvement in an activity is a necessary precondition for fully perceiving the nature of the activity. In de Grazia's words, "From infancy to old age, the law that involvement precedes perception seems to rule men's actions." [25] If we wait until we are certain that we fully understand everything, we may end up understanding, and accomplishing, very little.

Conclusion: Leadership and Political Feasibility

In this book we have focused on the political nature of the policy implementation process. Far from being institutionally neutral and isolated from political pressures, the implementation of public policies can be understood fully only in terms of the power relationships that shape the probabilities of success or failure.

Political concerns are central to policy implementation because the administration and execution of policies involves the reconciliation of the potentially conflicting values of leaders and followers at all levels. In a thoughtful discussion of the role of *Leadership in Administration*, Philip Selznick identifies four functions of institutional leadership—each of which involves the exercise of significant value choices—as being essential to carrying out "critical decisions": [26]

- The definition of institutional mission and role (i.e., "the creative task of setting goals").
- The institutional embodiment of purpose (i.e., the capacity "to build policy into an organization's social structure").
- The defense of institutional integrity (i.e., "maintaining values and institutional identity").
- The ordering of internal conflict (i.e., reconciling "the struggle among competing interests").

The preceding discussion of leadership styles indicates that personality preferences and ideological concerns have a profound impact on the types of value choices different leaders make in selecting both their policy goals and the means to be used in implementing those goals. The key to effective implementation is to protect the basic integrity of policy goals while exercising flexibility in the means employed to carry out these goals.

Because the implementation process is highly susceptible to political pressures, it is essential for leaders to analyze the political feasibility of different policy options as part of the goal selection process. As Duncan MacRae and James Wilde point out, this type of feasibility analysis poses a very demanding challenge:

> Choosing a course of action that will help to put your proposed policy into effect is usually the most difficult part of policy analysis. It requires personal skill, detailed knowledge of political institutions and personalities, and often luck as well.[27]

Since feasibility analysis involves speculation about a host of hypothetical unknowns that are extremely difficult to predict with any degree of precision and accuracy, there is no simple or foolproof formula to guide this type of endeavor. Political scientist Arnold Meltsner has suggested that "one way of organizing political information on policy alternatives is to write a scenario [that] depicts a policy's political feasibility,"[28] a strategy that we attempted to outline in chapter 7.

Another approach could involve the construction of a checklist of political feasibility that should, at a minimum, cover the following types of questions:

- *Political climate.* (What does the political terrain look like in the implementation environment? Who are the key actors? What are their major interests and concerns? Which actors can provide the kind of task leadership most appropriate to the policy goals? Does the policy under consideration permit a tight implementation scenario (i.e., "classical," technical)? Or is it more conducive to a decentralized and diffuse approach (i.e., bargaining, experimental)?

- *Resource base.* (What leverage and/or inducements are available to move actors in desired directions? Are existing resources—knowledge, funding, political energy, etc.—sufficient to promise reasonable returns in terms of policy objectives? Is the policy important enough to warrant high-priority follow-through at the possible expense of other important goals?

- *Mobilization potential.* (What are the key sources of opposition and support? What alternative strategies are available in terms of trade-offs, compromises, etc., to achieve results without sacrificing essential policy objectives? Is it more feasible to work directly through key actors, or to employ bypass tactics (e.g., appeals to public opinion) in an effort to secure support?

- *Assessment indicators.* (How can program activities be evaluated in terms of overall goals? What indicators are useful for monitoring the progress of implementation? What criteria are most appropriate to employ in assessing "success" or "failure" or in determining the need to mobilize additional support?)

The basic purpose of any such checklist is to achieve the type of leadership effectiveness that Fred Fiedler and associates advocate in the "leader match concept" by "matching the situation with your leadership style." [29]

If any such match is to be successful, it requires an accurate diagnosis of alternative implementation options that encompasses two different types of value judgments:

1. Choosing the *most appropriate scenario* to implement diverse policy goals.
2. Choosing the *most appropriate remedies* to correct breakdowns within this scenario if it begins to get off the track.

In the area of health care policy, for example, it is all well and good to prefer a tightly organized, hierarchical implementation approach. The political reality, however, is that America's health care delivery system is highly decentralized and fragmented. In the public sector, all three levels of government—federal, state, and local—exercise various degrees of authority over health care policy. In the private sector, responsibilities are divided among a host of different professional groups, including doctors, nurses, hospitals, nursing homes, and the like. Finally, the system is highly susceptible to pressure group influence by some very powerful actors such as the American Medical Association, the major insurance carriers, the drug and medical supply companies, health consumer organizations, and a host of others. Under these circumstances it is impossible to rely exclusively on a tightly structured "classical" implementation scenario. Instead, if health care policies are to be implemented at all, their implementers must take a complex negotiating–bargaining–experimental approach that involves heavy use of intermediary implementers and a skillful effort to reconcile potentially divisive conflicts.

The second challenge, employing appropriate remedies to deal with internal breakdowns, requires a diagnostic ability to recognize the differences between the various implementation scenarios. Unless these differences are recognized. inappropriate remedies will be employed unsuccessfully.

A case in point involves the diverse resources that could be used in an effort to secure implementer compliance in carrying out policy directives. As noted in chapter 4, political leaders can call upon a wide range of potential resources in an effort to secure compliance. These include material rewards (e.g., monetary incentives), symbolic rewards (e.g., status recognition), negative coercion (e.g., penalizing or firing noncomplying implementers), and so on. The diagnostic challenge involved in any given implementation scenario is to employ a compliance strategy that promises to achieve the desired results. To return to the area of health care policy, federal policy makers may be able to secure the compliance of other implementers through the use of financial incentives. It is virtually impossible, however, for federal policy makers to use negative coercion, since many of the key implementers occupy autonomous positions in state and local governments or within the medical professions, and federal officials have little or no authority to fire or penalize such implementers. In addition, federal policy makers are dependent on the cooperation and professional expertise that many of these intermediaries must bring to bear on the implementation process if it is to be successful. Hence, once again, coercive sanctions do not serve a useful function in this scenario.

In the final analysis, it is impossible to recommend any easy or automatic approach to policy implementation or any single "best fit" scenario that is guaranteed to ensure success in all cases. To the contrary, it is obvious that each of the implementation scenarios described in chapter 7 represents a different range of opportunities and constraints in terms of both political and practical feasibility. The "classical" and "instructed-delegate" approaches present the fewest potential political pressures because a general consensus exists on. the desirability of common policy goals. However, they may also encompass a more limited range of options in terms of the policy goals they are designed to accommodate. The negotiating, bargaining, and experimental scenarios, on the other hand, are characterized by higher potential for conflict and disagreement and require more sophisticated analysis of their political, as well as technical, feasibility. However, they may provide the only practical options for implementing more innovative policy goals.

The challenge that faces policy leaders is to evaluate these different approaches in order to integrate their preferred methods of doing things (which grow out of their own personalities and styles) with the political realities of the policy implementation environment. Policy makers must gain an overview of the potential sources of resistance and/or opportunity as part of the formulation of policy choices. They must then identify the key actors who will be responsible for carrying out their policy goals. Finally, they must, when appropriate, be prepared to monitor, intervene in, and adjust program activities so that they remain consistent with these policy goals.

All of these tasks involve the types of judgments and value choices that constitute the essence of effective political leadership, which is as crucial in the area of policy implementation as it is in any other field of political endeavor.

Postscript

This book has attempted to spell out the political dimensions of the policy implementation process by analyzing the complex types of linkages and interrelationships that characterize the policy system. As a result, we have exposed a variety of mishaps and failures involving many different implementation efforts, especially in chapter 7, where we attempted to explicitly examine and illustrate the various kinds of breakdowns that can plague the implementation process.

Before concluding our observations, we would like to clarify our personal views on policy implementation. As noted in the opening chapter, a variety of new implementation studies have appeared in recent years, and most, if not all, of them have chronicled a series of misfortunes and mistakes. In effect, they raise the question of whether governments are capable of implementing any policies at all.

During the same period, the national political arena has been subjected to growing pressure from the right, (witness the success of California's Proposition 13 and related measures) which has chastised governmental incompetence and called for a return to a free-market system for the delivery of many public services. Economist Milton Friedman, one of the leading advocates of this position, has asserted that the view that government is the problem, not the cure, and that the invisible hand of private cooperation through the market is far more effective than the visible hand of the bureaucrat is a sophisticated, subtle view . . . The inefficiency and failures of government have become so blatant, so far-reaching that even the blindest are hard put to deny them . . . One result has been an increasing number of intellectuals who have come to recognize the threat that growing government offers to a preservation of human freedom. Another result—ultimately perhaps more far-reaching—has been the awakening of the public at large to the true situation, so socialist snake oil no longer sells so readily.[30]

Although it is difficult to digest this kind of rhetoric, we think it is healthy for many critics to question the capacity of government to solve all of our social problems. Since the earliest years of the New Deal, the United States has witnessed an increasing degree of governmental intervention in virtually every facet of society, despite the fact that a growing number of studies have indicated that governmental authorities—like their private sector counterparts—possess only finite and limited ability to formulate and implement social policies.

Even if we recognize these limitations, however, we feel that it is useful and desirable to make two observations about the current negative reaction to public sector policies.

First, most critics of these policies are not calling for the abolition of all government. Instead, they are advocating selective cutbacks that will protect, and perhaps enhance, those policies which they feel are important at the expense of other policies which they feel are not so important. Hence, many of those who call for less government also want higher defense expenditures, more subsidies for selected industries (to strengthen the free-enterprise system), and more governmental intervention in selected social issues, such as abortion. This call for selective cutbacks is, of course, what politics is really all about. In the forward to this study we referred to David Easton's definition of politics as "the authoritative allocation of values for a society."[31] Politics exists as a means to resolve public conflict precisely because people disagree over policy goals and the values that stand behind those goals. If we are disillusioned because public policies cannot resolve everything, this does not mean that they cannot resolve anything. Nor does it mean that we should always abandon the newest, and perhaps most innovative, experimental policies just so that the programs that have been around longest can prosper and possibly expand.

Second, it is important to recognize that much of our more recent disillusionment with various public policies, and especially with the implementation of these policies, has grown out of the fact that we have developed a more sophisticated understanding of the nature of the policy process. In a perceptive commentary in a paper titled "In Search of a New Public Philosophy," Samuel Beer has observed that the use of new scientific methodologies to formulate and evaluate public policies has contributed to more skeptical questioning of these policies. In Beer's words, "When science-based policy has fallen short of its promises of social control, critics have been able to perceive and measure these failures thanks to the methods of behavioralism itself." [32]

Once again, there is nothing terribly new about this development if it is viewed in its larger perspective. Advances in every field of knowledge have always tended to reveal weaknesses in preexisting theories and perceptions, and they have also broadened our understanding of the limits of the phenomenon under investigation. We are not expected to commit suicide every time a new finding of medical and biological research uncovers a previously unknown illness.

The key, then, is to analyze a new field of inquiry openly and honestly, and not to despair if this analysis indicates a high degree of complexity and raises a host of new questions. Our analysis has indicated that the policy implementation process is characterized by a complex series of diverse linkages among policy makers, implementers, and evaluators, and that a high degree of political judgment and leadership is required to tie this system into an integrated whole. The point is not that any one of the different implementation scenarios that we have described is automatically guaranteed to produce the most successful results. Rather, taken as a whole they represent a diversified array of options to deal with the promise and problems of policy implementation. The promise is to be found in using the appropriate types of linkages to achieve different policy goals. The problems are to be found in emphasizing any one approach to the exclusion of all others or concluding that the implementation of public policies is too complicated to be carried out with any reasonable degree of effectiveness.

Notes

1. Richard Neustadt, *Presidential Power* (New York: Wiley, 1960), p. 9.
2. Louis W. Koenig, *The Chief Executive* (New York: Harcourt Brace Jovanovich, 1964), p. 170.
3. Commission on Intergovernmental Relations (Kestenbaum Commission), *A Report to the President for Transmittal to the Congress*, June 1955, p. v.
4. Joseph E. Kallenbach, *The American Chief Executive* (New York: Harper & Row, 1966), pp. 466–468.
5. Koenig, *The Chief Executive*, p. 172.

6. Dale Vinyard, *The Presidency* (New York: Scribner's, 1971), p. 135.

7. Douglas Yates, "The Roots of American Leadership: Political Style and Policy Consequences," in Walter D. Burnham and Martha W. Weinberg, eds., *American Politics and Public Policy* (Cambridge, Mass.: M.I.T. Press, 1978), p. 152.

8. Aaron Wildavsky and Jack Knott, "Jimmy Carter's Theory of Governing," in Burnham and Weinberg, *American Politics and Public Policy*, pp. 55–76.

9. David S. Broder, "President Pulls Off Acrobatic Summitry," *Washington Post*, March 18, 1979.

10. James Fallows, "The Passionless Presidency," *Atlantic Monthly*, 243, no. 5 (May 1979), 39.

11. Rochelle Jones and Peter Woll, "President Carter vs. the Bureaucracy: The Interest Vested in Chaos," in Peter Woll, ed., *American Government Readings and Cases*, 6th ed. (Boston: Little, Brown, 1978), pp. 455–461.

12. Fallows, "The Passionless Presidency," p. 39.

13. James D. Barber, *The Presidential Character* (Englewood Cliffs, N.J.: Prentice-Hall, 1972), pp. 7–10.

14. Douglas Yates, "The Roots of American Leadership: Political Style and Policy Consequences," in Burnham and Weinberg, *American Politics and Public Policy*, pp. 140–168.

15. James D. Barber, *The Lawmakers* (New Haven, Conn.: Yale University Press, 1965).

16. John P. Kotter and Paul R. Lawrence, *Mayors in Action* (New York: Wiley, 1974).

17. Francis E. Rourke, *Bureaucracy, Politics and Public Policy*, 2nd ed. (Boston: Little, Brown, 1976), p. 27.

18. Martha Derthick, *New Towns In-Town* (Washington, D.C.: Urban Institute, 1972), pp. 3–4.

19. Ibid., pp. 15–19.

20. Ibid., p. 83.

21. Bernard J. Frieden and Marshall Kaplan, *The Politics of Neglect* (Cambridge, Mass.: M.I.T. Press, 1975), p. 195.

22. James Fallows, "The Passionless Presidency: Part II," *Atlantic Monthly*, 243, no. 6 (June 1979), 76–79.

23. Peter Bachrach and Morton S. Baratz, *Power and Poverty: Theory and Practice* (New York: Oxford University Press, 1970).

24. Albert O. Hirschman, *Development Projects Observed* (Washington, D.C.: Brookings, 1967), pp. 9–35.

25. Alfred de Grazia, "Nature and Prospects of Political Interest Groups," *Annals*, 319 (September 1958).

26. Philip Selznick, *Leadership in Administration* (New York: Harper & Row, 1957), pp. 56–64.

27. Duncan MacRae, Jr., and James A. Wilde, *Policy Analysis for Public Decisions* (North Scituate, Mass.: Duxbury Press, 1979), p. 10.

28. Arnold J. Meltsner, "Political Feasibility and Policy Analysis," *Public Administration Review*, no. 6 (November–December 1972).

29. Fred E. Fiedler and Martin M. Chemers, *Improving Leadership Effectiveness: The Leader Match Concept* (New York: Wiley, 1976), pp. 134–151.

30. Milton Friedman, "Preface," in William E. Simon, *A Time for Truth* (New York: Berkley Books, Reader's Digest Press, 1978), xiv–xvi.

31. David Easton, *The Political System* (New York: Knopf, 1953), pp. 128–130.

32. Samuel H. Beer, "In Search of a New Public Philosophy," in Anthony King, ed., *The New American Political System* (Washington, D.C.: American Enterprise Institute, 1978), p. 33.

Bibliography

Abt, Clark, ed. *The Evaluation of Social Programs.* Beverly Hills: Sage, 1976.

Ackoff, Russell L., and Fred E. Emory. *On Purposeful Systems.* Chicago: Aldine-Atherton, 1972.

Anderson, James E. *Public Policy-Making.* New York: Praeger, 1975.

Anderson, James E., ed. *Cases in Public Policy-Making.* New York: Praeger, 1976.

Anderson, Martin. *Welfare.* Stanford, Calif.: Hoover Institution, 1978.

Appleby, Paul. *Policy and Administration.* University, Ala.: University of Alabama Press, 1949.

Bachrach, Peter, and Morton S. Baratz. *Power and Poverty: Theory and Practice.* New York: Oxford University Press, 1970.

Barber, James D. *The Lawmakers.* New Haven, Conn.: Yale University Press, 1965.

———. *The Presidential Character.* Englewood Cliffs, N.J.: Prentice-Hall, 1972.

Bardach, Eugene. *The Implementation Game.* Cambridge, Mass.: M.I.T. Press, 1977.

Barnard, Chester I. *The Functions of the Executive.* Cambridge, Mass.: Harvard University Press, 1938.

Bennis, Warren G. *Changing Organizations.* New York: McGraw-Hill, 1966.

Blau, Peter, and Marshall W. Meyer. *Bureaucracy in Modern Society.* 2nd ed. New York: Random House, 1971.

Bothun, Douglas, and John C. Comer. "The Politics of Termination: Concepts and Process." *Policy Studies Journal,* 7 no. 3 (Spring 1979), 541.

Broder, David S. "President Pulls Off Acrobatic Summitry." *Washington Post,* March 18, 1979.

Brown v. *Board of Education of Topeka,* 347 U.S. 483, 1954.

Burnham, Walter D., and Martha W. Weinberg, eds. *American Politics and Public Policy.* Cambridge, Mass.: M.I.T. Press, 1978.

Campbell, Donald. "Reforms as Experiments." *American Psychologist,* April 1969.

Caro, Robert A. *The Power Broker.* New York: Vintage, 1975.

Cohen, David, and Michael S. Garet. "Reforming Educational Policy with Applied Social Research." *Harvard Educational Review,* February 1975.

Congressional Budget Office. *Federally Assisted Programs Impacting on State and Local Governments.* Washington, D.C., Winter 1978.

Cook, F. J. *The FBI Nobody Knows*. New York: Macmillan, 1964.

Cook, Thomas D., et al., eds. *Evaluation Studies Review Annual*. Beverly Hills: Sage, 1978.

Coons, John, William H. Clune, and Stephen D. Sugarman. *Private Wealth and Public Education*. Cambridge, Mass.: Belknap, 1970.

Costain, Anne N. "Eliminating Sex Discrimination in Education: Lobbying for Implementation of Title IX." *Policy Studies Journal*, 7 no. 2 (Winter 1979), 189–195.

Dahl, Robert A. *Modern Political Analysis*. 3rd ed. Englewood Cliffs, N.J.: Prentice-Hall, 1976.

de Grazia, Alfred. "Nature and Prospects of Political Interest Groups." *The Annals*, (September 1958).

De Leon, Peter. "Public Policy Terminations: An End and a Beginning." *Policy Analysis*, Summer 1978.

Derthick, Martha. *New Towns In-Town*. Washington, D.C.: Urban Institute, 1972.

Dolbeare, Kenneth M., ed. *Public Policy Evaluation*. Vol. 2. Beverly Hills: Sage, 1975.

Dorvee, Stephen M. "An Implementation Study of the Tennessee Valley Authority." Dartmouth College, Government 83, 1978.

Downs, Anthony. *An Economic Theory of Democracy*. New York: Harper & Row, 1957.

———. "Why the Government Budget is Too Small in a Democracy." *World Politics*, 12, no. 4 (July 1960), 544–563.

Easton, David. *The Political System*. New York: Knopf, 1953.

Edwards, George C., and Ira Sharkansky. *The Policy Predicament*. San Francisco: W. H. Freeman, 1978.

Elmore, Richard F. "Organizational Models of Social Program Implementation," *Public Policy*, no. 2 (Spring 1979), 186–228.

Etzioni, Amitai. *Modern Organizations*. Englewood Cliffs, N.J.: Prentice-Hall, 1964.

———. "Societal Overload," *Political Science Quarterly*, Winter 1977–78, p. 626.

Fallows, James. "The Passionless Presidency," Part 1. *The Atlantic Monthly*, 43, no. 5 (May 1979), 39.

———. "The Passionless Presidency," Part 2. *The Atlantic Monthly*, 43, no. 6 (June 1979), 76–79.

Fiedler, Fred E., and Martin M. Chemers. *Improving Leadership Effectiveness: The Leader Match Concept*. New York: Wiley, 1976.

Frieden, Bernard J., and Marshall Kaplan. *The Politics of Neglect*. Cambridge, Mass.: M.I.T. Press, 1975.

Goffman, Erving. *The Presentation of Self in Everyday Life*. New York: Doubleday, 1959.

Goodman, Paul S. and Johannes M. Pennings, eds. *New Perspectives on Organizational Effectiveness*. San Francisco: Jossey-Bass, 1977.

Gulick, Luther. "Twenty-Fifth Anniversary of the American Society for Public Administration." *Public Administration Review*, 25, no. 1 (March 1965), 3.

Gulick, Luther, and Lyndall Urwick, eds. *Papers on the Science of Administration.* New York: Institute of Public Administration, 1937.

Hargrove, Edwin C. *The Missing Link.* Washington, D.C.: Urban Institute, 1975.

Haveman, Robert H., ed. *A Decade of Federal Antipoverty Programs.* New York: Academic Press, 1977.

Hayakawa, S. I. *Language in Thought and Action.* 4th ed. New York: Harcourt Brace Jovanovich, 1978.

Hirschman, Albert O. *Development Projects Observed.* Washington, D.C.: Brookings Institution, 1967.

Horst, P., J. Nay, J. Scanlon, and J. Wholey. *Program Management and the Federal Evaluator.* Reprint 162-0010-6. Washington, D.C.: Urban Institute, August 1974.

Ingram, Helen. "Policy Implementation Through Bargaining." *Public Policy,* 25, no. 4 (Fall 1977), 449–501.

Joyce, David R. "Formulation and Implementation of School Desegregation Policy in Corpus Christi, Texas." Dartmouth College, Government 83, 1979.

Kallenbach, Joseph E. *The American Chief Executive.* New York: Harper & Row, 1966.

Kaufman, Herbert. *The Forest Ranger.* Baltimore: Johns Hopkins University Press, 1960.

———. *Are Government Organizations Immortal?* Washington, D.C.: Brookings Institution, 1976.

Kearns, Doris. *Lyndon Johnson and the American Dream.* New York: Signet, 1976.

Kestenbaum Commission (Commission on Intergovernmental Relations). *A Report to the President for Transmittal to the Congress.* June 1955.

King, Anthony, ed. *The New American Political System.* Washington, D.C.: American Enterprise Institute, 1978.

Kingdon, John. *Congressmen's Voting Decisions.* New York: Harper & Row, 1973.

Kirp, David L. "Race, Politics, and the Courts: School Desegregation in San Francisco." *Harvard Educational Review,* November 1976, pp. 572–611.

———. "Law, Politics, and Equal Educational Opportunity: The Limits of Judicial Involvement." *Harvard Educational Review,* May 1977, pp. 117–137.

Koenig, Louis W. *The Chief Executive.* New York: Harcourt Brace Jovanovich, 1964.

Koppes, Clayton R. "Public Water, Private Land Origins of the Acreage Limitation Controversy, 1933–53." *Pacific Historical Review,* 47 (November 1978).

Kotter, John P., and Paul R. Lawrence. *Mayors in Action.* New York: Wiley, 1974.

Krasner, M. A., S. G. Chaberski, and D. K. Jones. *American Government Structure and Process.* New York: Macmillan, 1977.

Laidlaw, Laurie J. "United States Immigration Policy: A Case Study in the Politics of Implementation." Dartmouth College, Government 83, 1979.

Lane, Robert, and David Sears. *Public Opinion.* Englewood Cliffs, N.J.: Prentice-Hall, 1964.

Levy, Frank S., Arnold J. Meltsner, and Aaron Wildavsky. *Urban Outcomes.* Berkeley: University of California Press, 1974.

Lewis, Anthony. *Gideon's Trumpet.* New York: Vintage, 1964.

Lindblom, Charles E. "The Science of Muddling Thorugh." *Public Administration Review,* 19 (Spring 1959), 79–88.

———. *The Policy-Making Process.* Englewood Cliffs, N.J.: Prentice-Hall, 1968.

Lipsky, Michael. "Standing the Study of Policy Implementation on Its Head." In Burnham and Weinberg, eds. *American Politics and Public Policy.*

Lowi, Theodore J. *The End of Liberalism.* New York: Norton, 1969.

Lowi, Theodore, and Alan Stone, eds. *Nationalizing Government: Public Policies in America.* Beverly Hills: Sage, 1978.

Luft, Harold S. "Benefit–Cost Analysis and Public Policy Implementation." *Public Policy,* 24, no. 4 (Fall 1976), 437–462.

Lupo, Alan. *Liberty's Chosen Home.* Boston: Little, Brown, 1977.

Maass, Arthur A. *Muddy Waters.* Cambridge, Mass.: Harvard University Press, 1951.

McConnell, Grant. *Steel and the Presidency.* New York: W. W. Norton, 1963.

———. *Private Power and American Democracy.* New York: Vintage, 1966.

McLaughlin, Milbrey. "Implementation as Mutual Adaptation: Change in Classroom Organization." In Williams and Elmore, eds. *Social Program Implementation.*

MacRae, Duncan, Jr., and James A. Wilde. *Policy Analysis for Public Decisions.* North Scituate, Mass.: Duxbury Press, 1979.

Mayhew, David R. *Congress: The Electoral Connection.* New Haven, Conn.: Yale University Press, 1974.

Mazmanian, Daniel A., and Jeanne Nienaber. *Can Organizations Change? Environmental Protection, Citizen Participation and the Corps of Engineers.* Washington, D.C.: Brookings Institution, 1979.

Meltsner, Arnold J. "Political Feasibility and Policy Analysis." *Public Administration Review,* no. 6 (November-December 1972).

Meltsner, Arnold J., et al. *Political Feasibility of School Finance Reform in California.* New York: Praeger, 1972.

Meltsner, Arnold J., and Robert T. Nakamura. "Political Implications of *Serrano.*" In John Pincus, ed. *School Finance in Transition.*

Meyer, John W., and Brian Rowan. "Institutionalized Organizations: Formal Structure as Myth and Ceremony." *American Journal of Sociology,* 83 no. 2 (1977), 340–363.

Monahan, Peter J. "The National Endowment of the Arts: A Study in Policy Implementation." Dartmouth College, Government 83, 1979.

Moore, Mark H., and Graham T. Allison, eds. *Public Policy.* Cambridge, Mass.: Harvard University, Kennedy School, Spring 1978.

Moss, Milton, ed. *The Measurement of Economic and Social Performance.* New York: Columbia University, National Bureau of Economic Research, 1973.

Moynihan, Daniel P. *Maximum Feasible Misunderstanding.* New York: Free Press, 1970.

———. *The Politics of Guaranteed Annual Income.* New York: Vintage, 1973).

Muir, William K. *Prayer in the Schools: Law and Attitude Change.* Chicago: University of Chicago Press, 1967.

Munger, Stephen R. "Implementation of Phase II Wage and Price Controls." Dartmouth College, Government 83, 1978.

Murphy, Jerome T. "Title I of ESEA: The Politics of Implementing Federal Education Reform." *Harvard Educational Review,* 41, no. 1 (February 1971).

Nakamura, Robert T. "Information and the Policy Process: Experts and the Formulation of School Finance Reform in California." Unpublished Ph.D. dissertation, University of California, Berkeley, 1974.

Nakamura, Robert T., and Dianne M. Pinderhughes "Changing Anacostia: Definition and Implementation." Paper delivered at the American Educational Research Association Meeting, Toronto, Canada, March 1978.

Neustadt, Richard E. *Presidential Power.* New York: Wiley, 1960.

Neustadt, Richard E., and Harvery V. Fineberg. *The Swine Flu Affair.* Washington, U.S. Government Printing Office, 1978.

Olson, Mancur. *The Logic of Collective Action.* Cambridge, Mass.: Harvard University Press, 1971.

Orfield, Gary. *Must We Bus?: Segregated Schools and National Policy.* Washington, D.C.: Brookings Institution, 1978.

Peters, Charles, and Michael Nelson. *The Culture of Bureaucracy.* New York: Holt, Rinehart and Winston, 1979.

Pincus, John, ed. *School Finance in Transition* (RAND School Finance Series). Boston: Ballinger, 1973.

Pressman, Jeffrey L., and Aaron B. Wildavsky. *Implementation.* Berkeley: University of California Press, 1973.

Radin, Beryl A. *Implementation, Change, and the Federal Bureaucracy.* New York: Teachers College Press, Columbia University, 1977.

Rein, Martin, and Francine Rabinovitz. "Implementation: A Theoretical Perspective." In Burnham and Weinberg, eds. *American Politics and Public Policy.*

Radway, Laurence I., and Arthur A. Maass. "Gauging Administrative Responsibility," *Public Administration Review,* 9, no. 3 (Summer 1949), 183.

Rawson, George E. "Implementation of Public Policy by Third Sector Organizations." Paper delivered at American Political Science Association Annual Meeting, New York, September 1979.

Redford, Emmette S., et al. *Politics and Government in the United States.* New York: Harcourt Brace Jovanovich, 1965.

Richards, Robert B. "Formulation and Implementation of Desegregation Policy in Boston." Dartmouth College, Government 83, 1978.

Rivlin, Alice, and P. Michael Timpane, eds. *Planned Variation in Education.* Washington, D.C.: Brookings Institution, 1975.

Roos, N. P. "Constrasting Social Experimentation with Retrospective Evaluation: A Health Care Perspective." *Public Policy,* 23 no. 2 (Spring 1975), 241-257.

Rosenbaum, Lee. "Money and Culture." *Horizon,* 21, no. 5 (May 1978), 24.

Rourke, Francis E. *Bureaucracy, Politics, and Public Policy.* 2nd ed. Boston: Little, Brown, 1976.

Rowland, Adam. "The Implementation of a Structural Innovation." Dartmouth College, Government 83, 1978.

Schlesinger, James. "Systems Analysis and the Political Process," *Journal of Law and Economics,* 1966.

Schpoont, Robert. "The Politics of Education: Project Head Start." Dartmouth College, Government 83, 1979.

Schubert, Glendon. *Judicial Policy-Making: The Political Role of the Courts.* Glenview, Ill.: Scott, Foresman, 1965.

Schulberg, Herbert C., et al., eds. *Program Evaluation in the Health Fields.* New York: Behavioral Publications, 1969.

Selznick, Philip. *Leadership in Administration.* New York: Harper & Row, 1957.

Simon, Herbert A. *Administrative Behavior.* New York: Macmillan, 1947.

Simon, William E. *A Time for Truth.* New York: Berkley Books, Reader's Digest Press, 1978.

Sindler, Allan P., ed. *Policy and Politics in America.* Boston: Little, Brown, 1973.

Smallwood, Frank. "The JCAE: Congressional 'Watchdog' of the Atom?" Paper delivered at American Political Science Association meeting, New York, September 1960.

Smallwood, Frank. *Free and Independent.* Brattleboro, Vt.: The Stephen Greene Press, 1976.

Smith, T. B. "The Policy Implementation Process," *Policy Sciences,* 4 (1973), 197–198.

Sorg, James D. "Extensions of Van Meter and Van Horn's Conceptual Framework of the Policy Implementation Process." Paper delivered at Northeastern Political Science Association Conference, Tarrytown, N.Y., November 9–11, 1978.

Steers, Richard M. *Organizational Effectiveness: A Behavioral View.* Pacific Palisades, Calif.: Goodyear, 1977.

Stevens, Robert and Rosemary. *Welfare Medicine in America.* New York: Free Press, 1974.

Suchman, Edward A. *Evaluation Research.* New York: Russell Sage Foundation, 1967.

Sullivan, Denis G., Robert T. Nakamura and Richard F. Winters. *How America Is Ruled.* New York: Wiley, 1980.

Taylor, Frederick W. *The Principles of Scientific Management.* New York: Harper & Row, 1911.

Texas State Advisory Commission on Civil Rights. *School Desegregation in Corpus Christi, Texas.* May 1977.

Thomas, J. Alan, and Robert K. Wimpelberg, eds. *Dilemmas in School Finance.* Chicago: Midwestern Administration Center, 1978.

Thompson, Victor. *Modern Organization.* New York: Knopf, 1961.

Timpane, P. Michael. "Educational Experimentation in National Social Policy," *Harvard Educational Review,* November 1978.

Tolchin, Martin. "An Old Pol Takes on the New President," *New York Times Magazine,* July 24, 1977.

U.S. Congress, Joint Economic Committee, Subcommittee on Economy in Government. *The Analysis and Evaluation of Public Expenditures.* Vol. 3, p. 948, 1969.

Van Meter, Donald S., and Carl E. Van Horn. "The Policy Implementation Process: A Conceptual Framework." *Administration and Society*, 6, no. 4 (February 1975), 449.

Vinyard, Dale. *The Presidency.* New York: Scribner's, 1971.

Waldo, Dwight. *Perspectives on Administration.* University, Ala.: University of Alabama Press, 1956.

Wasby, Stephen. *The Impact of the United States Supreme Court: Some Perspectives.* Homewood, Ill.: Dorsey Press, 1970.

Weber, Max. *From Max Weber: Essays in Sociology.* H. H. Gerth and C. Wright Mills, eds. New York: Oxford University Press, 1946.

Weiss, Carol H. *Evaluation Research.* Englewood Cliffs, N.J.: Prentice-Hall, 1972.

———. "The Politics of Impact Measurement." *Policy Studies Journal*, Spring 1975, p. 181.

———. "Research for Policy's Sake." *Policy Analysis*, Fall 1977, p. 534.

Wendell, Jonathan. "Implementation of Title II of the 1970 Clean Air Act Amendments." Dartmouth College, Government 83, 1978.

Wessels, Maja. "HEW and Title IX Implementation." Dartmouth College, Government 83, 1979.

Wildavsky, Aaron B. "The Analysis of Issue Contexts in the Study of Decision-Making." *Journal of Politics*, November 1962.

———. *The Politics of the Budgetary Process.* Boston: Little, Brown, 1964.

Williams, Walter. "Editor's Comments: Special Issue on Implementation." *Policy Analysis*, 1, no. 3 (Summer 1975), 458.

Williams, Walter, and Richard F. Elmore, eds. *Social Program Implementation.* New York: Academic Press, 1976.

Williams, Walter, and John Evans. "The Politics of Evaluation: The Case of Head Start." *Annals, American Academy of Political Science*, July 1969.

Wilson, John O. "Social Experimentation and Public Policy Analysis." *Public Policy*, 22, no. 1 (Winter 1974).

Wilson, Woodrow. "The Study of Administration." *Political Science Quarterly*, 2 (June 1887), 212.

Wolfinger, Raymond E., ed. *Readings in American Political Behavior.* Englewood Cliffs, N.J.: Prentice-Hall, 1970.

Woll, Peter, ed. *Behind the Scenes in American Government.* Boston: Little, Brown, 1977.

———. *American Government Readings and Cases.* 6th ed. Englewood Cliffs, N.J.: Prentice-Hall, 1970.

Yates, Douglas. "The Roots of American Leadership: Political Style and Policy Consequences." In Burnham and Weinberg, eds. *American Politics and Public Policy.*

Yoshii, Michael J. "The Implementation of Affirmative Action." Dartmouth College, Government 83, 1978.

Zeller, Mitchell. "Neighborhood Housing Services Program." Dartmouth College, Government 83, 1978.

Index

Accountability, 11, 12, 33, 67, 80, 83
Adams, Sherman, 166
Administration
   "classical" model of, 7–12, 18–19,
     111, 112, 117, 118
   integration of politics and, 11, 13, 14
   separation of politics and, 8
Administrative distance, 54–55
Administrative Management,
   Commission on, 157–158
Affirmative action programs, 62–63
Allison, Graham T., Jr., 2
Ambiguity, 33, 34, 37, 39, 119
   of court decisions, 89, 90
   of legislation, 11, 12, 17, 62
Anderson, James, 59
Anderson, Martin, 134–135
Appellate court, 87, 88, 92, 95
Appleby, Paul, 10–11
Appropriations committees,
   congressional, 71
   House, 157
Army Corps of Engineers, 140–141
Atomic Energy Act, 113
Atomic Energy Commission, 116
Authority, 8, 12
   of implementers, 11, 111, 118, 127,
     128
   See also Control; Power

Bachrach, Peter, 174–175
Banfield, Edward C., 34
Baratz, Morton, 174–175
Barber, James David, 169–170
Bardach, Eugene, 15–17, 41, 43, 55, 57

Bargaining (bargaining scenario),
   122–127, 150, 167–168, 179
   balanced power resources and,
     125–126
   Eisenhower and, 165
   greater implementer power and,
     126–127
   greater policy maker power and,
     123–125
Barnard, Chester, 10
Bayh, Birch, 130–131
Beer, Samuel, 181
Beliefs, court decisions and, 91–92
Bennis, Warren, 11
Bethlehem Steel, 125
Blau, Peter, 59
Blough, Roger I., 123, 125
Boston, Massachusetts, school
   desegregation in, 100–101, 103
Bothun, Douglas, 80–82
Bradford, Amory, 56
Broder, David S., 168
Brown, Harold, 135
Brown v. Board of Education of
   Topeka, 89, 90, 92–93, 95–97, 166
Bureaucracy (bureaucratic
   organization)
   power of, 57
   Weber's "ideal," 7–8
Bureaucratic entrepreneurship,
   133–142, 151
   bureaucratic resistance, 135–136
   control of information and, 134–135
   Eisenhower and, 166
   entrepreneurial initiatives, 136–142

Bureaucratic norms, 57–59
"Bureaucratic process model,"
    Elmore's, 54
Bureaucratic-rational imperative, 17,
    18, 23, 58
Busing, 98–103
  in Boston, 100–101
  in Corpus Christi, 101–103
  in San Francisco, 99–100

Cabinet government, 164, 166, 168, 169
Califano, Joseph A., Jr., 131
California State Supreme Court, 89, 95,
    103, 104
Campbell, Donald, 43
Campbell, John P., 145–146
Caro, Robert, 137, 141
Carter, Jimmy (Carter administration),
    135, 140–141, 147
  leadership style of, 167–169, 171, 174,
    175
Caution, constraints of undue, 173–175
Centralized authority. See "Classical"
    model of administration;
    "Classical" technocracy
Ceremonial rules, 58
Character of president, 170
Chicago School District, 126
Circularity of policy process, 19, 26
  Rein and Rabinovitz's principle of,
    17–18, 23, 27, 54, 142
Cirneros v. Corpus Christi
    Independent School District, 101
Civil Rights, Office of, 62, 63
Civil Rights Act (1964), 16–17, 49, 62,
    126
Clarity of policy statements, 33–34
  constraints on, 34–39
    coalition building, 38–39
    conceptual complexity, 36–38
    technical limitations, 34–36
  court decisions, 90
"Classical" model of administration,
    7–12, 111, 112, 117, 118
  challenges to, 10–11, 18–19
  decision-making steps in, 9

implementation steps in, 9
"Classical" technocracy, 112, 113,
    116–118, 167, 178–179
  Eisenhower and, 164, 167
  evaluation and, 148, 152
Clean Air Act (1970), 36
Clientele responsiveness, 150–151, 157
Coalitions, building, 38–39
Collective goods, evaluation of policies
    providing, 148
Comer, John, 80–82
Commission on Administrative
    Management, 157–158
Communications (communications
    linkages; communications
    networks), 23–25, 27–28
  in implementation environment,
    59–65
  judicial implementation and, 88–94
    clarity of decisions, 90
    cues as to permanence of decision,
      90–91
    decisions and beliefs, 91–92
  organizational, 54
  pitfalls in, 24–25, 33
Community Action Agencies (CAAs),
    51, 129–130
Community Action Program, 34, 36,
    129
Complexity
  conceptual, 36–38
  in organizational structure, 55
Compliance (compliance linkages;
    compliance mechanisms), 23,
    48, 59–65
  diffuse performance criteria and,
    61–63
  by intermediaries, securing, 60–61,
    178
  with judicial decisions, 90, 92–98,
    101, 104–106
  legitimacy, 63–65
Comprehensive Employment and
    Training Act (CETA), 55
Conceptual complexity, 36–38
"Conflict and bargaining model,"
    Elmore's, 54, 55

Congressional appropriations
    committees, 71
    House, 157
Congressmen, piecemeal appraisal by,
    69
Consensual imperative, 17, 18, 23, 120
Consortium for Longitudinal Studies,
    The, 155
Constituency satisfaction, 149–150
Constituents (constituency groups), 32,
    49–50
    monitoring by, 40–41
    monitoring feedback from, 68–71
"Consumer implementation," 50–51
Consumer satisfaction, 150, 157
Control, 8, 60, 83, 90, 113, 119, 133
    Bardach on, 16
    of information, 134–135
    scope of governmental, 11–12,
    179–180
Cooper, Dr. Theodore, 129
Co-optation, McLaughlin's concept of,
    15
Coordinating Council of Community
    Organizations, 126
Corpus Christi, Texas, school
    desegregation in, 101–103
Costain, Anne N., 132
Court decisions (judicial orders), 87
    communication of, 25, 88–94
    implementation of. *See* Judicial
        policy implementation
Courts
    appellate, 87, 88, 92, 95
    lower, 92, 94, 95, 97–99
    See also Judicial policy
        implementation; Supreme
        Court
Credit claiming, 42, 69

Dahl, Robert, 60
Daley, Richard J., 126–127
Dartmouth College, affirmative action
    policy of, 62–63
Data, gathering, 77–78
Davison, F. Trubee, 138

Decision making, 9–11, 55
    "classical," 9
    incrementalism in, 10, 36, 106, 128
Defendants' rights, 95, 105–106
Defense, United States Department of,
    135
De Grazia, Alfred, 175
Delegation, instructed. *See* Instructed
    delegation
DeLeon, Peter, 26, 80–81
Derthick, Martha, 12, 172
Desegregation. *See* School
    desegregation
Directives. *See* Policy statements
Discretionary experimentation
    (experimental scenario),
    127–133, 151, 154–155, 157, 167,
    168, 173, 179
    Eisenhower and, 165–166, 174
Discretionary powers of implementers,
    111–112, 113, 118, 120, 127, 128,
    130
"Divide-and-conquer" strategy,
    139–141
Dorvee, Stephen, 50
Downs, Anthony, 10, 148
"Due process," 87

Easton, David, 3, 180
Economic Development
    Administration (EDA), 13, 56,
    64, 120–121
Economic Opportunity, Office of, 129,
    154
Economic Opportunity Act (1964), 26,
    50–51, 129
Economic policy implementation, 52
EDA (Economic Development
    Administration), 13, 56, 64,
    120–121
Education, Office of, 127
Education Act Amendments (1972), 62,
    130–132
Educational finance. *See* School
    finance
Edwards, George C., 24, 25

Efficiency, 8
Efficiency criteria, evaluation by,
    148-149, 152, 157-158
Eisenhower, Dwight D. (Eisenhower
    presidency), 163-167, 171, 174,
    175
  bargaining and, 165
  bureaucratic enterpreneurship and,
    166
  "classical" technocracy and, 164, 167
  discretionary experimentation and,
    165-166, 174
  instructed delegation and, 164-165,
    167
Elementary and Secondary Education
    Act (ESEA), 39, 41-42, 56
Elmore, Richard, 54, 55
Entrepreneurship, bureaucratic. See
    Bureaucratic entrepreneurship
Etzioni, Amitai, 8, 11, 36, 43, 60, 63
Evaluation
  of intermediary performance, 61-63
  policy. See Policy evaluation
Executive Order 10925 (1961), 62
Executive Order 11246 (1965), 62
Experimentation, discretionary. See
    Discretionary experimentation

Fallows, James, 168-169, 174
Family assistance plan, Nixon's,
    134-135
Feasibility analysis, 175-179
Federal Bureau of Investigation, 136,
    137, 141
Feedback, monitoring, 68-71, 150
Fiedler, Fred, 177
Fineberg, Harvey, 129
Fiscal neutrality, 95, 104, 105
Foley, Eugene P., 56
Follow-up mechanisms, absence of, 25,
    172-174
Ford, Gerald (Ford administration),
    129
Frieden, Bernard J., 173
Friedman, Lawrence M., 129
Friedman, Milton, 179-180

Funding, 56
  See also Money

Game metaphor, Bardach's, 16
Garbled messages, 24
Garrity, Judge Arthur, 100, 101
Gerry, Martin, 63
Goal attainment evaluation, 146-148,
    152
Goals
  characterizing program activities in
    terms of, 75
  identification of, 73-75
  means outstripped by, 34, 36
  multiple, 155-158
  redefinition of, 81-82
Governmental intervention, scope of,
    11-12, 179-180
Great Society legislation, 11, 12, 24, 25,
    36, 50, 154, 171, 173
  See also specific Great Society
    legislation
Green, Edith, 131
Green v. Board of Education of New
    Kent County, 97-98
Gulick, Luther, 8, 157-158

Hargrove, Erwin C., 1, 12
Harris, Patricia R., 131-132
Hayakawa, S. I., 24
Head Start program, 154-155
Health, Education and Welfare, United
    States Department of (HEW), 37,
    56, 97, 121, 127, 135
  Radin on, 16, 49
  Social Security Administration of,
    42, 120
  Title IX of Education Act
    Amendments of 1972 and,
    130-132
Hierarchy. See "Classical" model of
    administration; "Classical"
    technocracy
Hirschman, Albert O., 175
Holmes, Peter, 62-63
Hoover, J. Edgar, 136-137, 141
House Appropriations Committee, 157

Housing Act (1949), 74–75
Housing and Urban Development,
United States Department of
(HUD), 51, 172–173

Ickes, Harold L., 139–140
Immigration and Nationality Act
(1952), 119
Immigration and Naturalization
Service (INS), 119, 120
Immigration policy, 119–120
Impacts, 76, 77, 146, 147, 155
Implementation. See Policy
implementation
Implementers. See Policy
implementers
Incrementalism, 10, 36, 106, 128
Influence relationships, 60
Information
control of, 134–135
limited, 36, 43
Information "overload," 25
Ingram, Helen, 125–126
Initiation of policy, 25–26
Inland Steel, 124–125
Instructed delegation, 118–122, 168,
178–179
Eisenhower and, 164–165, 167
evaluation and, 148, 149, 152
Instructions. See Policy statements
Integration. See School desegregation
Interest groups, 32, 39, 49–50
court decisions and, 93, 94
monitoring by, 40–41
monitoring feedback from, 68–70
Interior Department, United States, 41
Intermediaries, 47–48, 55
judicial implementation and, 85,
89–91, 93–95, 104–106
securing compliance of, 60–61, 178
compliance legitimacy, 63–65
diffuse performance criteria, 61–63
Interstate Commerce Act (1887), 11
Intervention by policy maker, 41–42
Irreversibility, 58

Johnson, Lyndon B. (Johnson

administration), 11, 41–42, 62,
77, 126–127, 147
leadership style of, 167, 171–174
Johnson v. San Francisco Unified
School District, 99
Joint Federal-State Action Committee,
165
Jones, Rochelle, 168
Joyce, David R., 101
Judges, 85, 88
Judicial decisions. See Court decisions
Judicial policy formation, 85–88
communication linkages and, 88–92
Judicial policy implementation, 85, 86,
88–107
communication linkages and, 88–94
defendants' rights, 105–106
examples of, 95–106
school desegregation. See School
desegregation
school finance, 103–105

Kaplan, Marshall, 173
Kaufman, Herbert, 11, 82
Kennedy, John F., 62, 113, 123–125, 137
Keppel, Francis, 42, 126, 127
Keyes v. School District No. 1, Denver,
Colorado, 98
Kirp, David L., 99
Knott, Jack, 167
Knowledge
limited, 34, 36, 43
power and, 57
Koenig, Louis, 164–166
Koppes, Clayton, 41
Kotter, John, 170–171

Labor Department, United States, 37,
62, 119–121
Laidlaw, Laurie, 119
Lanterman, Frank, 41
Lawrence, Paul, 170–171
Lazar, Irving, 155
"Leader match concept," 177
Leadership, continuity of, 13
Leadership styles, 163–181
comparative, 167–169

Eisenhower's, 163–167
overextension, 171–173
personal component of, 169–171
political feasibility and, 175–179
undue caution, 173–175
Legal imperative, 17, 23
Legislation
ambiguous, 11, 12, 17, 62
See also specific legislation
Legislators
Barber's classification of, 170
See also Congressmen
Levy, F. S., 76
Lindblom, Charles E., 9, 10, 36–38, 128
Linkages in policy process, 14, 21,
    23–26, 48, 181
See also Communications;
    Compliance; Policy
    evaluation linkages; Policy
    implementation linkages
Lipsky, Michael, 19
Lobbies, administrative, 49–50
Local intermediaries
delegation of responsibility to, 47–48
securing compliance of, 60–61, 63–65
Long Island State Park Commission,
    138
Lowi, Theodore, 11–12
Lukens Steel Company, 125

Maass, Arthur A., 111
"Machine" analogy, 7, 16
McLaughlin, Milbrey, 15
McNamara, Robert, 125
McPherson, Harry, 173
MacRae, Duncan, 176
Managerial leadership, 167, 168, 174,
    175
Manpower Development and Training
    Act, 121
Marmor, Theodore, 135
Mayhew, David, 69
Mayors, 171
Mazmanian, Daniel, 141
Means, goals that outstrip, 34, 36
Measurement of program effects, 76–77,
    146–149, 155

Media, 51–53
Medicaid, 42, 56, 60, 61, 65
Medical Services Administration, 42, 56
Medicare, 42, 60, 61, 65
Meltsner, Arnold J., 76, 176
Meyer, John W., 58
Meyer, Marshall, 59
Milliken v. *Bradley*, 98
Misinterpretation, 24–25, 39
Model Cities Program, 34, 36, 173
Monahan, Peter, 156–157
Money
allocation of, 55, 56
as compliance incentive, 64
Monitoring
constituency, 40–41
of feedback from constituents, 68–71,
    150
Moore, Mark H., 2
Morgan v. *Hennigan*, 100
Moses, Robert, 137–139, 141
Moynihan, Daniel, 12, 26, 34, 37,
    132–135
"Muddling through," Lindblom's
    concept of, 10
Munger, Stephen, 52–53
Murphy, Jerome T., 12, 41–42, 56, 61
Mutual adaptation, McLaughlin's
    concept of, 15

NAACP Legal Defense Fund, 94
National Collegiate Athletic
    Association, 131
National Defense and Interstate
    Highway Program (1956), 164
National Endowment for the Arts
    (NEA), 156–157
"Natural systems" perspective, 151
Negotiations, unsuccessful, 119, 121,
    122
Neighborhood Housing Services
    Program, 51
Nelson, Michael, 58
Neustadt, Richard E., 1, 129
Newlands Reclamation Act (1902), 41
Newman, Howard, 42
Newsweek (magazine), 155

New Towns In-Town program,
172-173
New York Times, 129, 135, 155
Nienaber, Jeanne, 141
Nixon, Richard M. (Nixon
administration), 52, 89, 134-135,
147, 154
Nonimplementation, 15
Nuclear power, 113, 116-118

Oakland, Calif., Pressman and
Wildavsky's study in, 13, 51-52,
56, 64, 120-122
Objective evaluation. *See* Technical
evaluation
Olson, Mancur, 148
O'Neill, Speaker Thomas P., "Tip,"
38-39
Opinion(s)
court decisions and, 91
judicial. *See* Court decisions
public, management of, 136-137
"Organizational development model,"
Elmore's, 54
Organizational structures, 53-59
Outcomes, 76, 146, 147, 155
Outputs, 76-77, 146-149, 155
Overextension, constraints of, 171-173
"Overload," information, 25

Performance indicators, 79
definition of, 75-78
Perrow, Charles, 150-151
Personality (personal component),
leadership style and, 169-173,
176, 179
Peters, Charles, 58
"Philadelphia plan," 62
Piecemeal feedback, 69-70
"Piling on," Bardach's concept of, 55
Piven, Frances Fox, 132-133, 151
Plessy v. *Ferguson,* 96
Policy
definition of, 31, 86-87
origin of, 25-26
termination of, 25, 26, 80-82

Policy directives. *See* Policy statements
Policy environments, 26-28
concept of, 21-23
See also Policy evaluation; Policy
formation; Policy
implementation
Policy evaluation, 23, 53, 67-83
judiciary and, 86
by political standards, 68-71
implementer's perspective, 70-71
policy maker's perspective, 68-70
technical. *See* Technical evaluation
termination and, 80-82
Policy evaluation criteria, 145-151
clientele responsiveness, 150-151
constituency satisfaction, 149-150
efficiency, 148-149
evaluation of implementation
scenarios and, 152, 157-159
goal attainment, 146-148
system maintenance, 151
Policy evaluation linkages, 145-159
evaluation criteria and, 145-151
evaluation of implementation
scenarios and, 152-159
"hypothetical unknowns,"
158-159
methodological obstacles, 154-155
multiple goals and cross-cutting
findings, 155-158
Policy formation, 13, 14, 22, 26, 31-44
actors and arenas in, 31-32
anticipating systems failure and,
42-43
instructions and directives and,
32-34
constraints on clarity, 34-39
signals and cues as to
interpretation, 39-42
judicial, 85-88
communication linkages, 88-92
Policy implementation, 23, 32, 46-65
actors and arenas in, 46-53
changing perceptions of, 7-19
"classical" model of
administration, 7-12
recent studies, 12-18

as circular, 19, 26
Rein and Rabinovitz's principle,
17–18, 23, 27, 54, 142
communications networks and
compliance mechanisms and,
59–65
definitions of, 1, 13–15, 17, 31
disillusionment with, 179–181
judicial. *See* Judicial policy
implementation
leadership styles and. *See* Leadership
styles
organizational structures and, 53–57
internal procedures, 54–55
psychological motivations and
bureaucratic norms, 57–59
resource allocation, 55–57
as unidirectional, 14
Policy implementation breakdowns,
112, 113, 119, 121–122, 129, 133
choice of appropriate remedy for,
177, 178
See also Systems failure
Policy implementation linkages,
111–144
See also Policy implementation
scenarios
Policy implementation scenarios
bargaining. *See* Bargaining
bureaucratic entrepreneurship.
See
Bureaucratic
entrepreneurship
choice of appropriate, 177–178
"classical" technocracy. *See*
"Classical" technocracy
discretionary experimentation,
127–133, 151, 154–155, 157,
167, 168, 173, 179
Eisenhower and, 165–166, 174
evaluation of. *See* Policy evaluation
linkages
instructed delegation. *See* Instructed
delegation
recognition of differences between,
178–179
Policy implementers, 15, 18, 23

authority (power) of. *See* Power, of
implementers
as bargainers. *See* Bargaining
as bureaucratic entrepreneurs. *See*
Bureaucratic
entrepreneurship
as "classical" technocrats. *See*
"Classical" technocracy
as discretionary experimenters. *See*
Discretionary
experimentation
evaluation and, 70–72, 78–81, 83
gathering data, 77–78
mobilizing support, 70–71
formal, 47, 53, 59
as instructed delegates. *See* Instructed
delegation
intermediary. *See* Intermediaries
linkages between policy makers and,
24, 33 (*see also* Policy
implementation linkages)
misinterpretation by, 24–25, 39
psychological motivations of, 57
receptivity of, 15, 25
resistance of. *See* Resistance
secondary. *See* Intermediaries
Policy makers, 15, 47
credit claiming by, 42, 69
evaluation and, 68–72, 78–81, 83
monitoring feedback, 68–70
formal, 22, 23, 31–32
intervention by, 41–42
leadership styles of. *See* Leadership
styles
linkages between implementers and,
24, 33 (*see also* Policy
implementation linkages)
power of. *See* Power, of policy
makers
See also Policy-making coalitions
Policy making. *See* Policy formation
Policy-making coalitions
building, 38–39
demonstrations of strength of, 40–42
"unrepresentativeness" of, 43
Policy process
as circular, 19, 26

Rein and Rabinovitz's principle,
17–18, 23, 27, 54, 142
conceptual overview of, 21–28
linkages, 23–26
origin and termination of policies,
25–26
policy environments, 21–23
as unidirectional, 14
Policy statements (policy directives;
policy instructions), 32–34
constraints on clarity of, 34–39
coalition building, 38–39
conceptual complexity, 36–38
technical limitations, 34–36
evaluation and determining intent
of, 74
judicial. *See* Court decisions
signals and cues as to interpretation
of, 39–42
credit claiming, 42
intervention, 41–42
monitoring, 40–41
vague, 34, 36–37, 39, 74–75, 79, 128
Politics, 180
integration of administration and,
11, 13, 14
separation of administration and, 8
Polsby, Nelson, 69
Power, 60
as administrative resource, 56–57
of implementers, 11, 111–112, 113,
118–120, 127, 130, 141
bargaining scenario, 122, 123,
126–127
evaluation, 68, 71, 83
shift from policy makers, 112, 128,
133–134, 142
of policy makers, 68, 71, 83, 113
bargaining scenario, 122–125
shift to implementers, 112, 128,
133–134, 142
Power Demonstration Reactor
Program, 116
Presidents, personality patterns of,
169–170
Press, the, 52, 53
Pressman, Jeffrey, 1, 12–14, 31, 51–52,

56, 64, 120–121, 147
Private sector intermediaries, 48
securing compliance of, 60–61, 63–65
Project Head Start, 154–155
Providers. *See* Intermediaries
Psychological motivations of
implementers, 57
Public opinion, management of,
136–137
Public Works and Economic
Development Act (1965), 120

Rabinovitz, Francine, 17–18, 23, 27, 54,
58, 142
Radin, Beryl, 12, 16–17, 49
Radway, Laurence I., 111
RAND Corporation, 1
Rational-bureaucratic imperative, 17,
18, 23, 58
Rawson, George E., 61
Receptivity, implementer, 15, 25
Recipients. *See* Consumer
implementation; Consumer
satisfaction
Rein, Martin, 17–18, 23, 27, 54, 58, 135,
142, 154–155
Resistance
bureaucratic, 135–136
to change, 15, 58, 59
to termination, 81–82
Resor, Stanley B., 135
Resources, allocation of, 55–57
Responsibility(-ies), 11, 33, 48
Responsiveness, 54, 128
clientele, 150–151, 157
Richards, Robert B., 100
Rockefeller, Nelson, 139
Rodriguez v. *San Antonio School
District*, 95
Roosevelt, Franklin D., 137, 158
Rourke, Francis E., 9, 49, 57, 58, 171
Rowan, Brian, 58
Rupp, Joseph, 101

San Francisco, California, school
desegregation in, 99–101, 103
Schlesinger, James, 36

School desegregation, judicial
implementation of, 95–103
in Boston, 100–101
in Corpus Christi, 101–103
in San Francisco, 99–100
School finance, judicial
implementation and, 95,
103–105
Schpoont, Robert, 154
Schubert, Glendon, 85
Selznick, Philip, 50, 176
Sencer, Dr. David J., 129
Serrano v. Priest, 89, 95, 103–105
Sharkansky, Ira, 24, 25
Simon, Herbert, 11
Smith, Al, 138
Smith, T. B., 8
Social Security Administration, 42, 120
Social security program, 157–158
Sorg, James D., 14
Specificity, 31, 33, 34
Staff resources, 56
State Council of Parks, 138
State Department, United States, 119,
120
State intermediaries
delegation of responsibility to, 47–48
securing compliance of, 60–61, 63–65
Steers, Richard M., 147
Stennis, John, 140–141
Stevens, Robert, 61
Stevens, Rosemary, 61
Strategic Air Command, 148–149
Strength, demonstrations of, 40–42
Style
leadership. See Leadership styles
presidential, 169, 170
Suchman, Edward A., 146
Supreme Court, California State, 89,
95, 103, 104
Supreme Court, United States, 40–41,
86, 87, 89–98, 105–106
Swann v. Charlotte-Mecklenburg
Board of Education, 98
Swine flu program, 129
System maintenance criterion, 151, 152,
158

Systems failure, 25
anticipation of, 42–43
See also Policy implementation
breakdowns
"Systems management model,"
Elmore's, 54
Systems overview of policy process,
21–28
elements, 21–23
linkages, 23–26

Taylor, Frederick W., 8
Technical difficulties, 113, 116–119,
121, 122
Technical discretion, 111, 112, 113
Technical evaluation, 72–83
methodological obstacles to, 73–78
characterizing program activities
in terms of goals, 75
defining indicators for program
performance, 75–76
gathering data, 77–78
identifying program goals, 73–75
outputs, outcomes, and impacts,
76–78
political obstacles to, 78–79
Technocracy, "classical." See
"Classical" technocracy
Tennessee Valley Authority, 50
"Tenn-Tom" project, 140–141
Termination of policy, 25, 26
evaluation and, 80–82
Third-sector organizations. See
Intermediaries
Time, allocation of, 55–56, 78
Truman, Harry S, 163

Unemployed, Pressman and
Wildavsky's study of EDA
program for, 13, 51–52, 56, 64,
120–122
Ungar, Sanford, 141
Unidirectionality of policy process, 14
See also "Classical" model of
administration; "Classical"
technocracy
United States Steel Corporation,

123-125
Urban Institute, Evaluation Group of,
    73-74
Urban Reinvestment Task Force, 51
Urwick, Lyndall, 8

Vagueness of policy statement, 34,
    36-37, 39, 74-75, 79, 128
Van Horn, Carl E., 1, 14, 57
Van Meter, Donald S., 1, 14, 57
Vendor payment schemes, 60, 61
Vermont Higher Education Planning
    Commission, 149
Visibility, 52-53

Waldo, Dwight, 7
War on Poverty, 34, 129
Water Resources Planning Act (1965),
    125-126
Weber, Max, 7-8, 57
Weigel, Judge, 99, 101
Weiss, Carol H., 71-73
Welfare dependency, 37-38
Welfare policy, 134-135

Wendell, Jonathan, 36
Wessels, Maja, 130, 131
Westinghouse Learning Corporation,
    154-155
White, Kevin H., 100
White, Sheldon, 154-155
White House Domestic Council, 37
Wholey, Joseph S., 147
Wildavsky, Aaron, 1, 12-14, 31, 51-52,
    56, 64, 71, 76, 120-121, 147, 167
Wilde, James, 176
Willes, Mark, 158-159
Williams, Walter, 46-48, 55
Wilson, Woodrow, 8
Woll, Peter, 117-118, 168
World Airways, 64, 121
World view, president's, 170

Yates, Douglas, 167, 170
Yates, Sidney R., 157
Yoshii, Michael, 62-63

Zeller, Mitchell, 51

aluih

$$38 -$$
$$15$$
$$52 -$$

$

70 - m
20 reg.
7 -
15 -
16 -
(5 -)   25   101
5 -   7   15
5 -   1 0 0

250
100
300

(5)

148 -   138 -   52 -   70
148   46
300 -   128   126
          75   190 -
          45

275
2)

                  75   75
          75   5.2
                           12 7

         100
         34   250

75   250

              70
              65   52   145
             130   148
48   293

        118   45
        20   75   4
        .7   120
       145 -